GEOFF THOMPSON
Lecturer in Applied Linguistics, University of Liverpool.

Introducing Functional Grammar

ARNOLD

A member of the Hodder Headline Group
LONDON • NEW YORK • SYDNEY • AUCKLAND

First published in Great Britain in 1996 by
Arnold, a member of the Hodder Headline Group,
338 Euston Road, London NW1 3BH
175 Fifth Avenue, New York, NY 10010

Distributed exclusively in the USA by
St Martin's Press, Inc.
175 Fifth Avenue, New York, NY 10010

British Library Cataloguing in Publication Data

A catalogue record for this book is available from the British Library

Library of Congress Cataloging-in-Publication Data

Thompson, Geoff, 1947–
    Introducing functional grammar / Geoff Thompson.
        p.   cm.
    Includes bibliographical references and index.
    ISBN 0-340-62535-X
    1. Functionalism (Linguistics)   I. Title.
    P147.T48 1996
    415–dc20   96-21668
                                                              CIP

ISBN 0 340 62535 X

Typeset in 10½/12½ Ehrhardt by
Mathematical Composition Setters Ltd, Salisbury, UK.
Printed and bound in Great Britain by
JW Arrowsmith Ltd, Bristol.

Contents

Foreword

This book arises directly from my experiences in introducing Functional Grammar to a number of different groups of students, teachers and researchers. Like any model that attempts to offer a global view of how language works, Functional Grammar is complex, and students may be understandably daunted not only by the seemingly abstruse explanations but simply by the amount of new terminology. What I have tried to do is to set out the approach from the point of view of readers who are not familiar with this way of looking at language, and who may, indeed, have little background in linguistic analysis generally. This involves describing the theoretical and practical aspects of the Functional Grammar model in as accessible a way as possible; but it also involves trying to make clear the reasons why the model is as it is, at all levels – from why a functional approach is adopted to why one particular analysis of a wording is preferable to another.

Throughout, the book tries to help readers to see that, on the whole, Functional Grammar explanations in fact correspond to things that they already know intuitively about language, and that the 'jargon' is merely necessary in order to systematise this knowledge. The constant aim is, without underestimating the initial difficulties, to encourage readers to realise that the fundamental assumptions of the model have an appealing simplicity and an intuitive validity. Once that step is achieved, it becomes easier to cope with the inevitable complexity of the details, and to see beyond the terminology to the important and useful insights offered by the approach.

The debt owed, at each stage of the conception and execution of this book, to Michael Halliday's work, especially his *An Introduction to Functional Grammar* (1985, 2nd edition 1994), will be obvious, even if it has not been feasible to signal explicitly all the points which are taken from that source. The book is consciously modelled on the *Introduction*, covering much of the same ground, though not necessarily in the same order or from exactly the same perspective. One way in which the present book can be used – which reflects its origins in the courses that I have taught – is as a preparation for reading Halliday's work. It can also be read as an independent introduction to the approach; but I hope that in either case it will tempt readers to go on to explore in greater depth the writings of Halliday and his colleagues.

In addition to the intellectual inspiration provided by Michael Halliday, the book naturally owes a great deal to many other people, of whom I am particularly grateful to the following. To my past and present colleagues in the Applied English Language Studies Unit at Liverpool – above all, Flo Davies, who first encouraged me to start teaching Functional Grammar, and who has been a constant source of ideas, insights and argument. To my students at the University of Liverpool, especially those on the MA/MEd course in Language Teaching and Learning over the last seven years, and to students and staff at the Pontifícia Universidade Catolica of São Paulo, the Universidad Central de Venezuela in Caracas and the Universidad del Norte in Barranquilla, Colombia: they had most of the material in the book tried out on them at various times, and their difficulties, comments and insights helped me to think through and clarify ideas that I had sometimes taken for granted; and they also provided many of the texts that are used in the book for analysis. To Naomi Meredith at Arnold, who has provided support and encouragement throughout the writing. And, above all, to Susan Thompson, who is, happily for me, always available to argue over interpretations and explanations, to identify confusions and evasions, and to suggest alternative ways of understanding or expressing the ideas. The completion of the book owes a great deal to her.

Acknowledgements

The publishers wish to express gratitude for permission to include extracts from the following copyright sources in the book:

Ellis Peters for an extract from *Monk's-Hood*; Addison Wesley Publishing Company, Inc. for an extract from *University Physics* (H.D. Young, 8th edition, 1992); Elizabeth Jennings and André Deutsch Ltd for an extract from 'Song to Autumn'; Gruner + Jahr AG & Co. for a letter and response from *best*, 14 November 1995; Express Newspapers plc for an extract from 'Bacon 'n eggs stop prison riot', *Daily Star*, 25 November 1992, and for extracts from 'Give sacked miners their jobs back, says Scargill' and 'Britain on the up', *Daily Express*, 9 April 1992; the Department of Health for an advertisement for nursing; Iris Murdoch for extracts from *The Philospher's Pupil*; Prentice Hall, Inc. for an extract from *Prentice Hall Science: Evolution* (1992); Lesley Milroy for an extract from *Observing and Analysing Natural Language*; Churchill Livingstone for an extract from *Clinical Orthopaedic Examination* (R. McRae, 3rd edition, 1990); MGN Ltd for an extract from 'Born into despair ... is today a new dawn for Julie and her little baby Paul?', *Daily Mirror*, 9 April 1992.

The author is also grateful to Sultan Al-Sharief and Johanna Jakabovicova for kindly providing data and allowing it to be used in this book.

1

The purposes of linguistic analysis

1.1 Starting-points

A man is driving through a part of the country he doesn't know, and he gets lost in what looks to him like the middle of nowhere, completely deserted. Finally, he sees an old man working in a field, and he stops the car and calls out to him, 'Excuse me, how do I get from here to ...?' (the town depends on which country you hear the story in). The old man thinks for a while, and then he says, 'Well now, if I were you I wouldn't start from here.'

I am deliberately starting this book from the wrong place for where I want to get to. This is not being perverse: it is that, in recent decades, there has built up an immensely influential view of what the study of language should involve which insists that there is only one proper place to start – from a view of language as an abstract set of generalised rules detached from any particular context of use. It would be possible to ignore this view and simply start with the approach that I will be setting out in the book, based on a view of how language functions as a system of human communication. However, a comparison of different possible approaches will help us to understand better not only the destinations that each approach allows us to head for but also the reasons why we might choose one of the approaches in preference to another. Therefore, in this chapter I will briefly outline the approach that has been dominant, showing why it has been so attractive but also showing why an increasing number of linguists feel that it does not make it easy for us to talk about many of the central features of language. I will then go on to introduce an alternative approach which focuses on those features, and which offers a more appropriate place to start from if we are interested in language in use.

We can begin by looking informally at a bit of language, selected more or less at random. This comes from an advertisement on nursing (we will look at the complete text in Chapter 4). Before reading on, can you decide what aspects of the sentence you might want to consider in providing a linguistic description of it?

> Of course, you're unlikely to be attracted to nursing because of the money.

When I have asked students to do this task, they mostly focus on issues such as who exactly 'you' is (since the writer is not addressing anyone face to face), and why the writer assumes this about 'you' so confidently ('Of course'). Some pick up on 'you're unlikely', which softens the possible arrogance of the writer telling 'you' about 'your' own feelings; others comment on the implication that 'you' are likely to be attracted to nursing for other reasons apart from money; and a few wonder why the writer decided not to say 'nursing is unlikely to attract you'. What all these points have in common is that they are concerned with the function of the sentence, what the writer's purpose is in writing the sentence – in other words, with the meaning. Underlying the points, though not usually made explicit, is also the idea of choice: that there are potentially identifiable reasons why the writer is expressing the message in this particular way rather than in other possible ways.

Other students (often those who have learnt English as a foreign language and therefore have more background in grammatical analysis) take a different tack. They label the parts of the sentence using terms like Subject and Verb, or non-finite verb and prepositional phrase. They comment on the fact that 'to be attracted' is a passive form, and that the understood Subject is 'you', carried over from the Subject of the preceding verb. Some mention that the structure 'be unlikely to be attracted' is not possible in some languages and that, in a way, it is an illogical structure (since it is not 'you' who are 'unlikely', but 'you being attracted to nursing'). What they are essentially focusing on is what the different parts of the sentence are and how they fit together – in other words, the form.

Both of these ways of looking at the sentence tell us something useful about it, and, in the informal descriptions given here at least, there is a good deal of potential overlap. Any full analysis of the sentence will inevitably need to take account of both the meaning and the form (and of the links between them). However, in order to make the analysis fairly rigorous rather than just an unordered list of points about the sentence, we need to decide on a reasonably systematic method; and in practice this involves choosing between form and meaning as our starting-point. This may at first seem simply a difference in emphasis, but, if carried through consistently, each approach in fact ends up with a strikingly different kind of description of language.

1.1.1 GOING IN THROUGH FORM

The most fully developed and influential version of the approach through form is that proposed by Noam Chomsky and his followers, generally known as the Transformational-Generative (TG) approach. Chomsky insisted that linguistics should go beyond merely describing syntactic structures, and aim to explain why language is structured in the way it is – which includes explaining why other kinds of structures are *not* found. He argued that, to do this adequately, it was essential to make language description absolutely **explicit**. Although the aim of TG is not to produce a computer program which can generate language, it is computers which provide the driving metaphor behind the approach. A computer is wonderfully literal: it cannot interpret what you mean, and will do exactly – and only – what you tell it to do. Therefore instructions to the computer have to be explicit and unambiguous: this includes giving them in exactly the right order so that each step in an operation has the required input from preceding steps, and formulating them so as to avoid triggering any unwanted operations by mistake. TG sets out to provide rules of this kind for the formation of grammatically correct sentences.

In order to do this it starts from another deceptively simple insight: that every verb has a Subject, and that understanding a sentence means above all identifying the Subject for each verb. In English, Subjects normally appear in front of the verb, so it might be thought that identifying them would be too easy to be interesting. However, there are many cases where the Subject does not appear in the 'right' position – or does not appear at all (we have already seen that the Subject of 'to be attracted' has to be carried over from a different verb). We are so skilled at understanding who does what in a sentence that we typically do not even notice that in such cases we have to interpret something that is not explicitly said. One famous example used by Chomsky was the pair of sentences:

John is eager to please. John is easy to please.

These appear, on the surface, to have the same structure; but in fact we understand that in the first case it is John who does the pleasing (i.e. is the understood Subject of 'to please'), while in the second it is an unnamed person or thing (and 'John' is understood as the Object of 'to please'). This game of 'hunt the Subject' can become even more complex and exciting – the kind of (invented) sentence that makes TG linguists salivate with delight is the following:

Which burglar did John say Mary thought had shot himself?

Here, we understand that the Subject of 'had shot' is 'which burglar', even though there are two other clauses ('did John say' and 'Mary thought') between the verb and its Subject. Adding to the excitement is the fact that we also understand that 'himself' refers to the burglar, even though 'John' is closer in the sentence, whereas, if we replaced it with 'him', it could not refer to the burglar.

But how do we understand all this? And how can the linguist show, in an explicit way, what it is that we actually understand? One problem is that, in order to label part of the sentence as 'Subject', we have first had to identify that part as a separate constituent (a noun phrase) – in other words, we have actually jumped over the initial stage. That means that our description is not in fact fully explicit. We need to work with labels that tell us what each constituent is in itself, not what it does in the sentence. At the same time, we also need to show where each constituent fits in the basic structure. Chomsky's famous first rule captures this:

S → NP VP

This is a non-verbal (and thus less ambiguous) way of saying that every 'sentence' in a language consists of a noun phrase followed by a verb phrase. If it does not show these features it is not a grammatically acceptable 'sentence'. Translated into functional terms, it means in effect that every verb must have a Subject. Using this rule, the underlying meanings of our 'burglar' example can be set out as follows (the inverted commas round the words signal that we are dealing with the abstract concepts that the words refer to rather than the words themselves):

$S_1 \rightarrow$ NP   VP
      ['John']   ['did say' (something)]

$S_2 \rightarrow$ NP   VP
      ['Mary']   ['thought' (something)]

$S_3 \rightarrow$ NP   VP
      ['which burglar']   ['had shot himself']

Note that this analysis also begins to elucidate why 'himself' refers to the burglar.

If we accept that this captures what we understand in understanding the sentence, our task now is to show how S_{1-3} combine into the sentence as we actually see it. Although this is immensely complex in practice, it is simple in theory: it turns out that we can identify not only a finite set of explicit rules governing the possible combinations (the complexity comes especially from the interaction between the rules), but, more crucially, an even more restricted set of underlying regularities in the type of rules that are possible. Just to give you a taste of how the analysis proceeds, one further rule (in a simplified form) is:

VP $\rightarrow$ V S

This means that one permitted kind of verb phrase can itself include not only a verb but another S (this is technically known as recursion). This may be easier to grasp if we revise the analysis of our example to take this new rule into account:

$S_1 \rightarrow$ NP   VP $\rightarrow$ [V   S]
      ['John']   [['did say']   ['S_2']]

$S_2 \rightarrow$ NP   VP $\rightarrow$ [V   S]
      ['Mary']   [['thought']   ['S_3']]

$S_3 \rightarrow$ NP   VP
      ['which burglar']   ['had shot himself']

I have concentrated so far on the Subject, but exactly the same kind of analysis can be done for Objects and other clause constituents that appear in the 'wrong' place or which govern the form and interpretation of other constituents (as 'which burglar' governs the interpretation of 'himself'). What are the S_{1-3} underlying this version of the example?

Which burglar did John say Mary told him she had shot?

It is perhaps surprising that, using such apparently marginal examples, the approach should have thrown so much light on how sentences are structured;

and yet the insights gained have been extensive and in some ways revolutionary. For our present purposes, however, it is less important to look at these discoveries in any detail than to consider where the approach leads us. The first thing to say is that TG is only interested in what we can call **'propositional meaning'**. The following two sentences have exactly the same analysis in terms of Ss:

John is eager to please.   Is John eager to please?

$S_1 \rightarrow NP$ VP
     ['John']   ['is eager to S_2']

$S_2 \rightarrow NP$ VP
     ['John']   ['pleases']

The difference in surface form ('John is' vs. 'Is John') results from rules which allow the auxiliary 'is' to move in front of the NP as the Ss transform into the sentence. On the other hand, the fact that a statement and a question serve entirely different functions in communication is regarded as irrelevant in the grammatical analysis – it is taken into account in a different part of the linguistic description (though there has so far been little interest in developing that part within TG). Chomsky made a principled decision to exclude how we use sentences in communication (e.g. as statements or questions): the model is not designed to show, for example, that one sentence functions as the answer to a preceding question. The aim is to discover the rules which govern how constituents can be put together to form grammatically correct sentences, and to formulate these rules in as general a way as possible (ideally, so that they apply to all human language rather than just individual languages); therefore each sentence is analysed in complete isolation, both from other sentences and from the situations in which it might be used. This limitation is self-imposed because TG linguists feel that it is only worth describing those aspects of language which can be described 'scientifically' (i.e. with absolute explicitness). The ways in which language is used are, unfortunately, too messy and are therefore ignored, at least until someone can find a way of describing them according to scientific general laws.

But if the path towards an examination of use is blocked off, where else can we go? The answer is inwards, into the mind. The fact that we as language users can make the complex transitions from Ss to sentences and vice versa, i.e. can identify the separate constituents in the sentence and assign them to their place in the structure of the appropriate S, tells us a great deal about how our minds must work. At the same time, the fact that we do not need to be explicitly taught how to do this means that we must in some way be born with the required mental capacities. Thus a rigorously formal approach to the description of language leads us towards psychology and genetics. Clearly, these are fascinating and worthwhile areas, but they do involve giving up any idea of looking at language in use.

1.1.2 GOING IN THROUGH MEANING

It may well be possible, and intellectually productive, to view language, as the TG approach does, as a system of abstract rules which are applied in order to end up with a grammatically correct sentence; but there are doubts about whether this view captures to any useful extent the psychological processes involved when users actually produce or understand language. More importantly, there is little doubt that it does not reflect how the users themselves view language. They respond above all to the meanings that are expressed and the ways in which those meanings are expressed. For the user, the following sentences have very different meanings because of the differences in the expected response (acknowledging, agreeing or informing):

> The UX fax machine has got a brilliant memory.

> The UX fax machine has got a brilliant memory, hasn't it?

> Has the UX fax machine got a brilliant memory?

Similarly, there are important differences between the following sentences because of the speaker's choice of a formal or intimate wording:

> Would you mind helping me with this?

> Gissa hand, will you?

The syntactic underpinning in the examples above is, of course, important in expressing the different meanings, but only as a tool which enables the primary function of language – communicating meanings in particular contexts – to be carried out. As always, the exact nature of the tool used depends on the task in hand. In linguistic terms, we can express this as the assumption that, since language has evolved for the function of communication, this must have a direct and controlling effect on its design features – in other words, the form of language can be substantially explained by examining its functions. Of course, we need to take into account the constraints of the 'raw materials': the predetermined (genetic) characteristics of the human mind which allow or encourage certain kinds of language forms, and disallow or discourage other kinds. TG provides a possible way of investigating those characteristics. But they clearly represent only half the story: we still need to examine the formative influences of the uses to which language is put. (We can see the contrast between the two approaches as a reflection of the old dichotomy of nature vs. nurture and, as always, the answer is most likely to lie in a combination of both.)

What happens, then, if we take the other tack and (like language users) start from meaning? The meanings that we may want to express, or the uses to which we may want to put language, are clearly 'messy': they appear so varied and so dependent on the infinite range of different contexts that it is difficult at first to see how we might impose some order on them. However, if we look at the grammatical options open to us, we can in fact relate those options fairly systematically to different kinds of meanings. Let us take just two examples of areas that we will examine in more detail later. We can relate the presence of modal verbs to the expression of the speaker's personal view of events and states in the external world. In the following example, the speaker evaluates 'this seeming strange at first' as only potentially valid ('may'):

> This *may* seem strange at first.

And we can relate the ordering of parts of the clause to the speaker's desire to signal how this message fits in with the preceding message(s). Compare what comes first in the second sentences in each of these pairs (and think about why the order is different, and whether the second sentences could be swapped):

> So, what do we mean by a miracle? *A miracle* is something exceedingly surprising that happens.

> So, what do we call these different phenomena? *Something exceedingly surprising that happens* is a miracle.

It may seem odd to say that ordering in the clause has 'meaning'; but it is only odd if we restrict meaning to 'propositional meaning', which, as I have suggested, is a narrower definition than we want (note that the three sentences about the fax machine above all have exactly the same propositional meaning: 'fax machine' + 'has' + 'brilliant memory'). If we take meaning as being the sum of what the speaker wants the hearer to understand – in other words, if we equate the **meaning** of a sentence with its **function** – then understanding how the present message fits in its context is clearly part of the meaning, just as the difference between a statement and a question is part of the meaning.

In describing the various kinds of meanings in this fairly general way (e.g. 'signalling how this message fits in with the preceding message(s)'), we are already beginning to set up categories of functions that we perform through language; and we can then go back to texts to see if there are other grammatical features which seem to be performing the same kind of function. But we are still in danger of ending up with a fairly random-seeming list of functions. Is there any way of arriving at an even more generalised grouping of meaning types, so that we can start to explain why we find the particular kinds of functions that we do? For this, we need to step back and, rather than looking at language structures, think about what we do with language. In the broadest terms, we use language to talk about things and events ('It's raining') and to get things done ('Sit down'). As we shall see, these are not mutually exclusive (the command 'Sit down' involves reference to the particular event of sitting rather than any other): indeed, the basic principle is that every time we use language we are doing both simultaneously. We will also see that we need to add a third major function, a kind of language-internal 'service function'; but, having simply established here that it is possible to identify a very small number of broad functions, we can leave further specification until, in Chapter 3, we start exploring how these major functions can be used to illuminate and explain the choices that are available in language.

I have at several points used the term 'choice' in discussing meanings. If we want to examine what a piece of language is intended to do (i.e. its function), we cannot avoid thinking in terms of choice. Clearly, speakers do not go round producing de-contextualised grammatically correct sentences: they have reasons for saying something, and for saying it in the way they do. To take a simple example, if you want to find out some information you are most likely to ask a question rather than make a statement; and, at a more detailed level, you are more likely to use an informal wording if you are talking to a friend rather than a formal one:

> What the hell was that noise?

But note that, in describing the example in this way, we have in fact set up two sets of context-dependent choices: question vs. statement, informal vs. formal. If you have reasons for doing (saying) one thing, the implication is that you could have done (said) something else if the reasons (the context) had been different.

Functional Grammar sets out to investigate what the range of relevant choices are, both in the kinds of meanings that we might want to express (or functions that we might want to perform) and in the kinds of wordings that we can use to express these meanings; and to match these two sets of choices. In order to identify meaning choices, we have to look outwards at the **context**: what, in the kind of society we live in, do we typically need or want to say? What are the contextual factors which make one set of meanings more appropriate or likely to be expressed than another? But at the same time we need to identify the linguistic options (i.e. the lexical and structural possibilities that the language system offers for use), and to explore the meanings that each option expresses. These are complementary perspectives on the same phenomenon, one, as it were, from the bottom up – from wording to context – and the other from the top down – from context to wording. Looking from the bottom up, the use of the 'the hell' in the question above means, i.e. has the function of expressing, informality (amongst other things): in other words, one thing that our grammatical description must account for is the lexical and structural means by which different degrees of formality are expressed. Looking from the top down, the fact that the speaker is talking to a friend makes appropriate the use of informal wordings: in other words, we need a description of the social context which includes degrees of familiarity between people interacting with each other as a relevant factor influencing language choices.

Note that the use of the term 'choice' does not necessarily imply a conscious process of selection by the speaker: what we aim to uncover through a functional analysis are the reasons why the speaker produces a particular wording rather than any other in a particular context (in some ways, it would almost be as true to talk of the wording choosing the speaker). In writing this book, there are certain choices that I am very aware of making, e.g. the decision to sometimes address 'you' directly rather than always avoiding this by using passives, etc. (both decisions are possible in a textbook, and I have consciously set out to sound 'interactive' in parts). But there are many 'choices' that I am constrained to make by the kind of context in which I am using language: except in quotes, and most probably in section 4.5 where I deal with swearing, is it likely that I will use the structures associated with swearing? It is only in self-conscious, contrived situations like the present discussion that such choices even present themselves as possible: but the choice not to swear has nevertheless been made (or, rather, made for me). These are deliberately crude examples; but the principle applies in every detail of the wordings that I 'choose'.

One important implication of the functional view of language is that context and language are interdependent. This might seem too strong a way of putting it: it looks as though language could be seen as dependent on context – because the speaker is in an informal context, he is likely to use informal language – but not necessarily the other way round. But note that the use of informal language also contributes to creating the informal context: if the example question above were uttered by, say, a TV journalist interviewing a government minister, it would sound odd precisely because it would conjure up an inappropriate context. We can use the term 'construe' to talk about this kind of reflexivity. The wording 'the hell' construes informality: that is, it simultaneously reflects and constructs an informal context. Similarly, 'the glass broke' construes a slightly different view of events from 'I broke the glass' and 'Sit down' construes a different relationship between the speaker and hearer from 'Would you like to sit down?'.

At a broader level, our experiences in the world clearly influence what we normally talk about and the way we talk about it: for example, we are not impassive observers of the world, and we typically evaluate events that we talk about (and the lexico-grammatical resources of the language therefore offer ways of performing this evaluation). At the same time, the way we normally talk about these experiences (and the way we hear other people talk about them) influences the way we see them: for example, in talking about history, school textbooks typically teach us to use terms like 'industrialisation', and we are thereby trained to view history as consisting of isolatable meaningful processes like these (as opposed to, say, 'denaturisation', or even a random sequence of accidental events, which, for all we know, might be an equally valid view of what has gone on).

By formulating our approach to linguistic description in the kind of terms used above – choices amongst relevant options in context – we are deliberately opening up the path towards grammatically based text analysis (where 'text' means any instance of language in use): at each stage, we can ask why the writer or speaker is expressing this particular meaning in this particular way at this particular point. I mentioned earlier that TG takes linguistics towards biology; functional grammar takes it towards sociology: the systematic study of relevant features in the culture and society which form the context in which language is used. Both approaches, through form and meaning, ask essentially the same question about language: how can we explain why language has the main features that it does? But whereas the form-based approach finds the answer in the way our brains are structured, the meaning-based approach finds it in the way our social context is structured. (Of course, the different answers depend very largely on the fact that each approach takes a different view of the 'main features' that need to be explained.) Although our focus in the rest of the book will be on choices within the grammatical systems, we shall be regularly looking outwards towards the wider contextual factors that are construed by these choices.

1.2 Language, context and function: a preliminary exploration

If it is true that language and context are inextricably linked, any stretch of language should, to a greater or lesser extent, come trailing clouds of context with it: we should be able to deduce a great deal about the context in which the language was produced, the purpose for which it was produced, and the reasons why it was expressed in the way it was. We can check this in a preliminary way by looking at a simple example. I have deliberately chosen one which conjures up a very clear context; but can you go from that to explain as much as possible about the language choices in terms of who the interactants are and what the speaker's purposes are? My commentary follows, but you will find it useful to try your own analysis before reading it.

> once upon a time, there was a big, bad bear

The context is obviously a fairy story, probably told by an adult to a young child. This is most clearly signalled by 'once upon a time', which is used almost only in fairy stories (so much so that, if used in another context, it imports the very specific fairy tale context, however fleetingly). The individual story-teller hardly needs to 'choose' this opening: he knows that this is how fairy stories start. However, it is worth considering why this type of narrative should have such an immediately recognisable opening. One important factor is the addressee: a relatively unsophisticated language user, for whom very clear signals of purpose are necessary. The conventional opening signals something like: 'I'm not going to tell you to do anything; I'm not going to tell you off; all you need to do is to sit back and enjoy the story that is coming up.' In addition, although the expression belongs grammatically to the group of adverbials which specify time ('Once', 'Yesterday', 'Three years ago', etc.), it clearly does not in fact specify a real time. It thus signals that the narrative is a fictional one rather than, say, an account of what the story-teller did last year.

The clause structure ('there was ...') is an existential one (see 5.2.4). It introduces one of the main characters without saying that the bear was involved in any particular action – the action will presumably start in the next clause. Thus it stages the information, building up the story in increments that are manageable to the inexperienced language processor to whom the story is addressed. What we are told about the bear apart from its existence is that it is big and bad. The alliteration is obviously striking here: it appeals to children's pleasure in incidental patternings of sound, rather like wordplay at a more sophisticated level (in adult texts we are more likely to rewrite something to remove alliteration if it happens to occur). At the same time, it serves to reinforce the non-real, poetic nature of the story, perhaps reducing the potential frighteningness of the animal (cf. the effect of 'an enormous, savage bear'). It is also worth commenting on the fact that the speaker evaluates the character as he introduces it. In sophisticated narratives such as novels, we expect to be skilfully guided towards an evaluation of characters without having the author's evaluation thrust upon us; but here the child is told in advance that the bear is bad. The adult takes on the responsibility of setting out the required set of values for the child, partly no doubt as a reflection of his assessment of the child's restricted ability to do the necessary inferencing for himself (we will see a similar lack of confidence in young language users' expertise in processing language in 7.4). In addition, the evaluation opens up generic expectations of how the story will unfold: the bear will somehow cause problems for the good characters who will be along in a moment, but will in the end be defeated. Children learn very rapidly to recognise conventional story lines, as long as the signals are clear enough.

These are only some of the main points that can be made about how this piece of language works in its context. I have not, for example, touched on the broader issues of the role of story-telling in the socialisation of children. I have deliberately outlined the points as informally as I can; but what I hope the discussion shows is the kind of thing that we want to be able to discuss in a more formalised way. The grammatical system that we set up should provide categories that relate to the communicative purposes and choices that we have identified. In the rest of the book, I shall be setting out a functional approach based closely on Michael Halliday's work, which allows us to do this in a systematic and satisfying way.

§   Refer to Exercise 1.1.

EXERCISE 1.1

Analyse the following extracts in the same way as the fairy story opening: identify as much as you can about the context from which the extract comes, and discuss any features of the wording (lexis and structure) that you can relate to that context. The lexis will often provide the easiest clues, but try to go beyond that to identify other features as well.

1 Day return to Liverpool, please.
2 Appearances can be deceptive. But not in this case. The new Mercedes E-class looks different. And is different. It has the most aerodynamic body we've ever built. The best in its class.
3 Well you see she wrote this letter saying that she'd been ringing and what we couldn't understand when we spoke to Liz was she knew you

were going to Peru and she knows you don't put the cats in the cattery when you go away so it was obvious where we were.

4   Old Brother Rhys was sitting up beside his neatly made bed, not far from the fire, nodding his ancient, grey-tonsured head. He looked proudly complacent, as one who has got his due against all the odds, stubbly chin jutting, thick old eyebrows bristling in all directions, and the small, sharp eyes beneath almost colourless in their grey pallor, but triumphantly bright.

5   While this handbook will give intending applicants the information they need, students must, in order to obtain up-to-date, full and official information about entrance requirements and courses, write direct to the institutions of their choice at least a year before they hope to begin their studies, so that they will have decided to which institutions they wish to seek admission, and obtained the necessary application form, well before the closing date for receipt of applications.

6   To make brown rolls divide the dough into 18 equal portions – each should weigh about 50 g (2 oz). On an unfloured surface roll each piece of dough into a ball inside your cupped hand. Press down hard at first, then ease up to shape them nicely.

7   In Section 37–2 we found the directions of maximum and minimum intensity in a two-source interference pattern. We may also find the intensity at *any* point in the pattern. To do this, we have to combine the two sinusoidally varying fields (from the two sources) at a point P in the radiation pattern, taking proper account of the phase difference of the two waves at point P, which results from the path difference.

8   But I am carried back against my will into a childhood where autumn is bonfires, marbles, smoke; I lean against my window fenced from evocations in the air. When I said autumn, autumn broke.

2

Identifying clauses and clause constituents

2.1 Breaking up the sentence and labelling the parts

At this stage, it is possible that the framework which I have set out in Chapter 1 will strike you as rather abstract, and the full implications of adopting the functional approach may not be easy to grasp. This is something of a Catch-22 situation: you can only really understand the reasons for taking a particular approach when you understand the approach as a whole; but in order to understand this you need a general framework into which you can fit the various aspects as they are introduced. This means that you may find it useful to re-read Chapter 1 after reading the rest of the book (and in the final chapter I will come back to some of the themes in the light of the intervening discussion).

In the present chapter I want to turn to some more concrete preliminaries: the ways in which we can split up the sentence into parts, so that we can later go on to look at the particular functions which each part serves. As well as reviewing the different kinds of elements which make up sentences, one of the main purposes of the chapter is to go rapidly over the basic terminology that I will be using. Technical terms which are specific to Hallidayan functional grammar, or which are used in a special sense, will be defined and explained as they are introduced in the book. However, there are other terms which I will be assuming are familiar to you but which I will look at briefly in this chapter, just so that we can confirm that we are on common ground. If you have done grammatical analysis before, you will probably find that most of this chapter tells you nothing new, and you can safely skim through it rapidly (but check section 2.2 on ranks, which organises the familiar topics in a possibly unfamiliar way).

2.1.1 RECOGNISING CONSTITUENTS

As a start, I assume that you will be familiar with the main terms for word classes: **noun, verb, adjective, adverb, preposition, auxiliary verb, modal verb, pronoun,** and **conjunction.** I also assume that you will be able to recognise them in text and to recognise when there might be some doubt. For example, in what ways might there be some hesitation over labelling the word class of the words in italics in the following examples?

I heard a *car* door slam.

Children ran *screaming* down the street.

Heller's music was new. *So* were many of the piano works composed by Schumann.

Other visitors, *however*, regret the lack of a residents' lounge.

It has a slightly old-fashioned air *apart* from the dining conservatory.

We came about nine years *ago*.

I am less interested here in deciding on a 'right' label than in showing that there are areas of uncertainty; but, for the record, these are my comments on the words in italics. 'Car' is a noun, but modifying another noun in a way that seems more typical of an adjective. 'Screaming' is a verb – and therefore counts as a clause by itself (see below) – but it could be analysed as an adjective (the adjectival aspects come out more strongly in 'screaming children'). 'So' is a pro-form (like a pro-noun), standing in for part of the clause: it may be called an adverb in grammar books, mainly because adverb is the ragbag category where words get put if they do not fit anywhere else. 'However' is generally classified as an adverb, for the same negative reason as 'so'. 'Apart' is most commonly used as an adverb, but here it functions with 'from' as a two-word preposition. And 'ago' belongs in a class of its own, since it behaves like no other word in English – but, as you might guess, it is usually thrown in amongst the adverbs.

At a more general level, much of the analysis will rest implicitly on the distinction between **open-set** and **closed-set** word classes. Nouns, verbs, adjectives, and, to a large extent, adverbs are open sets in that it is not in principle possible to draw up a complete list of each set. For example, the number of nouns in English is open-ended: not only is the number very large, but new nouns may be added at any time by affixation, etc. (when I used 'frighteningness' in Chapter 1, the spell-checker on my word-processor did not recognise it). These sets are also called lexical words or 'content' words, in that they typically refer fairly clearly to entities and events in the world outside language – that is, they express the propositional content of the message. Closed-set word classes – also called grammatical words or 'form' words – consist of a relatively small and stable number of items. For example, a definitive list of the English pronouns can be easily drawn up, and changes in the list happen rarely (though they are not unknown: at the moment, as a consequence of the increasing use of 'they' as the gender-neutral singular third-person pronoun, a new reflexive form, 'themself', seems to be entering the language, e.g. 'In such cases, a student may nominate themself'). The words in closed sets are typically described as having a grammatical function: rather than expressing the propositional content of the message, they link parts of the message to each other (e.g. conjunctions, prepositions), or express 'subsidiary' aspects of the message (e.g. auxiliary verbs can indicate when the event expressed by the main verb takes place), and so on. As we shall see, within Functional Grammar such functions are actually treated not as subsidiary but as a crucial part of the meaning. Some grammatical systems such as transitivity (see Chapter 5) involve mainly open-set words, whereas other equally important systems such as conjunction (see Chapter 7) involve mainly closed-set words.

Moving up from individual words, we will be looking explicitly at **groups** (especially in Chapter 9), but you will find the discussion easier to follow if you are familiar with the idea that the words in a clause can often be grouped together into separate components of the clause each consisting of more than one word. This is obvious with words like 'the', which form a unit with the following noun; but can you identify the parallels between the following sentences in terms of groups?

Charity is business.

The ordinary little North Bavarian town used to be one of the main iron-mining centres of the region.

This comfortable family-run old farmhouse on the unspoilt southern shore of Ullswater has been a long-time favourite of Guide readers, particularly walkers and climbers.

One aspect of Trollope's reputation that can find no place in the present study is his fame as a writer of travel books.

If you are familiar with groups, you will have seen that each of the four sentences consists of three groups: the middle group in each case comprises a form of the verb 'be' ('is', 'used to be', 'has been', 'is'); everything before the verbal group forms a single nominal group (i.e. a group centred around a noun), and so does everything after it. What I am calling groups here are sometimes called phrases (in Chapter 1, I mentioned noun phrases – NPs – in discussing TG). In Hallidayan grammar, on the other hand, a clear difference is made between groups and phrases: the latter is only used to refer to prepositional phrases (see 2.2 below).

One distinction within groups that we need to make is that between **finite** and **non-finite verbal groups** (these are sometimes confusingly referred to as finite and non-finite verbs). This distinction will be discussed briefly in 4.3.5, but it is important particularly in relation to clauses (see next paragraph). A finite verbal group is traditionally defined as one which shows tense, whereas a non-finite group does not. Since tense is often shown in the auxiliary rather than in the main verb, this helps to explain why I have said that finiteness is a property of the group rather than just of the verb. Can you identify the verbal groups in the following sentences and decide if they are finite or non-finite? Are there any doubtful cases?

> She would start with them, ticking off their names after each call.

> Mr Howard does his best to out-sentence Mr Straw.

> The jobs pay £350 a week and have been created as the plant gears up for the production of new V8 engines for a range of Jaguar cars to replace the ageing XJS.

> Anna's career was also closely bound up with the Ladies' Land League, and she was persuaded by Fanny to return to Ireland at the end of 1880 and organise the League there.

The clear cases are as follows. Finite groups: 'would start'; 'does'; 'pay', 'have been created', 'gears up' (a phrasal verb); 'was persuaded'. Non-finite groups: 'ticking off' (another phrasal verb); 'to out-sentence'; 'to replace'; 'to return', '(to) organise'. The doubtful cases are 'ageing' ('adjectives' like this derived from a non-finite verbal form have an uncertain status between verbs and adjectives, but for most purposes they are best taken as adjectives), and 'was ... bound up' (this could be a passive verbal group, but here it seems better to analyse it as 'was' = finite verbal group, 'closely bound up' = adjectival group − contrast this with 'was persuaded', which is clearly a passive form).

Following on from this point about verbal groups, I will also be assuming on the whole that you can identify the boundaries of clauses. For our purposes, a **clause** is (potentially) any stretch of language centred around a verbal group. Thus, the following example has four clauses:

> Bedrooms are individually decorated, and while you are having dinner your room is tidied and the beds folded down.

You might like to verify this by identifying the verbs and then marking the clause boundaries (note that the final clause is elliptical, in that the auxiliary 'are' is understood as carried over from 'is' in the preceding clause; and there is the same doubt about 'are decorated' as about 'was bound up' above − again, the passive reading is less appropriate). Sometimes it is said that a clause must have a finite verbal group and that, if there is a non-finite group, we call it a phrase. However, in Hallidayan grammar clauses may be either finite or non-finite, depending on whether the verbal group is finite or non-finite. Can you therefore identify the clause boundaries in the four sentences above that we analysed for finite and non-finite verbal groups?

You should find two clauses in the first sentence (one finite, one non-finite), two in the second (ditto), four in the third (three finite, one non-finite) and four in the fourth (two finite, two non-finite). But what about these sentences (one of which you saw above)?

Today, however, she is struggling to finish a sentence, which is not something that ever happens to her in the television studio, because she is crying.

One aspect of Trollope's reputation that can find no place in the present study is his fame as a writer of travel books.

In the first sentence, we have 'is struggling to finish'. This includes two verbal groups, one finite ('is struggling') and one non-finite ('to finish'). However, they are not analysed as two clauses: instead they form one **complex verbal group** – a concept that will be discussed more fully in 9.3. In the second sentence, we have a clear finite clause 'that can find no place in the present study', but it is 'inside' something that we have already identified as a single nominal group. This is in fact an embedded clause – a concept that will be discussed more fully in 2.2 below and again in 9.1.1. There is also an embedded clause in the first sentence ('that ever happens to her in the television studio').

So far we have simply counted the clauses in a sentence; but we can also look at the relations between the clauses. There is a traditional distinction between **main** and **subordinate clauses**, and between **coordination** and **subordina-tion**. Can you identify the main and subordinate clauses in these examples? And can you see any differences in the various cases of coordination?

Bedrooms are individually decorated, and while you are having dinner your room is tidied and the beds folded down.

Anna's career was also closely bound up with the Ladies' Land League, and she was persuaded by Fanny to return to Ireland at the end of 1880 and organise the League there.

Although the back door of the cottage could be locked and they had left her the key, an intruder could easily break in through a window.

In the first example, you should find three coordinated main clauses and one subordinate clause ('while ...'); in the second, two coordinated main clauses and two coordinated subordinate non-finite clauses ('to return ... and organise ...'); and in the third, one main clause and two coordinated subordinate clauses ('Although ... and ...'). One thing that the analysis shows is that coordination can occur at different levels: between main or subordinate clauses, and between finite or non-finite clauses. This is a point we will come back to in Chapter 10.

2.1.2 STRUCTURAL AND FUNCTIONAL LABELS

So far in this chapter, I have avoided using some terms that you might have expected to see, like Subject and Object. This is deliberate, because it is essential in a functional approach to have different sets of labels according to whether we are describing the structure of a stretch of language or its function. Most of the rest of the book focuses on functional labels, for obvious reasons, so I will not spend long on them here; but it will be useful at this point to set out the distinction as clearly as possible. To show the difference, how can you label the following bit of language?

> their subsequent affair

You should be able to see that it is a nominal group; but is it Subject or Object? The answer, of course, is that it can be neither until it is used in a clause; and in a clause it can be either:

> *Their subsequent affair* climaxes in a showdown across the House divide. [= Subject]

> The death of his children overshadows *their subsequent affair*. [= Object]

It can also form part of a different type of clause constituent, an Adjunct:

> She got a divorce *because of their subsequent affair*.

As you will see, we are making a distinction between what it is (a nominal group) and what it does (e.g. Subject in the clause). Its structural label remains the same, whereas its functional label is dependent on the context in which it appears.

One image that will crop up several times in the book is that of **slots** and **fillers**. We can see the clause as having a number of functional slots, such as Subject, which can be filled by elements (groups) with certain kinds of structural qualities. For example, the Subject and Object slots are normally both filled by a nominal group; and so on. We can show this as in Figure 2.1 for the sentence:

> He paid his bill very casually.

Types of group ⇓	*nominal group* *e.g.* [1] He [2] his bill	*verbal group* *e.g.* paid	*adverbial group* *e.g.* very casually
Clause functions	NG [1] └────┘ *Subject*	VG └────┘ *Predicator*	NG [2] AG └────┘ └────┘ *Object* *Adjunct*

Fig 2.1 Functional slots and structural fillers

One reason for using this approach is that it allows us to show how the functional slots may in fact be filled by different structural constituents. Most obviously, the Adjunct slot is often filled by a prepositional phrase rather than an adverbial group:

> He paid his bill *by credit card*.

But we can also find, for example, the Subject slot sometimes filled by an adverbial group or an embedded clause:

Tomorrow is another day.

To lose one parent, Mr Worthing, may be regarded as a misfortune.

The traditional labels for the functional slots in the clause give the abbreviation SPOCA: Subject, Predicator, Object, Complement, Adjunct. (Sometimes 'Verb' is used instead of Predicator, but that is mixing a structural label with the functional ones.) Whereas, in traditional terms, the Object is the entity that the Subject 'does' the Predicator to, 'Complement' is used to label a nominal or adjectival group which refers to the same entity as the Subject, or describes the Subject. The Predicator in these cases is a linking verb such as 'be':

Joan is *something of a saint*.

The first prize is *a trip to the Bahamas*.

An Adjunct is typically an adverbial group or a prepositional phrase giving some kind of background information about the event expressed by the Predicator (e.g. when, where, how or why it happened). Just to check, can you label the functional parts of these clauses?

Charity is business.

During dinner your room is tidied.

In my maths classes I am on the horns of another dilemma.

Their subsequent affair climaxes in a showdown.

London could no longer supply milk for her population.

On the first day I wept bitterly.

The analyses are: SPC; ASP; ASPC; SPA; SP(A)OA (the brackets indicate that 'no longer' is an A which appears in the middle of the P 'could supply'); ASPA. In Chapter 4, I will be setting out a slightly modified version of these labels; but, more importantly, I will be introducing a range of other types of functional labels, reflecting the fact that clauses do not express only one kind of meaning (or perform only one kind of function). To reiterate what I have emphasised above, the main point to take from this section is the difference between the two types of labelling: structural and functional. In TG, as I explained in Chapter 1, functional labels are avoided as much as possible, since they are too closely associated with context and therefore introduce undesirable fuzziness into the description. In functional grammar, on the other hand, we obviously rely primarily on functional labels, but structural labels are used in exploring exactly how different meanings are expressed. To help keep the distinction clear in the discussion to come, I will follow Halliday's custom of using an initial capital letter for all functional labels such as Subject.

2.2 Ranks

So far we have been referring in a fairly informal way to the different parts of sentences that we can identify. It will be useful at this point to set up a more systematic approach to looking at the constituents on which our analyses are going to be based.

One way of doing this is by using the theoretical concept of the **rank scale**. This is based on the assumption that we can split any meaningful unit at one rank, or level, into smaller units of a different kind at the rank below. Thus, for example, we can divide the following clause into three groups:

[Tensions at work] [could undermine] [your usual sunny optimism].

This analysis represents an explicit claim that we can identify two different ranks – clause and group – and also an implicit claim that the distinction is analytically useful: that the concept of ranks captures something about the way this stretch of language is put together, and that we need a rank between the intuitively identifiable ranks of clause and word. This seems justified on a number of grounds: for example, we can move the groups around as complete units in different grammatical structures while keeping recognisably the same propositional meaning (although, of course, the functional meaning will change):

[Your usual sunny optimism], [tensions at work] [could undermine]

What [could undermine] [your usual sunny optimism] is [tensions at work]

[Your usual sunny optimism] [could be undermined] by [tensions at work]

The groups themselves can clearly be divided further, into **words**, for example:

[{your}{usual}{sunny}{optimism}]

This division is intuitively necessary (we do, after all, separate words by spaces in writing, which indicates that we see them as separate elements), but, equally importantly, it corresponds to identifiable functional divisions: each word clearly contributes a distinct element to the meaning of the group. We can in fact go below the word and identify meaningful units which make up words. These are not, as one might perhaps expect, letters or sounds, or even syllables: those are not in themselves meaningful (the letter 'i' and the syllable 'ti' in 'optimism' do not mean anything), and they need to be dealt with in a completely different part of the description of the language. The smallest meaningful units are **morphemes**. For example, 'sunny' can be analysed as the lexical morpheme 'sun-' plus the grammatical morpheme '-(n)y' (which changes the noun into an adjective, compare 'fun/funny'). In a similar way 'optimism' can be analysed as 'optim-' plus '-ism': 'optim-' is not a free lexical morpheme as 'sun' is, but it combines with several grammatical morphemes such as '-ist', '-ise' and '-al' and makes a similar contribution to the meaning of each resulting word. We therefore have a rank scale consisting of the following four ranks: clause, group, word, morpheme.

There are two important aspects of the rank scale hypothesis which need to be made explicit. The first is that units at each rank can be made up only of units from the rank below: a clause is therefore taken to consist of groups, not of words. Of course, a group, for example, may consist of a single word:

[{Christmas}] [{starts}] [{here}]

Nevertheless, it is as a group that each unit functions in the clause (each group here could be expanded: e.g. 'Our Christmas will start right here.'). The second is that the analysis is, in principle, exhaustive: every element is accounted for at each rank. We cannot have 'spare bits' floating around in the clause. Every word has a function as part of a group and every group has a function as part of a clause (as we shall see, this principle has to be relaxed in practice).

You may wonder why there is no 'sentence' rank above clause. The main reason is that we can adequately account for sentences by introducing the concept of **clause complexes**: two or more clauses linked by coordination and/or subordination in a larger structural unit. This sounds very like the traditional description of a sentence. However, as you will know if you have ever tried to transcribe an informal conversation, the sentence is an idealisation of the written language which it is often difficult to impose on spoken language. We also find that full stops, which mark the boundaries of sentences in writing, may be used between clauses which are grammatically dependent on each other:

> Ticket agencies then resold them for $400. Thus capitalising on the unique skill of this specialised workforce.

The term **'sentence'** is therefore best reserved to label stretches of written text bounded by full stops or the equivalent. Typically, written sentences correspond to clause complexes – but not always (the example above comprises two sentences but one clause complex). A more theoretical reason for not including the sentence as a separate rank is the fact that two clauses may be combined into a complex unit, but the choices (slots) available in the second clause are basically the same as in the first. As we move from group to clause, the set of options is very different: in the group we have no equivalent, for example, of the Subject slot in the clause (see 9.1.1 for an outline of slots in nominal groups). But there is no such clear-cut change as we move from clause to clause complex: the same SPOCA slots recur. An image that I find useful is that of a tandem: it is different from a bicycle – it has two crossbars, two seats and two sets of handlebars – and yet functionally it is still the same sort of machine as a bicycle (not least because it consists mainly of the same structural elements like handlebars).

The idea of complexes is perhaps more straightforward at group rank. In a clause like the following, it is reasonably easy to accept that we have only one Subject (in italics):

A huge sofa and two armchairs surrounded the fireplace.

But the Subject consists of two nominal elements, either of which could be Subject on its own, with a third element ('and') linking them into a single complex unit. The clause complex is simply a parallel phenomenon at the next rank up. As one might predict, it is also possible to identify word complexes (e.g. 'These play an *essential though unexplained* role') and morpheme complexes (e.g. 'pro- and anti-marketeers'); but these are linguistic resources which are not as regularly drawn on in expressing meanings as complexes at the two upper ranks are, and we will not deal with them in any further detail.

Figure 2.2 gives an overview of the rank scale as outlined so far (the reasons for the number of slashes around clauses will become clear in Chapter 10).

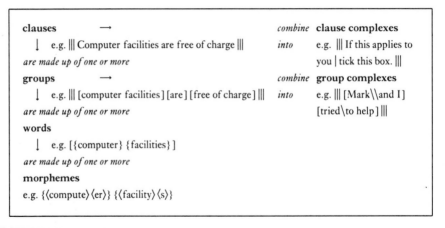

Fig 2.2 The rank scale

This deceptively simple picture needs two main additions to make it fit most of the observable phenomena. The first is the inclusion of **prepositional phrases**. We will look in more detail at how and why these are different from groups in 9.2; but for the moment, I will simply slip them in as an extension of the rank scale. They lie at roughly the same level as groups, though Halliday (1994: 215) points out that they have arrived there from different directions: the group is like a 'bloated word' (I mentioned above that it may in fact consist of a single word), whereas the phrase is more like a 'shrunken clause' (it must consist of at least two different parts, the preposition and the nominal group dependent on it). The prepositional phrases in the following examples are in italic:

Her education had been completed *in Switzerland.*

We drove *for a couple of hours into the mountains* and arrived *at a hotel.*

The second addition is the concept of **embedding**. This is a general principle which allows a unit to be expanded by the inclusion of another unit from a higher rank or, in some cases, the same rank. This is a phenomenon which will crop up at several points (e.g. in discussing the identification of the Subject in 4.3.2), so I will only give a few examples here. The main site for embedding is the nominal group (see also 9.1.1). Very frequently, this has a prepositional phrase embedded in it:

> [Her attitude *to emancipation*] was probably not far different from the Queen's.

> [Experiments *in the dehydration and evaporation of milk*] were also taking place at this time.

Since a prepositional phrase itself includes a nominal group, that nominal group may have another prepositional phrase embedded in it (e.g. 'of milk' in the second example above) and the embedding can obviously be repeated again, certainly more than once without sounding odd:

> ... has put forward [a proposal *for the doubling of the assisted places scheme for independent schools in the area*].

A nominal group may also have a clause embedded in it:

> It is impossible to trace [all the influences *which led to the Gothic revival in architecture*].

> But [the idea *that this new method could bring profits*] soon drew other manufacturers into the field.

> They showed [no disposition *to chat*].

An embedded clause may function by itself as the equivalent of a nominal group:

> [*That there had soon been a reconciliation*] was due to Albert.

> [*What really happened*] cannot be definitely established.

> She never knew [*what had happened between the two men*].

There are other types of embedding, but, once the principle is grasped, they are mostly straightforward to deal with. Note that the term 'ranking clause' is used to distinguish non-embedded from embedded clauses. If we mark the clause boundaries with slashes, we can see that the first example below consists of one ranking clause, whereas the second consists of two (and thus forms a clause complex):

> ||| That there had soon been a reconciliation was due to Albert. |||

> ||| He argues | that the banks have taken advantage of a naturally docile workforce. |||

There are certain problems with the rank scale as a way of looking at the structure of clauses. We do not need to go into most of them, since we will only be using the rank scale as a practical starting-point and can overlook theoretical objections. However, there is one which will come up, especially in Chapter 4. The rank scale prioritises the view of the clause in terms of constituents but there are times when we will want to examine elements in the clause that do not fit easily in the scale. I said above that only groups, not words, have a function at the level of the clause; but in Chapter 4, for example, we will be focusing on the Finite, which has a crucial function directly at clause level, but which does not constitute a group (or even a word in some cases). Similarly, in a sentence like the following:

He felt *certain* there *must* be a clue he had forgotten.

both 'certain' and 'must' are clearly contributing to expressing the same meaning – his attitude towards the validity of there being a clue – and yet they are very different kinds of constituents which the rank scale will separate, thus obscuring their functional symbiosis.

Nevertheless, despite drawbacks like these, the rank scale provides an extremely useful and systematic basis for the initial analysis of clauses into their constituent parts. Once we have a fairly secure picture of what the main parts are, we can move on to a functional analysis, if necessary adapting or discarding the divisions made according to the rank scale.

§   Refer to Exercise 2.1.

EXERCISE 2.1

The first text below is a letter to the medical advice column of a general magazine, and the second is the answer. Divide the texts into their constituent clauses and groups (and phrases). Identify any clause or group complexes, and any embedded clauses. Label the groups/phrases in terms of their function in the clause – SPOCA.

1   Recently, I've had a very painful shoulder which makes lifting my arm almost impossible. My GP diagnosed a 'frozen shoulder', prescribed painkillers and told me to stay off work for a week. What causes it and will it get better?

2   Frozen shoulder can result from muscle sprain or wear and tear. It may happen after surgery to the chest, or a heart attack. Movement is usually painful and difficult.

It can be treated with pain-killers, anti-inflammatory pills, or – in severe cases – a steroid injection in the shoulder. Physiotherapy aids recovery. Recovery time varies from a week to over a year.

(*best*, 14 November 1995, 45/95, p. 26: data collected by
Sultan Al-Sharief)

3

An overview of Functional Grammar

3.1 Three kinds of meaning

I pointed out in Chapter 1 that in functional approaches to grammar we essentially equate meaning with function. It is worth exploring in a little more detail what this involves. Suppose, for example, that we want to explain to a foreign learner of English what this sentence means:

And he was indifferent, are you saying?

We might get by in this case simply by focusing on what we can call the dictionary meaning of 'indifferent' and assuming that the learner understands the rest. But what about the following sentence? Before reading on, can you think of how you would explain it?

It's not as if I'd been rude to him.

Here we will almost certainly need to resort to more circumlocution, perhaps something along the lines of 'The speaker is saying that the man's behaviour would be understandable if she had been rude to him, but she wasn't: in other words, we say "it's not as if" when we are talking about a situation that we are unhappy about for some reason, and we want to suggest a possible excuse for the people involved but to say that the excuse isn't valid.' Note that what this admittedly clumsy explanation focuses on is the way in which expressions like the one in the example are used, i.e. their function. The meaning is the use.

You could argue that this different approach to the explanation is only because 'it's not as if' is an idiom where the meaning is more than the sum of the individual words. But, if we look back at the first example, we can see that there is in fact a good deal we could say about that sentence along the same kind of lines. For instance, we could point out that the speaker there wants to check whether s/he has understood what the other person means by offering a wording that the other person has not used ('indifferent') to see if the other person accepts it. The other person's response shows that this is how the speaker's message is interpreted:

'And he was indifferent, are you saying?' 'I wouldn't say indifferent.'

The reason why the explanation in terms of function might seem less necessary is that the grammar appears more 'transparent': for example, questions are typically used to find out or to check on information, so it could be thought that we do not need to comment on this feature of the sentence. However, if, as linguists, we want to make our explanation more explicit – to explain as exactly as possible how the sentence comes to have the form that it does – we need to talk about all the functions of the sentence, including the most obvious ones. We then explain how those functions are performed by particular choices of wording. By 'wording', I mean not just the individual words chosen, but all aspects of the way the meanings are expressed: for example, the placing of 'are you saying' at the end of the sentence expresses a slightly different meaning from placing it at the beginning. Thus the meaning is *always* more than the sum of the individual words – it is just that this is more obvious in the case of idioms.

This raises the question of how we can frame a grammatical description which includes an explanation of the meanings of whole messages rather than just individual words. In order to find an answer, we can rephrase the question in the kind of terms that were introduced in Chapter 1: how do we go about relating in a systematic way the functions performed by speakers to the wordings that they choose? I suggested that we can group types of meanings or functions into a relatively manageable number of categories. For example, we can identify a group of meanings relating to what the speaker expects the hearer to do (e.g. the functional difference between a statement and a question); and we can match these with sets of grammatical resources for expressing the meanings, including different choices in the ordering of elements in the verbal group ('you are' vs. 'are you?'). Another group is meanings relating to the speaker's assessment of the validity of his/her proposition; these meanings are typically expressed by the use of the modality resources of the language ('may', 'possibly', etc.). A further grouping is related to signalling how the message fits in with (makes sense in relation to) what else is said around it; these meanings are expressed, amongst other things, by the ordering of the constituents of the clause.

So far, then, we have considered meaning differences like those exemplified in the following rewordings:

Reid packed his bags.	vs.	What did Reid pack?
Reid packed his bags.	vs.	Reid may have packed his bags.
Reid packed his bags.	vs.	It was his bags that Reid packed.

I have deliberately not yet paid much attention to meaning differences like the following:

Reid packed his bags.	vs.	Reid packed his toothbrush.
Reid packed his bags.	vs.	Reid saw his bags.

These are probably the kinds of differences in meaning that spring most easily to mind: different wordings used to refer to different things and events in the world.

These differences are obviously very important and need to be accounted for in the grammar. The reason why I have appeared to downplay them is that they are sometimes taken to represent the only, or at least the dominant, kind of meaning that needs to be considered; but within Functional Grammar, they represent only one of three broad types of meanings that are recognised. It is important to understand that each of the three types contributes equally to the meaning of the message as a whole. It is also important to understand that each of the three types of meaning is typically expressed by different aspects of the wording of the clause. If we only take account of the different things or events referred to ('bags' vs. 'toothbrush', or 'packed' vs. 'saw'), we end up with an impoverished one-dimensional view of meaning.

We can summarise the three kinds of meanings that we have so far identified in an informal way as follows:

1. We use language to talk about our experience of the world, including the worlds in our own minds, to describe events and states and the entities involved in them.
2. We also use language to interact with other people, to establish and maintain relations with them, to influence their behaviour, to express our own viewpoint on things in the world, and to elicit or change theirs.
3. Finally, in using language, we organise our messages in ways which indicate how they fit in with the other messages around them and with the wider context in which we are talking or writing.

It might well be possible to establish other sets of categories: for example, some theoreticians have suggested functions such as 'expressive' (expressing one's own feelings and view of the world) as a separate category rather than including it in a broader category as I have done. In Hallidayan Functional Grammar, however, the three categories above are used as the basis for exploring how meanings are created and understood, because they allow the matching of particular types of functions/meanings with particular types of wordings to an extent that other categorisations generally do not.

3.1.1 THE THREE METAFUNCTIONS

All the more specific functions can be assigned to one or other of the three broad functions outlined above; and hence we refer to these broad functions as **metafunctions**. The labels for each of the metafunctions are reasonably transparent: the first is the **experiential**; the second is the **interpersonal**; and the third is the **textual**.

The grammar – that is, the description of the specific matches of function and wording – reflects this three-strand approach, in that it consists of three **components**, each corresponding to one of the metafunctions. For example, the interpersonal component of the grammar is the part where we describe all the options that we have in expressing interpersonal meanings. Thus each component has its own **systems** of choices: to stay with the interpersonal as the example, the system which includes the choice between interrogative meanings (questions) and declarative meanings (statements) belongs to the interpersonal component of the grammar. The result of a series of choices from any system is a **structure**. As we shall see in Chapter 4, if the speaker chooses the interrogative option, this will typically result in the structure Finite^Subject ('^' means 'followed by'), e.g. 'are you?', whereas the declarative option results in the structure Subject^Finite, e.g. 'you are'. When we put together the structures resulting from choices in all the relevant systems in each of the three components, we end up with a wording, a message.

This is a deliberately brief outline that it is probably difficult to take in fully as yet, but a simplified example may help to make things a little clearer. Let us suppose that a child in class complains that someone has taken her calculator while she was not looking. In that context, the teacher is expected to identify the child responsible and make him or her return the calculator. There are obviously many options open to him as to how he goes about this, but let us assume that he takes a fairly direct one. In experiential terms, he wants to refer to the action that has happened (taking) and the thing that the action was done to (the calculator); and he also wants to refer to the unknown doer of the action. He will thus opt for an experiential structure which expresses the event, the doer and the done-to: we can symbolise this as 'X/has taken/her calculator'. Simultaneously, in interpersonal terms, he wants his addressees, the children, to supply the missing information in his description, and he will therefore opt for an interrogative structure with the appropriate WH-word: 'who?' The WH-word is Subject, and therefore the ordering is Subject^Finite rather than the Finite^Subject ordering used for other interrogatives (for reasons that will be discussed in Chapter 4): 'Who has (taken her calculator)?' In textual terms, his starting-point is the missing element 'who', which is presumably uppermost in his mind; so he has no reason to move the WH-Subject from its most natural position at the beginning of his utterance. As a result of these choices (and others not included here), he produces the wording: 'Who's taken her calculator?'

It is important to emphasise that this is not intended as a description of successive steps in a process that the speaker goes through: I have to set it out step by step simply because of the linear nature of written language. We unpack the choices for analytical purposes, but the choices are usually all made – consciously or, in the main, unconsciously – at the same time. There are times when the process may become more staged and more conscious: for example, in redrafting written text I sometimes find myself deciding that a new starting-point will make the sentence fit in more clearly, which may mean that I also have to alter the wording in the rest of the sentence. But typically a functional description brings to light and separates closely interwoven decisions that we are not aware of making about how to word what we want to say. It also throws light, at a higher level, on how we decide to say what we do. I will come back to this briefly in 3.2 below.

3.1.2 THREE KINDS OF FUNCTION IN THE CLAUSE

In the discussion so far, I have gone from what the speaker (the teacher) wants to say to how he says it. However, we can also move in the other direction, starting from the utterance 'Who's taken her calculator?' and explaining retrospectively the choices that are embodied or 'realised' in the utterance. This is probably easier to grasp in practice, because we are starting at the concrete end, with an actual wording. Thus we can ask, for example, why he ordered the constituents in the way he did; what meaning he was expressing by the choice of a WH-word as Subject; and so on. This is generally the direction that the analyses in this book will take, not only because it is conceptually simpler in most respects but also because this is a book about grammar and the main aim is to describe the range of structures available and the meanings that they construe if they are chosen.

In doing the analysis from this end, we work with three different sets of labels, corresponding to the three different kinds of **functional roles** that the elements in the clause are serving. To give you a preliminary idea of what is involved, we can look at analyses of the calculator example from each of the three perspectives, and compare them with the analyses of possible rewordings. Try not to be put off by all the unfamiliar labels that will be appearing: I will not explain them in any detail here, since that will be the function of the three following chapters. The aim is simply to indicate what a three-strand functional description looks like.

Figure 3.1 shows the analysis of the clause in experiential terms.

Who	's taken	her calculator
Actor	*Process*	*Goal*

Fig 3.1 Analysis from the experiential perspective

To label 'Who' as Actor, for example, indicates that it has the function of expressing the (unknown) 'doer' of the action expressed in the process: in other words, we are looking at the clause from the experiential perspective of how entities and events in the world are referred to (in crude terms, who did what to whom and in what circumstances). From this perspective, 'Who' remains Actor even if we reword the example as in Figure 3.2.

Who	has	her calculator	been taken	by?
Actor		*Goal*	*Process*	

Fig 3.2 Experiential analysis of a passive clause

Figure 3.3 shows an analysis in interpersonal terms (this is only a partial analysis, but it is sufficient for our present purposes).

Who	's	taken	her calculator?
Subject	*Finite*	*Predicator*	*Complement*

Fig 3.3 Analysis from the interpersonal perspective

When we say that 'Who' is Subject, we are looking at the clause from the interpersonal perspective of how the speaker negotiates meanings with the listener (this function of Subject is a tricky concept, but I will be discussing it more fully in 4.3.3). Note that the passive rewording this time results in a change of Subject – see Figure 3.4 ('by who' forms an Adjunct which has been split up).

Who	has	her calculator	been taken	by?
Ad–	*Finite*	*Subject*	*Predicator*	*–junct*

Fig 3.4 Interpersonal analysis of a passive clause

Finally, Figure 3.5 shows the analysis in textual terms.

Who	's taken her calculator?
Theme	*Rheme*

Fig 3.5 Analysis from the textual perspective

To say that 'Who' is Theme means that we are looking at the clause from the textual perspective of how the speaker orders the various groups and phrases in the clause, in particular, which constituent is chosen as the starting-point for the message. With the simple example above, it is difficult to think of a natural rewording which would not have 'Who' as Theme (the passive version still keeps the same Theme); but we could imagine the teacher recounting the event later and starting by referring to the context in which his story took place – see Figure 3.6.

It is important to see that the different labels, even for the same constituent, identify different functions that it is performing in the clause. This multi-functionality is in fact the norm for clause constituents: typically, they are all

In the maths lesson today	someone took Gillian's calculator.
Theme	*Rheme*

Fig 3.6 Starting with a contextualising Adjunct

doing more than one thing at once – they are all contributing in different ways to the different kinds of meaning being expressed in the clause. The examples also show that, though there are tendencies for certain functions to be performed by the same constituent, e.g. Actor tends to be Subject, and Subject tends to be Theme, they can all be performed by different constituents. This reinforces the need for the three-dimensional analysis.

3.1.3 THREE KINDS OF STRUCTURE IN THE CLAUSE

I have focused above on individual functional roles (Actor, Subject, Theme); but note that each perspective has in fact identified a different kind of structure for the clause. The label 'Actor', for example, represents one function in the experiential structure Actor + Process + Goal. Typically, there is a fair amount of overlap in the way in which the three perspectives divide up the clause into parts, although there are significant differences. We can see this if we put together the three analyses of the original example, as in Figure 3.7.

Type of structure	Who	's	taken	her calculator?
Experiential →	*Actor*	*Process*		*Goal*
Interpersonal →	*Subject*	*Finite*	*Predicator*	*Complement*
Textual →	*Theme*	*Rheme*		

Fig 3.7 Three kinds of structure in the clause

The vertical lines show that many of the divisions are the same in two or all three of the structures. But note that the Theme + Rheme structure is simpler: it is only the first constituent which plays a crucial role in this structure, and the rest of the clause can be treated as a single unit. Note also that the experiential perspective is 'blind' to the separate existence of the Finite: in very simple terms, from this perspective we are only interested in what action is referred to, not in the time of the action in relation to the time of talking about it (the tense). Once we move on to more complex clauses, we will find that such differences in terms of which parts of the clause are highlighted from each perspective become greater.

3.1.4 BRINGING IT ALL TOGETHER

The combination of the three analyses in Figure 3.7 is a useful reminder that, although we separate the three perspectives for the purposes of grammatical analysis, there must be a point at which we bring them together again. The meaning of the clause comes from all three types of meaning simultaneously. We have seen a fairly simple example above (Figures 3.1 to 3.4), where a passive rewording means that the same element remains Actor and Theme but is no longer Subject. The change in wording, as always, reflects a change in meaning, though in this case it is quite difficult to pin down exactly what the difference is. Another example of related wordings, where the differences in meaning are perhaps more obvious, is the following (the original version is the first). What is the effect of each? What can you guess about the context of each, i.e. the sentences around them?

> No war had disturbed the country since 1815.

> Since 1815 the country had not been disturbed by any war.

> The country had not undergone any war since 1815.

The analyses are given in Figure 3.8. Use them to help you identify how the different meanings emerge (focus just on Actor, Subject and Theme). Which of the three seems the most neutral, i.e. the one that would fit into a wider range of contexts?

Here is my own brief commentary. With (a), the writer has emphasised in the preceding sentence that the general situation in Britain was peaceful; thus 'no war' is now the starting-point, the Theme. In the paragraph as a whole the topic is the effects of peace (the writer uses the pattern 'peace/war affected the country' several times); hence 'no war' is also Subject and Actor. In (b), the choice of 'since 1815' as Theme implies a time-scale as the framework: the Theme of the next sentence might well be something like 'In 1857, (however)'. The choice of 'the country' as Subject suggests that the discussion concerns the state of Britain in general; and the choice of 'any war' as Actor in the final slot of the sentence suggests that the concept of 'war' is likely to be picked up in the next sentence (quite possibly as Subject as well: e.g. 'the Indian Mutiny [= war] ended this peaceful period'). In (c), 'the country' is Actor, Subject and Theme, which suggests that we are in the middle of a discussion of the state of Britain, in which peace is probably just one aspect to be covered. We might well expect the next sentence to begin with 'it' [= 'the country'], or a variation of the same concept such as 'the British people'. Version (c) is perhaps the most neutral: (b) splits up the three functions of Actor, Subject and Theme, which suggests specific communicative pressures on the writer to balance the general topic (the country), the framework (dates) and the possible incoming sub-topic (war); while (a), though it also combines Actor, Subject and Theme, has a less expected element in these functions ('no war' is quite an odd concept to have as

(a)

	No war	had	disturbed	the country	since 1815
Experiential	*Actor*	*Process*	*Goal*	*Circumstance*	
Interpersonal	*Subject*	*Finite*	*Predicator*	*Complement*	*Adjunct*
Textual	*Theme*	*Rheme*			

(b)

	Since 1815	the country	had not	been disturbed	by any war
Experiential	*Circumstance*	*Goal*	*Process*		*Actor*
Interpersonal	*Adjunct*	*Subject*	*Finite*	*Predicator*	*Adjunct*
Textual	*Theme*	*Rheme*			

(c)

	The country	had not	undergone	any war	since 1815
Experiential	*Actor*	*Process*		*Goal*	*Circumstance*
Interpersonal	*Subject*	*Finite*	*Predicator*	*Complement*	*Adjunct*
Textual	*Theme*	*Rheme*			

Fig 3.8 Analyses of alternative wordings

Actor and Subject when you think about it), which suggests that the writer is covering a specific topic in a broader discussion.

As you can see, even with relatively simple examples it is hard to juggle all three perspectives at once. In the main section of the book, formed by Chapters 4, 5 and 6, we will in fact be examining each perspective in turn, with only occasional cross-references to the other perspectives, usually in the analyses of texts in the latter part of each chapter. Chapter 8, on grammatical metaphor, will start to draw the perspectives together; and in the final chapter I will discuss some aspects of how the three sets of choices interact in a particular text.

3.1.5 A FOURTH METAFUNCTION

Although I have not so far said it explicitly, I have implied at a number of points that the book will mostly be focusing on choices in the clause. This is not to say that we cannot identify similar kinds of choices at lower levels – in Chapter 9, we will be looking at what happens within groups. Nevertheless, it is in the clause that the main functional choices operate: just as Subject is a functional slot in the clause (see 2.1.2), so are Actor and Theme. The clause is the main resource through which we express meanings.

However, there is one further issue which we need to consider: what happens when clauses are combined into clause complexes? For this, we need to look at the types of relationships which can be established between clauses; and this involves bringing in a fourth metafunction: the **logical** metafunction. It is the logical component of the grammar that handles the similarities and differences in the way that the following pair of clauses can be combined:

> Estimates of the soot produced by the fires vary, *but* it is probably about 500,000 tonnes a month.

> *Although* estimates of the soot produced by the fires vary, it is probably about 500,000 tonnes a month.

Whereas the other three metafunctions relate mainly to the meanings that we express in our messages, the logical metafunction relates to the connections between the messages, and to the ways in which we signal these connections.

This formulation suggests that the logical metafunction may operate at levels other than just between clauses; and, indeed, there are clearly similarities between the combinations of clauses above and the following rewording with two separate sentences/clause complexes:

> Estimates of the soot produced by the fires vary. *However*, it is probably about 500,000 tonnes a month.

We can even go the other way and recognise functional similarities with the following rewording, where the meaning of one of the clauses is expressed in a prepositional phrase:

> *Despite* variations in the estimates of the soot produced by the fires, it is probably about 500,000 tonnes a month.

The logical metafunction will be explored more fully in Chapter 10.

3.2 Register and genre

In Chapter 1, I mentioned that socio–cultural factors influence or determine the kinds of things that we try to do through language, and thus the kinds of things that we say. So far in this chapter, on the other hand, I have talked only about the choices in how we say things; and in the rest of the book this will remain the focus of attention. 'How we can say things' is a very simplistic description of what the grammar of a language covers, but it does indicate the role of the grammar in offering conventionally accepted wordings to express our meanings. A more formal way of putting this is to describe grammar as the set of linguistic resources available to us for making meanings.

I have already suggested that the kinds of wordings which are available are themselves determined by the uses to which we want to put them; in other words, the linguistic resources are determined by the meanings that we want to make. In 1.1.2, I talked about 'wordings choosing the speaker': a crucial part of our language ability is knowing how things are typically – or even obligatorily – said in certain contexts. We can extend this to talk of 'meanings choosing the speaker': we also know what things are typically – or obligatorily – said in certain contexts. Although I will not be looking in any systematic way at the issue of what the broader contextual factors are and how they determine meanings, it will be useful to mention some of these factors particularly when we analyse texts.

The way in which these factors are accounted for in Functional Grammar is particularly by invoking the concepts of register and genre. **Register** is defined by Halliday (in Halliday & Hasan, 1985/89: 41) as 'variation according to use': that is, we typically use certain recognisable configurations of linguistic resources in certain contexts. There are three main dimensions of variation which characterise any register: what is being talked about (this is called the 'field'); the people involved in the communication and the relationship between them (the 'tenor'); and how the language is functioning in the interaction, e.g. whether it is written or spoken (the 'mode'). The fact that there are three areas is not accidental since each of them corresponds to one of the metafunctions: the field mainly determines the experiential meanings that are expressed; the tenor mainly determines the interpersonal meanings; and the mode mainly determines the textual meanings. In Exercise 1.1, you were in fact being asked to identify informally the register of the extracts – the context from which they come and the linguistic features which are typical of that context.

Genre, in very simple terms, can be seen as register plus purpose. That is, it includes the more general idea of what the interactants are doing through language, and how they organise the language event in order to achieve that purpose. As an example, we can take the following extract from a newspaper report (from the *Daily Star* for 25 November 1992):

Bacon 'n eggs stop prison riot

Prison officers broke up a jail riot yesterday – with bacon and eggs.

The aroma of hot breakfasts tempted 140 inmates out of a barricaded wing after an 11-hour, £2 million wrecking spree.

They were led off to a dining hall.

An insider said: 'The smell of bacon and eggs was too much to bear.'

Rescued

Prisoners went on the rampage at Highpoint prison, Suffolk, after warders foiled an escape bid by two of them.

This shows easily recognisable features that mark it as belonging to the register of journalism: at word level, the use of items like 'foiled', and set phrases like 'went on the rampage'; at group level, the dense packing of pre-modifiers in 'an *11-hour*, *£2 million wrecking* spree'; at clause level, the inclusion of a direct quote from someone involved, and, again, the foregrounding/backgrounding effect in the second sentence of the report, where the riot is referred to in a prepositional phrase, relegating it to providing the background for the main event of tempting the inmates with the smell of food. Beyond this, however, we can also point to generic features of how the text goes about its business. These include the headline and sub-heading – the former intended to be eye-catching, the latter typically uninformative and apparently intended simply to break up the text visually. They also include the staging of the text, starting with an expansion of the headline in the first sentence; followed by a further expansion in the next three sentences still focusing on the most 'newsworthy' aspect of the story; followed by the details, mostly about the riot, starting after the subheading and continuing for a further five sentences (not included here). At a less concrete level, we could also see the purpose of the story as being determined by the cultural expectations of the writer and readers: the bacon and eggs incident is more newsworthy than the riot itself, and the text as a whole reflects this.

This is only a very brief indication of the broader socio-cultural orientation of the functional approach that I will be setting out. I have included it here just before we begin the detailed examination of clause-level grammatical choices in order to re-emphasise that these are only part of the story, and that they can only be fully understood in the wider context.

4

Interaction in the clause: the interpersonal metafunction

4.1 Introduction

As emphasised in the previous chapter, one of the main purposes of communicating is to **interact** with other people: to establish and maintain appropriate social links with them. If we try to view language simply as a one-way system for telling other people things, we end up with a very distorted view of how language works, because we are overlooking the fact that we use it to **exchange** meanings, that communication is inherently two-way. We tell other people things for a purpose: we may want to influence their attitudes or behaviour, or to provide information that we know they do not have, or to explain our own attitudes or behaviour, or to get them to provide us with information, and so on. I have already said that a functional approach to investigating language is based on the assumption that the language system has evolved (and is constantly evolving) to serve the functions that we need it for. Therefore, the fact that interaction – having a purpose for saying things to other people – is an inherent part of language use means that there must be aspects of the grammar which can be identified as enabling us to interact through language. Some of the grammar of the clause must be attributable to its role in the exchange of meanings between interactants. In this chapter, we will be looking at some of the most important lexico-grammatical systems which we rely on to express our messages in such a way that our hearers have a good chance of understanding why we are saying something to them.

We can start with a relatively simple analysis that should help to show the kind of aspects that we will be concerned with. Take the following example:

> Might I ask you if you could recommend a couple of nice books on taboo language?

What 'content' would you identify in this sentence? It is fairly clear that the message is 'about' books and recommending. Presumably we would accept 'you' as part of the content, as the person involved in the recommending. However, it is not so clear whether the content includes the event of asking: 'might I ask you if' seems to be functioning less to talk about events in the world than to negotiate politely with the reader for the right to ask a question. If we look back at the recommending, 'could' refers not to the event of recommending in itself but to some kind of assessment by the writer of how likely the event is to happen – and again the issue of politeness comes up. The phrase 'on taboo language' gives us information about the characteristics of the books and belongs under the content, but 'nice' refers more to the writer's feelings about the books. Finally, we can note that listing the 'content' does not allow us to mention the vital fact that this is a question to the reader, not a statement or a command. It is possible to separate the cores of the two different kinds of meaning that we have identified as follows:

'CONTENT'	[I ask you]	you	recommend	books on taboo language
'INTERACTION' Might I ask you if		could	nice	?

(Of course, this is over-simple, but it captures enough of the difference for the moment.)

We can now express what we have done here in the terms introduced in the previous chapter: we have separated the experiential meanings (the 'content') from the interpersonal ones (the 'interaction'). The interpersonal meanings relate to the fact that the clause is interrogative (a question), that it expresses the writer's assessment of probabilities and her attitude, and that it explicitly signals the writer's negotiation with the reader. In the rest of this chapter, we will look at how each of these kinds of meanings is encoded in the clause, under the headings of Mood, modality, evaluation and negotiation. However, we first need to provide a general framework for looking at the clause in terms of its function in the communicative exchange of meanings.

4.2 Roles of addressers and audience

I have mentioned above a number of purposes that we might have in entering into a communicative exchange. In one sense, these purposes are clearly unlimited: we may want to order, apologise, confirm, invite, reject, evaluate, describe, and so on. However, in order to be in a position to make useful general statements about the grammar, we need to identify a more restricted range of purposes as a basis to work from. The most fundamental purposes in any exchange are, of course, **giving** (and taking) or **demanding** (and being given) a commodity of some kind. If we look at this from the point of view of a speaker in a verbal exchange, the commodity that the speaker may be giving or demanding is **information**. In such cases, the speaker's purpose is carried out only, or primarily, through language: the speaker makes a statement to give information, or asks a question to demand it; and the exchange is successful if the listener receives (understands) the information that the speaker gives or provides the information demanded (answers the question).

But this clearly does not describe what is happening if the speaker says something like:

Look up the words in a dictionary to find more uses.

Here, the exchange will only be successful if a non-verbal action is carried out – if the listener obeys the command. For such cases we need to include another 'commodity' that is being exchanged: what Halliday (1994: 68) calls 'goods-&-services'. We then end up with four basic speech roles: giving information, demanding information, giving goods-&-services and demanding goods-&-services. The usual labels for these functions are: statement, question, offer and command. Figure 4.1 shows these options, with an example of each.

role in exchange ↓	commodity exchanged →	(a) goods-&-services	(b) information
(i) giving		offer I'll show you the way.	statement We're nearly there.
(ii) demanding		command Give me your hand.	question Is this the place?

Fig 4.1 Basic speech roles

Note that three of these basic functions are closely associated with particular grammatical structures: statements are most naturally expressed by declarative clauses; questions by interrogative clauses; and commands by imperative clauses. These are the three main choices in the mood system of the clause. From this perspective, offers are the odd one out, since they are not associated with a specific mood choice (though they are strongly associated with modality). Halliday (1994: 70) suggests that this is because here 'language is functioning simply as a means towards achieving what are essentially non-linguistic ends' (although, as he says, this is also true of imperatives, which are associated with specific grammatical resources). As we shall see below, we can investigate these interactive functions by focusing on a particular element of the clause, which we shall call the Mood.

Of course, to match function and structure as simply as in Figure 4.1 represents an idealised view of what actually happens. We can, for example, demand goods-&-services by means of a clause which is grammatically declarative, i.e. a statement:

You'd better come in.

However, such uses differ from the basic speech functions precisely because they express one purpose in terms of another. The effect of, say, a declarative-functioning-as-command (as opposed to an imperative) comes from the blending of the meanings associated with declaratives and commands. We will come back to this issue in Chapter 8 when we examine grammatical metaphor.

4.3 Mood

4.3.1 THE STRUCTURE OF THE MOOD

One very distinctive feature of English is the kind of responses illustrated below:

> 'They've all gone.' '*Have they?*'
>
> 'I thought very highly of him.' 'So *you did, did you?*'
>
> 'One goes on looking.' 'Yes, I suppose *one does*. Or at least *some of us do.*'
>
> 'It's different for you, you can earn your own living.' 'So *can anyone.*'
>
> 'Do you remember that case?' '*Should I?*' 'Well, I thought *you might.*'

What is happening here is that part of the first speaker's message is being picked up and re-used, sometimes slightly adapted, in order to keep the exchange going. However, it is not just any part: in each case, the core of the response consists of the same two elements. One is the **Subject**, e.g. 'they' in the first example. The other is traditionally called an auxiliary verb (e.g. 'have' in the same example); but this does not identify its function precisely enough, and in our approach the term **Finite** is used instead. Together, the Subject and Finite make up a component of the clause that is called the **Mood**. This component plays a vital role in carrying out the interpersonal function of the clause as exchange in English.

The Subject is a familiar term from traditional grammar, although it should be remembered that here it is being reinterpreted in functional terms. The Finite is the first functional element of the verbal group. It is most easily recognised in yes–no questions, since it is the auxiliary which comes in front of the Subject. In the following examples, the Finite is in italics. Note that in the last example there are two auxiliaries ('may have'), but only the first is the Finite.

> *Did* you see him that day?
>
> *Didn't* he come home last night?
>
> You *can* imagine his reaction.
>
> What *were* you doing?
>
> Someone *may* have heard the shot.

One reason why the concept of the Finite is probably less familiar than that of Subject is that in many cases it is '**fused**' with the lexical verb. This happens when the verb is used in the simple present or simple past tense (which are in fact the two most frequently occurring verb forms in English):

> Linguists *talk* of marked and unmarked terms.

> She *sat* at the big table.

Despite the absence of an overt marker of the Finite in forms like 'talk' or 'sat', it is useful to see them as consisting of two functional elements, the lexical verb itself and the Finite. For one thing, the Finite becomes explicit as soon as we ask a question ('*Did* she sit ...'), or use the negative ('She *didn't* sit ...'), or if we use an emphatic form ('Linguists *do* talk of marked forms.'). In addition, as we shall see, one of the main functions of the Finite is to mark tense, and this is still identifiable even in fused forms.

4.3.2 IDENTIFYING SUBJECT AND FINITE

It is usually relatively easy to identify the Subject, and only a little less difficult to identify the Finite, but in cases of doubt (at least in declarative clauses) we can establish exactly what the Subject and Finite of any clause are by adding a **tag question** if one is not already present. For example:

> There, that didn't hurt, *did it?*

A tag question repeats the two elements in the Mood at the end of the clause: the Finite is made explicit, even if it is fused with the lexical verb in the clause, and the Subject is picked up by the pronoun in the tag. Figure 4.2 shows the links.

She	was	shopping in town	wasn't	she?
Ted	wouldn't	have married her	[would	he?]
Running a hotel	isn't	as easy as it might look	[is	it?]
These two quotes	[*present*]	exemplify many of the points	[don't	they?]
Subject	**Finite**		**F**	**S**

Fig 4.2 Tags showing Subject and Finite

One implication of this method of identifying the Subject is that it leads us to include certain things that are not traditionally called Subjects, especially 'empty it' and 'there' in clauses like those shown in Figure 4.3.

Most of the Subjects in the examples so far have been relatively simple; but the nominal group functioning as Subject may be much more complex, especially in certain genres such as academic articles. For example, there may be a complex nominal group consisting of more than one constituent functioning

Subject	Finite		F	S
It	's	pouring down outside	isn't	it?
It	was	half past seven	wasn't	it?
There	should	be another one like this	[shouldn't	there?]

Fig 4.3 'It' and 'there' as Subject

together as Subject (the Subject is in italics):

> *The loss of his father's fortune and his father's subsequent death, along with the general decline in the family's circumstances,* decrease the number of servants in the household [don't they?]

The nominal group may include a postmodifying embedded clause:

> *Those who read these stories in the order in which they are printed* will observe the growing proliferation of his style [won't they?]

The Subject function may also be performed by an embedded clause on its own, functioning as the equivalent of a nominal group:

> *To remark of* Brooksmith *that 'the scaffolding of this tale rests upon the existence of a class-stratified society'* is silly [isn't it?]

With regard to this last example, it is worth noting that, when the Subject is an embedded clause, it is actually far more common to find an **anticipatory** 'it' in the normal Subject position, with the embedded clause itself appearing at the end of the clause of which it is Subject. In this case, both 'it' and the embedded clause are labelled as Subject:

> In general, however, *it* is best *to modernise only the spelling.*

> *It's* a real pain *having to shave in cold water.*

> *It* has been found *that a significant number of children turn up at school being able to read.*

> *It* was from that sort of nonsense *that he escaped the following year.*

> *It* is this latter question *which is often ignored.*

As we shall see when we examine Theme in Chapter 6, there are in fact two different structures involved here, but they both share the function of placing certain kinds of information in different positions in the clause for primarily thematic purposes (see 6.4.2 and 6.4.3).

Whereas the Subject function may be carried out by any nominal group of the kinds illustrated above, the Finite is drawn from a small number of verbal **operators**. These can be divided into two main groups: those which express tense ('be', 'have' and 'do', plus 'be' as the marker of passive voice) and those which express **modality** ('can', 'may', 'could', 'might', 'must', 'will', 'would', 'shall', 'should', 'ought to'). 'Will' and 'would' can be included in the tense as well as the modality group, because of their particular uses in signalling the future (see 9.1.2). There are some less central operators, e.g. 'used to' for tense and 'have to' and 'needn't' for modality; and a few marginal ones that tend to be restricted to semi-idiomatic uses, e.g. 'dare' is Finite in 'How dare you talk to me like that?'. If present, the negative marker 'n't' is included as part of the Finite, for reasons that will be explained below.

§   Refer to Exercise 4.1

4.3.3 MEANINGS OF SUBJECT AND FINITE

I mentioned at the beginning of this section that Mood plays a special role in carrying out the interpersonal functions of the clause. In order to understand what this role is, we need to examine the meanings expressed by the Subject and Finite, and then to see how they work together as Mood.

In traditional terms, the Subject is the entity of which something is predicated in the rest of the clause. This is a powerful insight which has been applied in most approaches to grammatical description. It is, for example, reflected in Chomsky's original idealisation $S \longrightarrow NP\ VP$ ('a Sentence consists of a Noun Phrase followed by a Verb Phrase') which makes the first 'cut' in the sentence between the first noun phrase, which is by definition the Subject, and the rest of the sentence. In such approaches, the sentence is seen as being 'about' the Subject. As was made clear in the preceding chapter, however, in a functional approach the choice of a particular entity as Subject expresses only one of three possible kinds of 'aboutness'. In what sense can we see 'aboutness' as an interpersonal meaning?

At this point it will be useful to return to the idea of Subject and Actor. In the following example, 'NatWest' (a banking company) is clearly the entity involved in the sacking – that is, 'NatWest' is the Actor.

She was sacked last week by NatWest.

Thus, if we think of the real-world event being described, the clause tells us about something that NatWest did. On the other hand, we can also look at the clause in terms of the exchange going on between the speaker and the listener. One way of doing this is by examining the kind of response that the listener can make to the information being given (since the response will show us how the listener is interpreting the purpose of the speaker's message). From this perspective, the speaker has put up for negotiation something about 'she', not about NatWest. If, for example, the listener disagrees with the validity of the statement, s/he can simply repeat the Mood elements with negative polarity:

No she wasn't.

What is 'carried over' here from one step of the exchange to the next is all the rest of the clause ('No she wasn't [sacked last week by NatWest]'), and therefore it may be any part of the message that the listener is disagreeing with (perhaps she resigned, or it happened two weeks ago, or it was a different bank that sacked her). What is important is that the listener cannot change the Subject without making a complete new message:

No, NatWest didn't sack her, Barclays did.

If this was the response that the listener wanted to make to the original statement, 'No they didn't' would not work, even though 'they' refers to the Actor.

What this means is that the Subject expresses the entity that the speaker wants to make responsible for the validity of the proposition being advanced in the clause. The listener can then confirm, reject, query or qualify the validity by repeating or amending the Finite (see below), but the Subject must remain the same: if that is altered, the exchange has moved on to a new proposition. In this sense, the clause is 'about' the Subject from the interpersonal perspective. This is obviously clearest in dialogue, where both sides of the interaction are explicit; it may be more difficult to grasp this kind of meaning in other kinds of discourse.

If the Subject is the entity on which the validity of the clause rests, what is the meaning of the Finite? To some extent, the answer has begun to emerge from the discussion of Subject: the Finite makes it possible to negotiate about the validity of the proposition. We can see the Subject as non-negotiable as long as the current proposition remains in play. Through the Finite, the speaker signals three basic kinds of 'claims' about the validity of the proposition, each of which in principle is open to confirmation or rejection by the listener:

1. For what time in relation to that of speaking the proposition is valid (tense).
2. Whether the proposition is about positive or negative validity (polarity).
3. To what extent the proposition is valid (modality).

The following examples illustrate each of the above claims being contested or amended in turn:

1. 'I thought I was a revolutionary. But I'm not.'
2. 'You know what I mean.' 'No, I don't, as a matter of fact.'
3. 'Look out – he might scratch you.' 'Too late – he has.'

Of course, in the majority of cases, propositions are not explicitly contested in this way, and the arguability of the Finite is not highlighted. Nevertheless, the basic function of the Finite is to orient the listener towards the kind of validity being claimed for the proposition, by relating it either to the here-and-now reality of the speech event or to the speaker's attitude. Either of these options may be expressed in positive or negative terms.

Thus from an interactional perspective we can see the declarative clause as doing something like the following: the speaker introduces an entity (the Subject) about which he or she wants to make certain claims; s/he then indicates the kind and degree of validity of the claims s/he is going to make in the Finite; and s/he then makes the claims in the rest of the clause. If we go back to the earlier example:

She was sacked last week by NatWest.

we can paraphrase what is going on as follows: 'The validity of the information I am giving you depends on your accepting that we are talking about something that happened to "she"; the validity I claim for the information is that it is valid for something in the past (not present or future tense), it is absolutely valid (not modalised) and that it is positively valid (not negative); and the information I want to give you about "she" is "sacked last week by NatWest". As long as you accept the validity of the information in these terms, we can proceed to the next step in this interaction.' Of course, set out like this it looks unmanageably cumbersome: the paraphrase is not in the least intended to reflect the conscious mental processes of those taking part in the interaction. But it does reflect the tacit, unconscious agreement on which the interaction is based; and it also reflects what the grammatical structure indicates about the way in which the exchange is proceeding. In looking critically at how speakers and writers attempt to achieve their purposes, to negotiate with – and to manipulate – their audience, it is often essential to make these validity claims explicit.

It is because this negotiation is done through the Subject and Finite, and is then taken as given for the rest of the clause, that the Mood is identified as a separate functional element in the clause. The importance and the relative detachability of the Mood within the meaning of the clause in English are shown by the fact that it can be used as a 'counter' for the whole proposition in responses ('No, she wasn't'), demands for acceptance of validity through tags ('wasn't she?'), and so on. In interpersonal terms, the Mood is the core of the exchange: the rest of the clause merely fills in the details.

4.3.4 MOOD IN NON-DECLARATIVE CLAUSES

We have been focusing on declarative clauses in order to establish the general meanings of Subject and Finite. However, as was mentioned earlier, the Mood also has a crucial function in signalling speech roles. The basic pattern is that the presence of Subject and Finite in the clause signals that the clause is indicative rather than imperative; and within this category, the ordering of the two elements distinguishes between declarative (Subject, then Finite: see Figure 4.4) and interrogative (Finite, then Subject: see Figure 4.5; but see the discussion of WH-interrogatives below).

Assessment	will	be by coursework.
We	[*present*]	take conversation for granted most of the time.
Subject	Finite	
Mood		

Fig 4.4 Mood in declarative clauses

Can	he	paint well enough?
Do	we	have anything in common?
Finite	Subject	
Mood		

Fig 4.5 Mood in yes/no interrogative clauses

In **yes/no interrogatives**, it is primarily the **polarity** of the message which the speaker wants the listener to specify ('He can or can't paint well enough?'), and, for thematic reasons (see 6.3.2), the speaker typically begins with the Finite, which is the part of the Mood where polarity is signalled.

In **WH-interrogatives**, there are two conflicting functions at work. The interrogative purpose is reflected in the fact that many WH-interrogatives have Finite preceding Subject in the Mood. However, the primary purpose of a WH-interrogative is to demand that the listener fill in a missing part of the message; and the WH-element signals which part is missing. For example, the question 'When is he leaving?' can be seen as a demand for the other person to complete the message 'He is leaving ... [time expression] ...'. Again for thematic reasons (see 6.3.2), the speaker typically begins with the WH-element (though we occasionally find so-called 'echo questions' where the WH-element remains in the place where the missing part would normally go: 'He's leaving *when*?'). In some cases, of course, it is the Subject that the speaker wants supplied; and thus the WH-Subject in fact appears before the Finite. These two orderings are compared in Figure 4.6 and Figure 4.7.

Exclamatives are like WH-interrogatives in that they have a WH-element, which typically comes first; but they have the Subject^Finite ordering of declarative clauses (remember that '^' is the symbol for 'followed by'). Figure 4.8 gives some examples.

In imperative clauses, the unmarked form has no Mood. The Subject of a command (the person responsible for carrying it out) is not specified, since it can

Why	did	the affair	end?
What	do	you	expect me to do?
How many	are	there?	
	Finite	**Subject**	
	Mood		

Fig 4.6 WH-interrogative with known Subject

Who	's	been sleeping in my bed?
What kind of idiot	would	do something like that?
Who	[*past*]	typed out that note?
Subject/WH-	**Finite**	
Mood		

Fig 4.7 WH-interrogative with WH-element as Subject

What an epitaph	that	would	make!
How simple	it all	[*past*]	seemed at the time.
	Subject	**Finite**	
	Mood		

Fig 4.8 Mood in exclamative clauses

only be the addressee ('you'). In interpersonal terms, an imperative is presented as not open to negotiation (which does not mean, of course, that the command will actually be obeyed), and thus most of the functions of the Finite are irrelevant: a command is absolute (there are no imperative forms of the modal verbs), and there is no need to specify time relevance since there is no choice (an imperative can only refer to an action not yet carried out, i.e. it can only refer to future time). The Finite may in fact appear in unmarked imperatives, but it has a restricted purpose: it is used only to signal negative polarity, see Figure 4.9.

There are, however, marked forms of imperatives in which the Subject may appear; and the Finite may also be used for emphasis, see Figure 4.10.

		Go away. Answer no more than three of the following questions.
Don't		look at me like that.
Finite	**[Subject]**	
Mood		

Fig 4.9 Unmarked imperative clauses

	You	listen to me, young man.
Do		hurry up, for goodness' sake.
Don't	you	take that tone of voice to me.
Finite	**Subject**	
Mood		

Fig 4.10 Marked imperative clauses

I have mentioned that the Finite here is not a 'normal' Finite with the normal range of functions; this is reflected in the fact that it is not the same form as appears if a tag is added at the end of an imperative clause:

Don't tell him anything, *will you?*

There is in fact a second kind of imperative clause, where the understood Subject is not 'you' but 'you and me': this is the **'let's'** form. Halliday (1994: 87) argues that 'let's' itself 'is best interpreted as a wayward form of the Subject'. In support of this, he mentions that there is an unmarked negative form 'don't let's' and an emphatic form 'do let's'. The suggested analyses are shown in Figure 4.11.

	Let's	call it a day.
Don't	let's	argue about it.
Do	let's	try and get it right this time.
Finite	**Subject**	
Mood		

Fig 4.11 'Let's' imperative clauses

The tag in these cases is 'shall we?'

4.3.5 THE RESIDUE

So far we have focused exclusively on Subject and Finite, without paying any attention to the rest of the clause. Although, as I have argued, much of the interactive work of the clause is performed by the Subject and Finite, it is useful to look at what else appears in the clause, not least in order to identify certain elements other than Subject and Finite which belong to the Mood. The general term for part of the clause that is not the Mood is the **Residue**. There are three kinds of functional elements in the Residue: the **Predicator, Complements,** and **Adjuncts**.

The Predicator is expressed by the rest of the verbal group apart from the Finite. There can be only one Predicator in any clause, and there must be a Predicator in any major clause (i.e. a 'major clause' means a clause which includes a Predicator). Since the Finite is not part of the Predicator, the Predicator itself is non-finite. This can be seen most clearly from the fact that there are non-finite clauses which have a Predicator but no Finite (they normally have no Subject either), for example, the clause in italics in this sentence:

Tim stood for a while *gazing at the cliff.*

(where 'gazing' is the Predicator in the non-finite second clause, while 'stood' is the Finite + Predicator in the first clause).

The Predicator obviously expresses the process – the action, happening, state, etc. in which the Subject is involved. In addition, it may perform three other functions. The first is to specify 'secondary tense', that is, time reference other than the immediate link to the time of speaking. For example (the Predicator is in italics):

Oh, we'll *have finished* by six o'clock for sure.

Here, the Finite ' 'll' indicates that the proposition is valid for a time in the future from the time of speaking; 'have (finish)ed', on the other hand, indicates that the event of finishing will take place at a time before the reference point in the future ('six o'clock') which has been set up – compare 'We'll finish at six o'clock', where there is no secondary tense expressed. For more detail, see the discussion of the verbal group in 9.1.2. The second function is to specify various other aspects of the process, such as starting, trying, achieving or continuing the process. For example:

He has *managed to charge* visitors for admission to the churches.

Here 'manage to', despite being the 'main verb' in traditional terms, is not the main process, which is expressed by 'charge' – it tells us that the process has been successfully carried out. For more detail, see the discussion of verbal group complexes in 9.3. Finally, the Predicator also specifies the voice: active or passive.

Another diplomat had *been shot* in Piccadilly.

It is worth mentioning that 'be' has a special status in that, strictly speaking, the simple present and past forms consist of Finite with no Predicator. Whereas other verbs need a separate verbal operator 'do' to express the Finite (e.g. in yes/no interrogatives) 'be' does not: we say 'Are you comfortable?' rather than 'Do you be comfortable?' For many (but not all) speakers of English, 'have' behaves in the same way when it means 'possess': 'Have you any wool?' and 'You haven't any wool, have you?'. However, other speakers will normally say 'Do you have' (treating 'have' as a normal Predicator with a separate Finite) or 'Have you got' (where 'have' is the verbal operator functioning as Finite, and the Predicator is 'got'); and many speakers, like myself, alternate between these three different options. In analysing 'be' and 'have' in the cases described here, it is simplest just to label the Finite and not have a slot labelled 'Predicator' – this is in fact the practice that has been followed so far in this chapter (see, for example, Figure 4.3).

The clause may include one or two Complements. Note that, as used here, the term includes both Objects and Complements in the more traditional sense. A Complement is an element in the Residue, typically realised by a nominal group, which could have been chosen as Subject, but was not. In the following groups of examples, the Complements are in italics in the first sentence, while the subsequent sentences in the group are reworded to show how the Complement could have been the Subject.

> He brought *her pamphlets on the Middle East situation*.

> She was brought pamphlets on the Middle East situation.

> Pamphlets on the Middle East situation were brought.

> Kate did not like *this* at all.

> This did not please Kate at all.

> The strongest shape is *the triangle*.

> The triangle is the strongest shape.

There is, however, one kind of Complement which cannot become Subject. This is the Attribute in a relational process (see 5.2.3):

> Interviewing politicians is always *entertaining*.

The positions of an attributive Complement and Subject may sometimes be reversed, but this does not affect their roles – the ordering is for thematic purposes (see 6.3.1). In the following example, 'the issue of rate of decay' remains the Subject:

> *Of greater interest* is the issue of rate of decay.

The clause may also contain one or more Adjuncts. Indeed, it may include quite a large number: it is relatively easy to find examples like the following, with six Adjuncts, which do not sound unnatural or unwieldy:

> *In an attempt to limit the potential damage*, John Prescott *yesterday* met *privately with suspended party members in Walsall over allegations of intimidation.*

The role of Adjunct is typically performed by an adverbial group or a prepositional phrase: in the above example, 'yesterday' and 'privately' are adverbial groups, while the remaining four Adjuncts are prepositional phrases. Adjuncts cannot in themselves be chosen as Subject – that is the main difference between Adjuncts and Complements. However, a prepositional phrase has its own internal structure, consisting of a preposition followed by a Complement; and this Complement may in certain circumstances be lifted out of the Adjunct to become Subject, leaving behind a truncated Adjunct consisting simply of the preposition:

> Had no one thought *of that?* Hadn't that been thought of?

In discussing WH-interrogatives above (4.3.4), I mentioned that the WH-element may **conflate** with (i.e. stand in for) the Subject. It may also conflate with Complement or Adjunct, that is, it may be asking the other person to supply the Complement or Adjunct in order to complete the message. In the first example below, 'what' is Complement, while in the second 'how far' is Adjunct.

> What would you have done?

> How far have you got to go?

The same in fact applies to other WH-elements, not just those in interrogatives. In the relative clauses in the following examples (in italics) 'who' is Subject in the first, while 'whose unpronounceable name' is Complement in the second:

> She thought all the time of Ben, *who was a prisoner somewhere.*

> There was a visiting American Professor, *whose unpronounceable name she immediately forgot.*

And in the following reported clause (in italics), 'why' is Adjunct (standing in for something like 'he chose history *for a certain reason*'):

> I don't know *why he chose history.*

In the exclamative clauses in Figure 4.8 above, the WH-element is Complement.
    Figure 4.12 gives some sample analyses of Mood and Residue together.

4.3.6 MODAL ADJUNCTS

There is one further step we must take before we have completed the identification of all the elements in the Mood–Residue analysis. In the discussion above, I have treated all Adjuncts as if they formed a single type of constituent

He	was	lying	on his back.
Subject	Finite	Predicator	Adjunct
Mood		Residue	

On the following day	he	did not	go	out	early.
Adjunct	Subject	Finite	Predicator	Adjunct	Adjunct
	Mood		Residue		

Why	did	you	leave	the convent	so suddenly?
Adjunct/WH-	Finite	Subject	Predicator	Complement	Adjunct
	Mood		Residue		

It	[past]	occurred	to me	on a recent conference trip	that my summary is destined to become truer than I thought
S-	Finite	Predicator	Adjunct	Adjunct	-ubject
		Residue			
		Mood			

Fig 4.12 Analysing Mood and Residue

for the purposes of the analysis. However, we in fact need to distinguish three types of Adjunct, each of which is treated differently. The Adjuncts in Figure 4.12 all contribute to the experiential meaning of the clause – they tell us things like when, or how, or where, or why the event happened. When we deal with the clause from the experiential perspective in Chapter 5 we shall be calling these 'circumstances'; and we can use the term **circumstantial Adjunct** here to differentiate them from the other two kinds. But there are Adjuncts to which the functional description given above clearly does not apply: for example, those which are in italics in the following sentences:

The punctuation, *on the other hand*, is reproduced with diplomatic faithfulness.

Unfortunately, I did not meet Paul Klee there or later in my life.

The first example here shows a **Conjunctive Adjunct**, while the second shows a **Modal Adjunct**.

Conjunctive Adjuncts (sometimes called 'discourse markers') have the function of signalling how the clause as a whole fits in with the preceding text. The meanings that they express are textual meanings, and we will be examining them in Chapter 6. They are not regarded as playing any part in the interpersonal meanings of the clause, and thus they do not form part of either the Mood or the Residue, see Figure 4.13.

The punctuation	on the other hand	is	reproduced	with diplomatic faithfulness
S	(Conjunctive)	F	P	A
Mo-		-od	Residue	

Fig 4.13 Conjunctive Adjunct

Modal Adjuncts, on the other hand, clearly do have an interpersonal function – 'unfortunately' in the example above tells us the writer's attitude towards the fact that he did not meet Paul Klee. These Adjuncts fall into two main groups. **Comment Adjuncts**, such as 'unfortunately', are relatively easy to identify: they typically comment on the clause as a whole rather than give circumstantial information about the event, and they are often separated off from the rest of the clause by commas. A list of the different types of Comment Adjunct is given in Table 3(3) in Halliday (1994: 49); and a fuller list is provided in Quirk *et al.* (1985: 612–31), where they are called disjuncts.

The second group of Modal Adjuncts are a little more difficult to identify, because most of them appear to be modifying the verb and may thus look like circumstantial Adjuncts. However, they are in fact most closely related not to the Predicator in the verbal group but to the Finite: they express meanings associated with tense, polarity and modality. Because of this link with the meanings associated with the Mood, they are called **Mood Adjuncts**. Generally, Mood Adjuncts feel intuitively more 'grammatical' than circumstantial Adjuncts, although in some cases it is, admittedly, difficult to see the difference. To take some clear examples, 'already' is related to tense, 'yes' is related to polarity, and 'maybe' is related to modality. Examples where the link with Mood meanings is perhaps less obvious include 'regularly' (related to temporal meanings) and 'at all costs' (related to modal meanings of obligation). A list of the main items which function as Mood Adjuncts is given in Halliday (1994: 82–3).

Both types of Modal Adjunct – Mood and Comment – are included in Mood when you do a Mood–Residue analysis. Figure 4.14 gives some sample analyses of clauses including Modal Adjuncts. Note that the final example includes a complex Predicator with elements marking secondary tense and modality, and passive voice.

Have	you	decided	on a colour	yet?
F	S	P	A	Mood Adjunct
		Residue		
		Mood		

Unfortunately	all too often	the amounts paid	aren't	reasonable.
Comment Adjunct	Mood Adjunct	S	F	C
Mood			Residue	

Surprisingly,	however,	this tendency	has	in fact	declined	since 1970.
Comment Adjunct	(Conjunctive Adjunct)	S	F	Mood Adjunct	P	A
M-		-ood			Residue	

The beams	are	obviously	going to have to be replaced.
S	F	Mood Adjunct	P
Mood			Residue

Fig 4.14 Modal Adjuncts

§   Refer to Exercise 4.2

4.4 Modality

4.4.1 MODALITY AND POLARITY

As we have seen above, the Finite expresses not only tense but also polarity and modality. Any Finite is inherently positive or negative in polarity. It is true that the negative forms have an identifiable added element ('n't' or 'not') in relation to the positive, but this is a reflection of the marked nature of negative meanings in general (we need a particular reason for talking about what is not rather than what is). In terms of the interaction carried out by the clause, polarity is a basic part of the meaning: as noted in 4.3.4, there is a specific grammatical structure, the yes/no interrogative, whose primary function is precisely to enquire about the polarity of a message.

Of course, polarity may also be expressed through Mood Adjuncts such as 'never' or 'hardly' (in which case, interestingly enough, the Finite is actually positive) – see Figure 4.15.

I	've	never	liked	him.
I	would	hardly	say	that.
Subject	Finite	Mood Adjunct	Predicator	Complement
Mood			Residue	

Fig 4.15 Mood Adjuncts expressing polarity

To go a step further, we can see that in fact the expression of polarity is not restricted even to the Mood. In the first example below, the Finite 'has' is clearly positive, and there is no Mood Adjunct: it is the Complement 'nothing' which expresses negative polarity.

He has said nothing to me about that.

He hasn't said anything to me about that.

As we shall see with modality, this freedom of movement is typical of interpersonal meanings as a whole: they tend to cluster around the Mood, but they are by no means confined to that part of the message. This helps to explain why, as mentioned in Chapter 2, Halliday has often argued forcefully against looking at language only in terms of 'constituents' – that is, breaking clauses into groups and then groups into words, and assigning each 'bit' an identifiable meaning. As a rule, interpersonal meanings are not inherently tied to specific constituents but spread over the whole clause; and they may well be cumulative, reinforced by being expressed at several points in the clause. This is especially clear when swearwords are used to express the speaker's evaluation – see 4.5 below. The choice of the particular place, or places, in the clause where an interpersonal meaning is expressed will be significant, but the range of options is typically very wide.

In the discussion so far, polarity has been treated as if it were absolute, and in one sense, of course, it is: a message is either positive or negative. The structural possibilities reflect this, in that the Finite must be formally positive or negative. However, semantically there are also intermediate stages – points between 'yes' and 'no' such as 'maybe' or 'sometimes' or 'supposedly' – which are expressed by modality. A simple starting definition of modality is that it is the space between 'yes' and 'no'. Figure 4.16 illustrates this concept by giving some examples of modality with an informal gloss in the right-hand column indicating the intermediateness of the proposition (note that the ordering of examples in the **'modal space'** is not intended to suggest that any of the examples are closer to the positive or negative poles).

+	She teaches Latin	
M S	She might teach Latin	perhaps yes, perhaps no
O P	She usually teaches Latin	sometimes yes, sometimes no
D A	She ought to teach Latin	at present no, but ideally in the future yes
A C	She'll teach Latin if you want	at present no, but in the future yes if you want
L E	She can teach Latin if she wants	at present no, but in the future yes if she wants
	She can teach Latin well	in principle yes, at present maybe yes or no
–	She doesn't teach English.	

Fig 4.16 Modal space

4.4.2 TYPES OF MODALITY

In order to understand more fully how modality works, we need to return to the distinction in speech roles that was set up at the beginning of this chapter (see Figure 4.1). If the commodity being exchanged is information, the modality relates to how valid the information is in terms of **probability** (how likely it is to be true) or **usuality** (how frequently it is true). Some of the basic points on the probability scale are: possible/probable/certain; on the usuality scale, they include: sometimes/often/always. If, on the other hand, the commodity is goods-&-services, the modality relates to how confident the speaker can be in the eventual success of the exchange. In commands, this concerns the degree of **obligation** on the other person to carry out the command (the scale for the demanded goods-&-services includes: permissible/advisable/obligatory), while in offers it concerns the degree of **willingness** or inclination of the speaker to fulfil the offer (the speaker may signal: ability/willingness/determination).

In order to distinguish these two basic types of modality, the first is called **modalisation**, whereas the second is referred to as **modulation**. Figure 4.17 shows the different types and sub-categories, with an example of each.

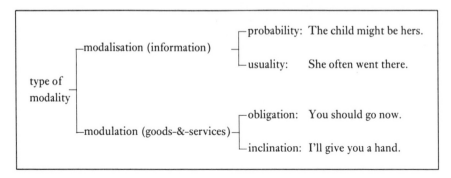

Fig 4.17 Types of modality

If we restrict ourselves for the moment to modality in Mood, there are a number of ways in which it can be expressed. The most obvious, and one of the main structural justifications for including modality as a function of the Mood in English, is through modal verbal operators. It was mentioned in 4.3.3 that the Finite related the proposition either to the here-and-now reality of the speech event (tense) or to the speaker's attitude (modality). This implied that tense and modality were alternative points of reference; but in fact it would be truer to say that, with a modal operator, tense is normally **neutralised** because the operator is inherently present tense. In most cases, a modal operator expresses the speaker's attitude at the time of speaking. This emerges clearly in forms such as the following where we have secondary tense after the Finite:

> He must have inspected the cottage.

This can be paraphrased as 'My best guess *is* that he *inspected* the cottage', which makes it clear that the 'pastness' signalled by 'have' relates to the event being talked about, but that the modality signalled by 'must' refers to the speaker's present opinion. This neutralisation of tense explains why forms such as 'might' and 'could', which historically are past tense forms (of 'may' and 'can'), typically do not function as past tense signals in modern English. In the following sentence, for example, 'may' could be substituted for 'might' with little difference in meaning:

> We might as well try for Cambridge.

There are certain contexts where the Finite does signal past tense in addition to modality, for example, when it is another person's modality in the past which is being reported. In such cases, the 'past tense' forms must normally be used:

> He explained that he *might* be late.

Apart from a modal verbal operator, modality may also be signalled in Mood by a Mood Adjunct: in fact this, rather than a modal operator, is the most normal way of expressing usuality. The following examples show Mood Adjuncts signalling probability and usuality respectively:

> Was that a hostel *perhaps?*

> People *usually* enquire after my sisters.

Probability in particular can be signalled by a combination of modal operator and Mood Adjunct – an example of the cumulative nature of interpersonal meanings mentioned above:

> But they *must surely* have realized what was happening?

With modalisation, there is the same choice between modal operators (e.g. 'must', 'will') and Mood Adjuncts (e.g. 'definitely', 'willingly'). Again, these two may be combined:

> You *really ought to* invite her.

> I *would willingly* carry a candle in one hand for St Michael and a candle for his Dragon in the other.

4.4.3 MODAL COMMITMENT

In 4.4.2, I talked about modality as involving degrees and scales. The speaker may, for example, signal a higher or lower degree of certainty about the validity of a proposition ('it will/may rain'); or a higher or lower degree of pressure on the other person to carry out a command ('you must/should leave'). It is possible to formalise this to some extent and to establish three basic values (Halliday, 1994: 358) or points on the scale: high, median and low. These are illustrated in Figure 4.18 for probability and obligation. Note that the figure shows permission, often expressed by 'can', as low value modulation: permission can be seen as the lowest degree of pressure, opening the possibility for the other person to do the action but leaving the decision to them.

	Modalisation	Modulation
HIGH ↑	I shall never be happy again.	You must ask someone.
MEDIAN ↑	They should be back by now.	You ought to invite her.
LOW	I may be quite wrong.	You can help yourself to a drink.

Fig 4.18 Modal values

It must be kept in mind that this is an idealisation, and that the three labels represent areas on a scale rather than absolute categories, with more delicate distinctions possible (e.g., in 'high' modalisation between 'That'll be the milkman' and 'That must be the milkman'). However, they are useful labels in investigating the question of the speaker's **commitment**: the degree to which the speaker commits himself or herself to the validity of what s/he is saying. This has important implications in a number of different areas of text analysis. For example, in an academic paper a writer has to judge very carefully the extent to which s/he advances a claim as certain or as still open to doubt; while in giving advice a speaker has to judge very carefully the extent to which s/he appears to be putting pressure on the other person.

4.4.4 MODAL RESPONSIBILITY

We have already seen that one type of interpersonal meaning, polarity, can be signalled at a number of places in the clause; and it is not surprising that the same is true of modality. The following examples have been invented to show something of the range of possibilities. The modality signals (in this case the modality is in the area of low or median value probability) are in italic.

He's ill.	He *may* be ill.
Maybe he's ill.	He's *quite possibly* ill.
In all probability he's ill.	*It's quite possible* that he's ill.
It could be that he's ill.	*There's a possibility* that he's ill.
I expect he's ill.	He's ill. *That's a possibility, anyway.*
The likelihood of his being ill isn't very great.	His *possible* illness is irrelevant.
I suppose it's possible that he *may well* be ill *perhaps*.	

Some of the ways of introducing modality exemplified here are beyond the scope of the present chapter: we will come back to them when we look at grammatical metaphor in Chapter 8. However, one thing that all these examples have in common is that they can be graded according to how far the speaker overtly accepts **responsibility** for the attitude being expressed. Essentially, the speaker may express his or her point of view in a way that makes it clear that this is his or her subjective point of view; or s/he may do it in a way that 'objectivises' the point of view by making it appear to be a quality of the event itself. This objectivisation is clearest in cases where the modality is expressed in a separate clause:

It's quite possible that he's ill.

Here, something referred to by the pronoun 'it' is described as 'quite possible'; and in the second part of the sentence (see 4.3.2) 'it' turns out to be the speaker's basic proposition, 'he's ill'. This proposition is thus being treated as a definable chunk of meaning, almost as if it were a kind of 'thing' in the world, which can have qualities attributed to it – in this case the quality of being possible. This way of expressing it disguises the fact that the quality of possibility is actually not something 'belonging to' the proposition but is the speaker's personal assessment of probability (see also the discussion of 'facts' in 10.4.2).

At the other extreme, the **subjective** nature of the assessment can be highlighted, again by expressing the modality in a separate clause:

> *I expect* he's ill.

Here the speaker's main clause in structural terms is 'I expect', which appears to be a proposition about himself or herself. In functional terms, however, the main proposition is still 'he's ill'. We can see this if we add a tag:

> I expect he's ill, isn't he?

Note that the tag here does not repeat the Mood of the 'main clause' (if it did, we would get 'I expect he's ill, don't I?', which sounds extremely odd). The tag in fact invites the other person to agree with the basic proposition 'he's ill'. Another feature which suggests that the 'main clause' does not really express the main proposition appears when the proposition is negative. In speech, it is more commonly the 'modal clause' which is negated:

> I don't expect he's ill.

Here it is almost as if the 'modal clause' is doing the job of the Finite in advance of the proposition, setting up the degree of validity and the polarity as a separate element of the message. Again the tag is revealing:

> I don't expect he's ill, is he?

Since tags normally reverse the polarity of the clause which they tag (positive Finite – negative tag, and vice versa), the tag here is clearly echoing a negative Finite, which must be 'he isn't ill'. The main function of these 'modal clauses' is in fact to make explicit the personal source of the modality. When the proposition is negative, we have another example of the 'non-constituent' character of polarity (see 4.4.1): it is natural that it should gravitate towards the part of the message where other interpersonal meanings are being expressed.

Between these two extremes, highlighting subjectivity or creating objectivity, there are intermediate ways of expressing modality. The two main ways have already been mentioned in 4.4.2: modal verbal operators and Mood Adjuncts. Of these, modal operators exploit the Finite slot and thus are firmly rooted in the interpersonal, subjective meanings of the clause; whereas Mood Adjuncts are a step closer to the objective end of the spectrum, in that they use one of the Adjunct slots which are typically used to express 'real-world' features of the event (e.g. 'He cleaned the mess up *rapidly*'). At around the same point on the scale as Mood Adjuncts we can also place what Halliday (1994: 89) calls an 'expansion of the Predicator': the use of passive forms such as 'supposed to' or 'obliged to', with a separate non-modal Finite, to express modality. In the following examples, there is a difference in the degree to which the speaker seems to be taking responsibility for the pressure on the other person: with 'supposed to' the feeling is that the pressure comes from another source, not directly from the speaker.

You're supposed to be doing your practising.

You ought to be doing your practising.

We have thus identified four main points on the scale of 'modal responsibility', in terms of the extent to which the speaker openly accepts responsibility for the subjective assessments being expressed. Figure 4.19 gives examples of each of the points for modalisation and modulation. (The term **'implicit'** is used when the modality is expressed in the same clause as the main proposition, while **'explicit'** is used when it is expressed in a separate clause; see Halliday, 1994: 355.)

	Modalisation	Modulation
Explicit subjective	*I'm sure* we should sell this place	*I don't advise* you to drink it
Implicit subjective	She *might* have written to me	I *mustn't* go there any more
Implicit objective	We *probably* won't repay it	A cathedral is *supposed* to be old
Explicit objective	*It's likely* that they've heard by now	*It's essential* that you leave at once

Fig 4.19 Modal responsibility

As with the scale of modal commitment (4.4.3), these are not absolute categories: there are intermediate points, and there is variation within each grouping. For example, prepositional phrases expressing modality lie somewhere between the explicit and implicit points exemplified above: on the subjective side, there are phrases like 'in my opinion' and 'to my mind', while on the objective side there are phrases like 'in all probability' and 'to some extent'. As always, it is the existence of the cline which is important rather than the exact location of points along it.

In looking at language in use, the issue of modal responsibility is often fascinating to explore, because writers and speakers may resort to various methods of masking their responsibility and presenting their viewpoint in an apparently objective way, for a number of reasons. For example, I recently found myself writing the following two sentences in letters to two students applying to come on one of our courses:

> Before we come to a final decision, however, *it will be necessary* for us to satisfy ourselves that your English level is sufficient to meet the demands of the course.

> *I will need to* write to your referees for their opinions, and *I will* contact you again as soon as I have heard from them.

It is fairly easy to guess which applicant had the better chance of being accepted on the course – and why I preferred the more objective wording in the less welcoming letter.

4.4.5 MODALITY IN TEXT

This has been a very brief overview of an area of English grammar which is extremely complex: Halliday (1994: 359) calculates that, once the different possibilities for expressing polarity with modality are included, the systems we have looked at so far (types of modality, values and degree of commitment) result in 144 categories of modality, and a more delicate analysis would show many others. Inevitably therefore many of the details have been missed out. What we have focused on have been the broad factors at work in the area of modality, particularly those which help in the analysis of spoken and written texts. One factor which has been implicit in what we have said about modality, but which is often the most interesting and revealing in text analysis, is the question of the **source** of the modality in a text. Any modality has a source, which is either directly the speaker or indirectly someone whose views are being reported by the speaker. In certain genres, the question of *whose* view we are being given may be crucial in understanding the text.

For example, writers of novels or short stories often use modality very subtly to indicate that we are seeing events not from the point of view of an omniscient narrator but from that of a character within the story. Since the character is not omniscient, we are given a restricted view of events, which opens up the possibility that as readers we may in fact be meant to see things differently. A classic example of this use of restricted point of view is the short story 'Clay', from James Joyce's *Dubliners*. In this paragraph from near the beginning of the story, the central figure, Maria, is looking forward to an evening off from her work.

> The women would have their tea at six o'clock and she would be able to get away before seven. From Ballsbridge to the Pillar, twenty minutes; from the Pillar to Drumcondra, twenty minutes; and twenty minutes to buy the things. She would be there before eight. She took out her purse

with the silver clasps and read again the words *A Present from Belfast*. She was very fond of that purse because Joe had brought it to her five years before when he and Alphy had gone to Belfast on a Whit-Monday trip. In the purse were two half-crowns and some coppers. She would have five shillings clear after paying the tram fare. What a nice evening they would have, all the children singing! Only she hoped that Joe wouldn't come in drunk. He was so different when he had a drink taken.

Although at first reading this may look like a description by the narrator, a closer inspection reveals that we are basically overhearing Maria's own train of thought. There are a number of modality signals which must have her as their source (since for an omniscient, neutral narrator there can be no 'may' or 'must': any signs of doubt or obligation either come from a character or represent an intrusion by the narrator into the telling of the story). Of these, only one is explicitly marked as reported ('she hoped that Joe *wouldn't* come in drunk'), and even that is a report of an internal mental event ('hoping' rather than 'saying'). Together with other signals of interpersonal interaction (e.g. the 'incomplete' second sentence, the exclamative sentence near the end), the modality helps to take us inside Maria's head and masks the narrator's role. As you will see if you read the rest of the story, this is crucial in suggesting that what we are actually told is not the whole story: Maria's view of her own life is far more determinedly (or desperately) positive than the one we as readers end up with.

Another genre where an investigation of modality is often rewarding is journalism. News reporting is usually supposed to be neutral, an objective setting-out of the facts as collected by the journalist. Any comment should be clearly signalled as that of the people involved, not of the journalist. If there is any modality, therefore, it should in principle have its source explicitly indicated (through reporting clauses, etc.). With that in mind, try looking at the modality in the following extracts from a 1992 report in a right-wing newspaper, the *Daily Express*, of a speech by the left-wing union leader, Arthur Scargill. Some of the modality is assigned to Scargill or other people – but not all. It is interesting to consider who the source of this unassigned modality is, and what the effect might be of slipping it into the article in this relatively unobtrusive way.

> Miners' leader Arthur Scargill took off his pre-election gag yesterday to present his list of demands on a Labour Government. First priority would be for miners sacked during the disastrous 1984–85 strike to be given their jobs back.
>
> Many of the 1,000 miners fired during and after the strike were dismissed for intimidation, violence and bully-boy tactics on the picket line. But Mr Scargill said Labour should reinstate them all with full back pay.
>
> That would cost the coal industry around £100 million and wipe out almost all the profit it is likely to make this year. ...

Labour leaders were desperately trying to distance themselves from the miners' £50,000-a-year president. The NUM [the union of which Mr Scargill is president] is understood to have contributed around £250,000 towards Labour's £7 million election fighting fund. Mr Scargill clearly hopes to become a powerful figure again if Mr Kinnock wins.

4.5 Evaluation

In discussing modality, we have moved from strictly grammatical issues (e.g. modal operators functioning as Finite) towards areas which are more difficult to pin down in structural terms – the list of examples of modality at the beginning of 4.4.4 illustrates this. With **evaluation**, we are even more on the edge of grammar: much of evaluation is expressed by lexical choices and there are few grammatical structures which can be seen as having evolved with a primarily evaluative function. The discussion here will therefore be brief; but it is important to note that evaluation is a central part of the meaning of any text and that any analysis of the interpersonal meanings of a text must take it into account.

Evaluation can be simply defined as the indication of whether the speaker thinks that something (a person, thing, action, event, situation, idea, etc.) is good or bad. The good/bad scale can be seen as the simplest and most basic one, but there are many other scales of evaluation, and it is revealing to see what kinds of values are established in any particular genre. For example, in the following sentence from an academic article on the effects of ageing, the scale used to evaluate the research findings is that of importance:

> The importance of this result is that it shows that age may affect the levels of performance which people attain at any point during an unusually prolonged experiment, but without also altering the rate at which they learn a complex skill.

What they are discussing is the way in which old age causes people to lose their faculties. For the old people involved, this process might be evaluated on a scale such as cheering/depressing; but for the scientific researcher the most prominent value (and the only one conventionally accepted in this context) is that of importance, i.e. the extent to which the findings help us to understand the area of research. The identification of the scales of evaluation is one way in to exploring the ethos of science, in which objectivity is prized above all. This may seem natural until we realise that, in the context of human sciences at least, 'objectivity' could in principle also be seen as 'lack of humanity': the choice of evaluation reflects and reinforces the ideological values of the culture (see the discussion of the texts in Chapter 11).

I mentioned above that evaluation does not have structures of its own: it is, in a sense, parasitic on other structural elements. There are, however, a number of cases where evaluation is, at the least, strongly associated with specific formal features. One of these is the structure illustrated in 4.3.2 above with an anticipatory 'it'.

> *It might be difficult* to find a more apt or prettier description of the romantic artist.

> *It's amazing* what nonsense people will believe.

In many cases, the introductory clause has the function of evaluating the information in the following clause (another typical function is to express modal meanings objectively; as we shall see below, modality is closely related to evaluation). For more discussion of this structure, see 6.4.3 on 'thematised comment'.

Another case is **swearing**. Within swearing, it is useful to distinguish between '**rude words**' and '**expletives**'. Rude words are socially stigmatised terms for activities and objects which are considered taboo, to a greater or lesser extent, within a culture: sex and excrement are the main sources of rude words in modern English. The taboo activities and objects can, of course, be referred to without rude words, by using scientific terms, euphemisms, etc. Expletives are mostly derived from rude words, but they have lost their reference to 'real-worlds' activities or objects, and have only retained the 'rudeness'. Compare:

> It's like pissing into the wind.

> I see he's pissed off home before I could ask him.

In the first example, 'piss' is a rude word for the action that in other contexts could be referred to as urinating; in the second, this reference is clearly irrelevant. The expletive 'piss' here contributes rudeness, probably to reflect the speaker's annoyance, while it is the whole collocation 'piss off' which means 'go'. The rudeness in this case could equally be provided by using another expletive such as 'bugger': the collocation 'bugger off' also means 'go'.

In functional terms, expletives have no experiential meaning: they have only interpersonal meaning. It is not surprising, therefore, that they appear in patterns which are to some extent unique. It is also not surprising that they show in an extreme form the mobility of interpersonal meanings within the clause (see 4.4.1 above): an expletive can appear at more or less any point, in the structural guise of a verb (e.g. 'piss off'), a noun ('bastard'), an adjective ('bloody') or an adverb ('damn well'). Here are some examples of the range:

> You can just *bloody well* wait your turn.

> Those tins are real *sods* to get open.

> *Screw* you, mate!

> What's the *bloody* use?

In analysing expletives, the constraints of applying constituent labels to interpersonal meanings become very clear, and we need to resort to 'translating' them into more constituent-like meanings. 'Pissed off' in the example above is clearly the Predicator, while 'real sods to get open' is Complement: note that in both cases we cannot actually indicate that these are expletives. With 'bloody well' and 'bloody' in the examples, we can follow Halliday's (1994: 85) suggestion of simply labelling them 'Expletive'; he points out that they are outside the Mood/Residue structure. 'Screw you' is an exclamation with no real internal structure (it appears to be an imperative, but is merely an imitation of one): we need to account for it as a step in an exchange (in this case it was a rejection of a request), but we do not need to assign it a grammatical analysis.

Evaluation is clearly related to modality, in that both relate to the speaker's attitude. As with modality (see 4.4.5), evaluation in a text always raises the question of **source**: the responsibility for evaluation may be disguised to a greater or lesser extent. It is also interesting to look at the ways in which evaluation is left open to negotiation or treated as unquestionable. You may have noticed in the text about Arthur Scargill in 4.4.5 that the 1984–85 strike was evaluated as 'disastrous': presumably the 'impartial' reporter is the source of this evaluation, which is slipped into the text in a way which treats it as accepted information and therefore makes it difficult to challenge.

4.6 Interaction and negotiation

Looking at the clause from an interpersonal perspective has naturally led us at several points to consider the wider context: the idea of the clause as exchange implies a minimum of two components (giving implies receiving, etc.). Since our approach to grammar is designed to allow us to look at how the grammar works in use, the next step is to formalise the links with the wider context as far as possible. This is potentially a huge undertaking, and it is not possible here to develop anything like a full set of systems for showing how particular choices at clause level affect the on-going interaction. What I would like to do is just to sketch in the lines of enquiry that can be followed in making the transition from clause to text in analysis.

One way into this is by looking back at the speech roles shown in Figure 4.1. For each role, we can set up the kind of response that the speaker expects. Of course, the other person is not bound by the speaker's expectations and is, in principle, free to choose what Halliday (1994: 69) calls the '**discretionary alternative**'. These two sets of responses are shown in Figure 4.20.

As the responses in square brackets indicate, some of the initiating speech functions do not need a verbal response (e.g. a command is successful if the action demanded is carried out), though in speech one is typically given. If the other person opts for the discretionary alternative in any case, this will in effect delay or cancel the success of the exchange, and is therefore less common on the whole (and typically needs a more elaborate form of response, in order to compensate for the interruption in the running of the exchange). The situation with written language is somewhat different because the interaction is not face-

	Initiation	Expected response	Discretionary alternative
give goods-&-services	offer	acceptance	rejection
demand goods-&-services	command	undertaking [action]	refusal
give information	statement	acknowledgement [non-intervention]	contradiction
demand information	question	answer	challenge

Fig 4.20 Responses in exchanges

to-face and therefore the reader's response cannot have the same function in contributing to the exchange as in speech. With statements (the function that written language lends itself to most easily since they do not in principle need any overt response), we are typically expected just to read on. We shall look at the effect of questions, etc. in written language when we analyse an advertisement, below.

The basic guideline for analysis is not only that the grammar of any particular clause will be at least partly determined by its intended role in the interaction, but that the meaning of the clause can only be understood by comparing its grammar to this intended role. For example, a question may be expressed by an interrogative Mood choice; but a declarative clause may be intended and interpreted as a question (a **'queclarative'**). The differences between choosing a queclarative and an interrogative in a specific context can be explored on the basis of the meanings typically associated with the declarative and interrogative structures in general. Similarly, an interrogative in written text may clearly not be expected to give rise to a response in reality, but its response-demanding function remains and is part of the reason why the writer has chosen an interrogative rather than a declarative at that point.

As an addition to this extension of the analysis from the clause to the exchange, it will be useful at this point to present an overview of the kinds of areas that can be explored in the analysis of interpersonal meanings. Figure 4.21 draws together the different areas that have been covered so far, dividing them into those which are primarily oriented towards the speaker's personal intervention and those which are primarily oriented towards the interaction between speaker and hearer.

Figure 4.21 introduces an area which has not been touched on so far: **projected roles.** This represents an area of overlap with transitivity, which will be dealt with in the next chapter, so at this stage only a brief outline will be given. In interacting with another person, the speaker will inevitably enact one

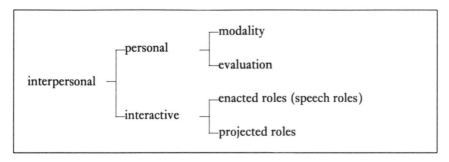

Fig 4.21 Aspects of interpersonal management

of the speech roles: anything s/he says will be intended and interpreted as a statement, question, command or offer. By acting out a role, s/he is simultaneously creating a corresponding role for the other person (even if the other person does not in turn carry out that role): in asking a question, for example, the speaker creates the role of answerer for the other person. However, the speaker may also project a role onto himself or herself or the other person by the way s/he talks about them. This is clearest with naming, where the way that the speaker names the other person indicates how s/he thinks of that other person:

> *Reader*, I married him.

> Can I help you, *sir*?

The message that the speaker is in effect conveying is: 'This is the kind of person that I expect you to be; and for the interaction to be successful you will normally have to agree to be that kind of person, at least for the duration of the interaction.' The most basic and general labels are 'I' and 'you': that is, simply, 'the person speaking' and 'the other person in this interaction'. But the labels can be varied and more specialised. You might like to consider the reasons why the following labels have been used for the interactants in each context:

> So, how are *we* today? (nurse to patient)

> *Students* may choose up to six units overall from these courses (from a University Department handbook for students)

> You see *Bosch* believe not just in building a better machine technically speaking, *we* insist it's easy on the eye too (in an advertisement for Bosch).

Figure 4.21 in some ways presents an oversimple picture, but it does show the areas which I have generally found it most rewarding to explore in the analysis of interpersonal meanings in text; and it provides a basis for the analysis that we will carry out now in 4.7.

4.7 Interaction in text

Here is the text of an advertisement (published by the Department of Health in 1989). Bearing in mind the issues raised especially in the last section, read the text and answer the questions following it (the orthographic sentences are numbered for ease of reference).

(1) **Do the financial rewards match the emotional ones?**

(2) Emotionally, nursing is one of the most satisfying of professions.

(3) Imagine how rewarding it is to nurse a stroke victim towards independence. (4) Or to watch a critically ill patient go into intensive care and come out of it in a stable condition. (5) Or being recognised and thanked by former patients.

(6) Of course these sorts of experiences are worth a great deal. (7) But you can't live off experiences any more than you can live off fresh air. (8) So what sort of money can you expect as a nurse?

(9) A nurse's salary is far from being the pittance of popular imagination. (10) The very least a newly qualified nurse can earn is £——— or £——— in Inner London. (11) (Those figures and the ones that follow exclude unsocial hours payment.)

(12) But the above salary is just the first rung on the pay ladder. (13) The pay structure in nursing is designed to reward the clinical skills and responsibilities of individual posts. (14) In other words, it's no longer necessary for a nurse to leave the patient's bedside in order to earn a higher salary.

(15) Even better, each step-up or grade gets an automatic increment every year for the first four years.

(16) But what does it all mean in real terms (or rather real money)?

(17) Well, more than three out of four staff nurses are currently in one of the higher grades. (18) They earn up to £——— or £——— in Inner London.

(19) And what's the money like if you go on to become a Ward Sister or (the male equivalent) a Charge Nurse?

(20) They can earn as much as £——— or £——— in Inner London.

(21) Not as bad as you thought, is it? (22) Of course, you're unlikely to be attracted to nursing because of the money. (23) But there's no reason in the world why you shouldn't be.

(24) **What did you do at work today?**

1. What is the main aim of this advert? What sort of person is likely to read it? What sort of person does the writer assume the reader will be?
2. What features of the language make the advert sound more like an informal conversation than a formal written text?
3. In a conversation, there are usually at least two people talking. Who are the two people in the conversation in the advert? Label which of the people says which parts of the conversation. Why do you think that the writer writes the text in this way?
4. How are the two main questions (the ones in bold) different from each other?
    What is the answer to each question? How do you know?
5. What do you notice about the pronouns 'you' and 'they' as used in the advert?
    Who exactly do they refer to?
6. What signals of modality are there in the text? What is their function?
7. What signals of evaluation are there in the text? How much of the evaluation is open to question? How does the writer encourage the reader to accept the evaluation as valid?
8. Are there any missing Subjects in the text? What is the effect of their absence?

The following is not intended as a complete analysis of the interpersonal meanings of the text. I shall simply be suggesting lines of enquiry that can be followed up in more depth. We shall be coming back to this text in each of the next three chapters to look at it from different perspectives; so by the end we should build up a fairly comprehensive picture of how the text works.

ANSWERS

1. The aim is to encourage people to become nurses. The readership is essentially self-selected, especially after an initial scan of the topic (i.e. someone thinking of changing their job is more likely to read through to the end). The writer assumes that the reader has a job which pays adequately, has 'normal' human emotions but also has 'normal' concerns about money, and believes that nursing is a badly paid job.
2. The following contribute to the informal conversational tone: the question and answer pattern; in (3), (4) and (5), the use of full stops to separate grammatically dependent clauses from each other in a way which mimics the afterthoughts of unplanned speech; the use of conjunctions such as 'But', e.g. (12) and 'So', e.g. (8) to start sentences; in (21) an elliptical clause and a tag question.
3. Presumably, the writer and the reader. The reader 'asks' the three questions in the body of the text about money – (8), (16) and (19) – and the writer 'answers' them. The writer asks the tag question (21) and

the closing question (24). It is ambiguous as to whether the first question, in the headline, is 'asked' by the writer or the reader. The rhetorical effect of writing the text in this way is complex, but one aspect is that the writer encourages the reader to accept him/her as able to ask questions on the reader's behalf, i.e. as familiar and trustworthy.

4. People usually ask questions in order to get information that they do not have. The two main questions are different from the others in that neither has a direct response in the text; and they are different from each other in that the first functions ambiguously whereas the second clearly functions as a question from the writer to the reader. The answer to the first question is conveyed by the whole text (which suggests that the question is meant to function as coming from the reader); but it is the reader who is actually invited to make the answer explicit when the writer asks 'Not as bad as you thought, is it?' (which suggests that the first question is meant to function as coming from the writer, inviting the reader's opinion in order to contradict it). The answer to the second question is outside the interaction: it is left hanging for the reader to consider. The kind of answer hoped for is clearly 'Something no better paid than nursing, and not as rewarding.'

5. In the main part of the text 'you' appears almost exclusively in the reader's questions, and is therefore partly equivalent to 'I' ('What sort of money can I expect as a nurse [if I become one]?'). 'They' and other 3rd-person forms are used in the answers to refer to nurses, and are therefore partly equivalent to 'you' ('You can earn as much as £———— or £———— in Inner London [if you become one]'). This 'pronoun-shift' is suddenly reversed at the end from (21) on, when 'you' becomes really 'you' – the addressee.

6. There is no modality in the parts of the text related to emotional rewards; those are presented as absolute and beyond qualification. All the modality is to do with the financial aspects – for example, what nurses 'can' earn. At the end, the writer uses objective modalisation to soften a statement about the reader's character ('You're *unlikely* to be attracted to nursing because of the money' – this is a flattering description, but the writer still has to avoid the appearance of being too confident in his/her knowledge of the reader). Moral obligation also appears, again in connection with money ('there's no reason in the world why you *shouldn't* be'). The modality here blurs the moral line between being attracted to nursing because of its emotional rewards and because of the money.

7. There is a clump of evaluation in (2) to (6) related to the emotional side of nursing: 'satisfying', 'rewarding', 'worth a great deal' (note the shift towards terms which could equally be applied in financial areas). These are potentially open to question, but the writer encourages agreement by expressing them as common ground ('Of course' in (6)), and in any

case the advert operates on the assumption that there will be no disagreement on these evaluations. The evaluations of the financial side ('far from being the *pittance* of popular imagination', 'Even better', 'not as bad as you thought') are justified by hard figures (it is assumed that the reader will agree that the figures represent a good salary, which indicates what the writer thinks the reader's present salary level is). These evaluations are mostly expressed in negative terms, reflecting the writer's assessment of the reader's own initial evaluations.

8. In (3) to (5) the Subjects are missing for 'Imagine', and the non-finite forms 'nurse', 'watch' and 'being recognised and thanked'. The understood Subject of the imperative 'Imagine' is 'you'; and, in non-finite clauses, Subject and Finite are normally assumed to be carried over from the finite clause on which they depend, i.e. the most natural Subject would be 'you'. However, this interpretation is not forced on the reader: as often happens in advertisements, there is an 'empty slot' which the reader is encouraged to step into mentally, but the writer does not insist on it (compare the effect of 'Imagine how rewarding it is *for you* to nurse ...'). This is a subtle variation on projected roles, which we will come back to when we look at transitivity in the text, in the next chapter.

§   Refer to Exercise 4.3.

EXERCISE 4.1

Identify the Subject and Finite in the following sentences. Where there is an embedded clause, ignore the Subject and Finite within that clause: simply analyse the main clause.

1   Kate didn't like this at all.
2   In that case, the universe should contain a number of regions that are smooth and uniform.
3   Tears streamed down his face.
4   In silence they went through the rooms on the top floor.
5   So the four we have don't count.
6   That might have been a different matter.
7   The other few items in the printing history of this work are easily summarised.
8   In the footnotes, the titles of works which we have had to cite fairly frequently have been abbreviated to the author's surname.
9   It is a matter of common experience that one can describe the position of a point in space by three numbers, or coordinates.
10   It isn't the money I'm worried about.

EXERCISE 4.2

Identify Mood and Residue in the following clauses, and label the elements in each: Subject, Finite, Predicator, Complement, Adjunct. For any Adjunct, decide whether it is circumstantial, textual, Mood or Comment. Do not analyse any non-finite clauses separately.

1   He picked up ideas about form from his teachers.
2   He had already been over the house.
3   Where have all the flowers gone?
4   Of course Tim could not really banish care.
5   The relatively well-educated and literate soldiers of these countries most willingly accepted their own death.
6   In her waking hours she would never let us out of her sight.
7   The union involved certainly has to face criticism for its lack of activity on health and safety over many years.
8   Put simply, you will probably find it difficult to find a job as a student.
9   Meanwhile, Bruce Grobbelaar's days at Liverpool could be over this week.
10 Right now, however, you might have to juggle your finances around.

EXERCISE 4.3

Here are three extracts from a consultation in a doctor's surgery. I have put in vertical strokes at 'natural breaks' to make it easier to follow. Analyse the Mood, modality, and interaction (e.g. look at who asks questions or gives information or instructions, when they do this, and how they do it). This text will be discussed in Chapter 11.

P   I can't bend forward and I can't like turn sideways | it's like the bottom of my spine it just feels like I'm sitting on a pin
D   so it's pain in the lower back
P   lower back just about there
D   ok how long did you say again
P   I mean all last night I couldn't turn on my side | I couldn't stand up | I couldn't go to the toilet
D   so it got worse overnight
P   yeh

D   so the first thing is rest | secondly I'll give you some painkillers | they don't speed up the healing | it's just to make life comfortable for you while it's healing | now it's
P   what is it | is it like a thing I've got with my spine or
D   it's a torn muscle in your back yeh | it should recover

P   you wouldn't think it was so painful would you

D   oh no it is | but it's all right as long as you don't move | as soon as you move it'll try and go into spasm to stop you using those muscles you've injured

P   how long will it take to um

D   I think you're going to be off work at least a week

P   a week

D   possibly two weeks

D   there's your note | the tablets I'm going to give you a common side-effect is indigestion so take them with food just to protect yourself | it's one three times a day | they don't make you drowsy | you don't have to finish the course | simply when your back is fine just stop them

P   ok

D   it's not like an antibiotic

(Recorded by Sultan Al-Sharief)

5

Representing the world: the experiential metafunction

5.1 Introduction

As well as using language to interact with people, we clearly use it to talk about the world, either the external world, things, events, qualities, etc., or our internal world, thoughts, beliefs, feelings, etc. When we look at how language works from this perspective, we are focusing primarily on the 'content' of a message rather than the purpose for which the speaker has uttered it (although it is not in practice possible to make a complete distinction: there are many alternative ways in which speakers can choose to represent the world, and their actual choice is dependent to a large extent on their purpose).

In Chapter 4, we have been examining the very different functions served by, for example, statements and questions. It is clear that the following two sentences are not in any way interchangeable in use:

Cats would choose Whiskas.

Would cats choose Whiskas?

But it is equally clear that 'cats' and 'Whiskas' have the same role in relation to each other and to the action of 'choosing' in both the statement and the question. Looking separately at the interpersonal meanings enables us to give them their full value in the overall meaning of the clause; but we do still need to account for the 'content' meanings. It is the role of the experiential perspective in the grammar to allow us to do this. It is worth emphasising again, however, that both perspectives are needed: the clause carries both kinds of meanings simultaneously, so at some point we need to bring the two analyses together.

From the experiential perspective, language comprises a set of resources for referring to entities in the world and the ways in which those entities act on or relate to each other. At the simplest level, language reflects our view of the world as consisting of 'goings-on' (verbs) involving things (nouns) which may have attributes (adjectives) and which go on against background details of place, time, manner, etc. (adverbials). Thus the following representation distinguishes not only a recognisable type of going-on ('unlocked') but also doers ('they') and 'done-to' ('the front door'), and a manner ('slowly').

They slowly unlocked the front door.

This will seem so obvious as hardly to need saying: but it is precisely because it is so natural-seeming that we can easily overlook what is going on. For one thing, it would clearly be possible to represent the 'same' going-on in different ways ('She took out the key. The door swung open in front of them.'), and we will want to be able to say something useful about exactly what the differences are. More importantly, this first step leads us towards a systematic and less immediately obvious categorisation of the kinds of goings-on, things, etc. that we can express through language.

If we use functional labels (i.e. labels which indicate the role played by each element of the representation), we can express what we have said about the 'content' of clauses in terms of **processes** involving **participants** in certain **circumstances**. The example above can then be analysed in a preliminary way as in Figure 5.1.

They	slowly	unlocked	the front door
Participant	**Circumstance**	**Process**	**Participant**

Fig 5.1 Process, participants and circumstance

The process is typically expressed – or realised – by the verbal group in the clause, and is the central component of the message from the experiential perspective. In some cases, the process can be seen as including another constituent apart from the verbal group proper. This is clearest with phrasal verbs, where the particle is usually best analysed as expressing part of the process (and see also the discussion of Range in 5.2.5 below):

He *found out* that she had high blood pressure.

He *didn't look at* her.

Every major clause normally includes at least one participant, which is normally realised by a nominal group. In interpersonal terms, this is usually Subject, while other participants, if there are any, will be Complements.

He began by translating *the programme*.

In some cases, a participant may not be explicitly mentioned but is understood as part of the experiential meaning: for example, 'you' is understood as the 'doer' participant in imperative clauses. With a small group of processes of a specific type – relating to weather – there may be no participant (even though there is a

Subject, 'it', this has no experiential meaning). The following example consists only of two processes in transitivity terms:

> It's raining, it's pouring.

Circumstances are typically realised by adverbial groups or prepositional phrases: they are circumstantial Adjuncts in interpersonal terms. Note that conjunctive and modal Adjuncts (see 4.3.6) do not contribute to the experiential meaning of the clause and are left out of the transitivity analysis (modal Adjuncts which appear next to or within the verbal group can simply be included with the process). Circumstances are often optional, reflecting their 'background' function in the clause – compare what was said about Adjuncts not easily becoming Subject in 4.3.5.

> *In 1923* two volumes were published.

However, in other cases, it may be more or less obligatory to include a Circumstance in the clause:

> The second great discovery took place *at about the same time.*

> She put the lamp *down on the floor.*

The process/participant/circumstance model is a start, which has the required advantage of matching structural and functional features. However, it is clearly still too general: in particular, we have no way of indicating the role of different participants ('doer' vs. 'done to', etc.). We need to establish a more delicate set of categories, bearing in mind that the categories must be based on grammatical as well as semantic differences. It turns out that there are two basic ways in which we can do this, each corresponding to a different way of representing the world, and each also corresponding to different structural possibilities. The first of these, which is the more general, involves an analysis in terms of transitivity: this starts from a classification of the different kinds of processes (see 5.2). The other involves analysing the clause in terms of ergativity: this centres on the kind of relationship that is set up between the process and the participants (see 5.3).

5.2 Transitivity

The term **transitivity** will probably be familiar as a way of distinguishing between verbs according to whether they have an Object or not. Here, however, it is being used in a much broader sense. In particular, it refers to a system for describing the whole clause, rather than just the verb and its Object. It does, though, share with the traditional use a focus on the verbal group, since it is the type of process which determines how the participants are labelled: the 'doer' of a physical process such as kicking is given a different label from the 'doer' of a mental process such as wishing (note that even at this informal level 'doer' seems less appropriate as a label in the case of the mental process).

In deciding what types of process to recognise, we resort to a combination of common sense and grammar: common sense to distinguish the different kinds of 'goings-on' that we can identify, and grammar to confirm that these intuitive differences are reflected in the language and thus to justify the decision to set up a separate category. We need to set up categories that are detailed enough to make us feel that we have captured something important about the meaning, but broad enough to be manageable as the basis for general claims about the grammar of English. In the following discussion, the grammatical justification for the categories will often be touched on only briefly, in order to keep things reasonably simple; but it should be borne in mind that the grammatical underpinning is there.

There are three basic questions that can be asked about any process and the clause of which it forms the nucleus:

1. What kind of process is it?
2. How many participants can/must be involved in the process?
3. What roles can/must those participants play?

You may well find that there is a rather bewildering amount of new terminology in this outline of transitivity. However, I hope that you will also see that the basic concept is simple: a relatively small number of types of process can be identified, and they each have their own types of participants. We need labels for each (and the labels are, admittedly, not always as transparent as they might be); but we are essentially going through the same kind of steps for each process type.

5.2.1 MATERIAL PROCESSES

One of the most salient types of processes are those involving physical actions: running, throwing, scratching, cooking, sitting down, and so on. These are called **material processes**. A traditional definition of a verb is 'a doing word', and this describes such processes reasonably well (but not, as we shall see, other types). The 'doer' of this type of action is called the Actor: any material process has an Actor, even though the Actor may not actually be mentioned in the clause. In many cases, the action may be represented as affecting or 'being done to' a second participant: this participant is called the **Goal**, since the action is, in a sense, directed at this participant. These labels for the participants are perhaps easiest to understand when the Actor is human and the Goal, if there is one, is inanimate, as in Figure 5.2. (NB: Some of the examples of processes include Circumstances; we will look at these separately in 5.2.6 below.)

However, the Actor may also be an inanimate or abstract entity, and the Goal may, of course, be human. Some examples are given in Figure 5.3.

It is possible to identify various sub-categories of material processes. One division is according to whether the process is **intentional** or **involuntary**.

Actor	Process: Material	Goal	Circumstance
He	had been shaving.		
The young girl	bounded		out of the gate.
Edward	was sawing	wood.	
Her mother	smashed	the glass.	

Fig 5.2 Material processes 1

Actor	Process: Material	Goal	Circumstance
The car	slithered		off the road.
Coarse grass	was growing		here and there.
The unhappiness	disappeared.		
The fire	had destroyed	everything.	
Scores of tiny brambles	scratched	him.	
The pounding rhythm	shook	walls and floor.	

Fig 5.3 Material processes 2

With involuntary processes, the Actor (in italics) often seems like a Goal in some respects:

> *The car* accelerated.

> *The affair* ended after a year.

> *She* tripped over the step.

If we want to find out about the events encoded in clauses like these, we are not likely to ask 'What did she do?'; instead it seems more appropriate to ask 'What happened to her?' The process here appears to affect the Actor – a description which recalls the way we defined the role of the Goal above. We will come back to this issue when we look at the clause from a different perspective in 5.3.

Another possible grouping would separate processes which are 'done to' existing Goals from those which bring Goals into existence (or the opposite).

> My Mum never eats *Christmas pudding*.

> I've just made *the Christmas puddings*.

This leads on to an area that is somewhat problematic in analysing transitivity: processes which encode an **outcome** without in themselves specifying what led to that outcome. In the following example, the process of 'achieving' seems to blend the ideas of 'doing something in order to have' and 'having'; in other words there is a blend of action and resulting state:

He achieved his lifetime ambition when he finally appeared on television.

The 'action' interpretation suggests that this is a material process, whereas the 'state' interpretation suggests that it is a relational process (see 5.2.3). In practice, I find that these are generally best coded as material processes, but that, if a number of the same blended process types appear in a text, it is often worth examining them separately as a sub-category which may give a particular 'tone' to the text as a whole. Another even clearer example of blending that occurs fairly frequently in certain types of text is one where the relational ('state') meaning is dominant but the wording brings in a material ('action') process colouring:

Hope Street *runs* between the two cathedrals.

This clearly expresses location, but the choice of a verb that normally encodes action gives the stative description a more dynamic tone, especially if there are a number of similar choices in that area of the text.

The most useful way of looking at such areas of uncertainty is to accept that the material process category has a core of **prototypical** processes which can be probed by questions like 'What did she do?'; around this core there are slightly less typical processes which are more easily probed by questions like 'What happened?'; and further out on the periphery there are processes for which the most appropriate probes are questions like 'What was the resulting state?'. This is in fact typical of all the categories: many examples fit smoothly into the categories as defined, while others seem to include less typical elements of meaning or to show a blend of two categories.

It was noted above in passing that all material processes have an Actor, but that the Actor may not appear explicitly in the clause. One of the main ways in which this can happen is by the choice of a passive clause:

The oil is added drop by drop.

Your son didn't kill himself. *He was murdered.*

In this case, the participant at which the process is directed is still coded as Goal, since its semantic relationship to the process has not changed; see Figure 5.4.

The oil He	is added was murdered.	drop by drop.
Goal	**Process: Material**	**Circumstance**

Fig 5.4 Passive material processes

Combining this analysis with the Mood analysis allows us to characterise passive material process clauses as those where the Goal is Subject. Note that we can normally discover the Actor in such cases by asking 'Who by?'. Passive clauses are, of course, marked in relation to active clauses (that is, there is usually a particular reason for choosing a passive clause, whereas an active clause is the natural choice when there are no particular reasons for not choosing it); and this is reflected in the fact that the most natural probe question is the one associated with more peripheral types of material processes: 'What happened to him?' – 'He was murdered.' It is worth noting in passing that the Goal may also be understood but not expressed in some cases: we can, for example, capture the difference between 'The fire's smoking' and 'He's smoking' by saying that, unlike the first clause, the second has an understood Goal (as the possible question 'What's he smoking?' shows).

5.2.2 MENTAL PROCESSES

I mentioned above that the simple functional description of a verb as 'a doing word' did not by any means fit all processes, which suggests that we need to establish other categories apart from material processes. Intuitively, **mental processes** form a viable semantic category: there are clear differences between something that goes on in the external world and something that goes on in the internal world of the mind; and there are many verbs which refer to these mental processes, of thinking, imagining, liking, wanting, seeing, etc. In addition, the terms Actor and, to a lesser extent, Goal seem inappropriate as labels for, say, the participants in this clause:

> *She* could hear *his voice.*

The person in whose mind the mental process occurs is not really 'acting' – if anything, she is 'undergoing' the process of hearing; and the process is not really 'directed at' the phenomenon. It seems as intuitively satisfactory to say that it is the voice which triggers the mental process of hearing. Thus a more appropriate set of labels are those shown in Figure 5.5.

She	could hear	his voice.
Senser	**Process: Mental**	**Phenomenon**

Fig 5.5 Senser and phenomenon

But what is the grammatical justification for placing these in a separate category? Halliday (1994: 114–17) gives five criteria for distinguishing between material and mental processes, which in fact help us to understand more fully how this area of language works. The first is that mental processes always involve at least one human participant: the participant who has the mind in which the process occurs. Even if an inanimate participant is represented as undergoing a mental process, a degree of humanness is bestowed on that participant by its involvement in the process (and the mental process also loses some of its 'mentalness'); for example:

> We used to have a car *that didn't like cold weather*.

The second, complementary, criterion is that the kind of entity which can fill the role of the other participant in a mental process – the **Phenomenon** – is less restricted than the entities which can act as participants in a material process. It can, of course, be a person, a concrete object, an abstraction, and so on, just as with material processes. We can say, for example:

> Did you notice *the key*?

However, in addition, the Phenomenon may be a 'fact': that is, a clause treated as if it were almost a thing:

> I see *that you've already met*.

> She doubted *whether you would find him on your own*.

> Do you regret *that she's left*?

A more precise definition of 'fact' will be given in Chapter 10; here it is sufficient to note that a clause like those in the examples cannot be a participant in a material process. Facts can be sensed – understood, felt, or perceived – but they cannot do anything or have anything done to them.

The third reason for differentiating between material and mental processes is **tense**. For material processes, the most natural present tense is the continuous form: 'He's mending the handle.' It is of course possible to use them in the simple form, but this needs some extra contextualisation: 'He mends the handle every week [but it keeps sticking].' For mental processes, on the other hand, the most natural present tense is the simple form: 'They like salmon'; and it is often difficult to construct a context in which the continuous form sounds natural. In Teaching English as a Foreign Language, this feature of mental process verbs is often presented as an odd exception; but in fact it is an inherent part of their grammar.

The fourth reason is that many (though not all) mental processes are 'reversible': that is, in talking about a mental process it is equally possible to have the Subject role filled either by the human participant in whose mind the process occurs or by the phenomenon which triggers the process. With material processes, the second participant, the Goal, can be Subject, but only in a passive clause (see Figure 5.4 above). With mental processes, this constraint does not apply. Figure 5.6 shows the analysis of examples we have already seen with Senser as Subject, while Figure 5.7 shows Phenomenon as Subject.

Did	you	notice	the key?
	I	see	that you've already met.
	She	doubted	whether you would find him on your own.
Do	you	regret	that she's left?
Process:-	**Senser**	**-Mental**	**Phenomenon**

Fig 5.6 Mental processes: Senser as Subject

This news	seemed to puzzle	her.
His lack of self-esteem	never worried	him.
The realisation	horrified	her.
Phenomenon	**Process: Mental**	**Senser**

Fig 5.7 Phenomenon as Subject

This reversibility emerges even more strongly in certain cases where we can identify pairs of verbs which refer to more or less the same kind of mental process but reverse the Senser/Phenomenon slots. In each of the pairs below, the first clause has Senser as Subject, while the second has Phenomenon as Subject (in the last example, the Subject is 'It/that she looked ill' – see 4.3.2).

She liked what he did.	What he did pleased her.
I admire his willingness to experiment.	His willingness to experiment impresses me.
He fancied her.	She attracted him.
He noticed that she looked ill.	It struck him that she looked ill.

Although each member of the pair is different in its choice of Subject (and Theme), in terms of the real-world event being talked about they are essentially the same; and the two participants remain in the same roles of Senser and Phenomenon. This follows from the semantics: as the formulation I have just given suggests, the process can be seen either as sensed by the human participant or as triggered by the phenomenon. Of course, it is also possible to use a passive clause, especially to bring the human Senser into Subject position. Figure 5.8 gives rewordings of the examples in Figure 5.7 to show this; note that this is one case where the passive sounds as unmarked and natural as the active.

The fifth reason for having a separate category for mental processes is that they need a different type of question from that used to probe core examples of material processes. For the examples in Figures 5.7 and 5.8, the most appropriate

She	seemed to be puzzled	by this news.
He	was never worried	by his lack of self-esteem.
She	was horrified	by the realisation.
Senser	**Process: Mental**	**Phenomenon**

Fig 5.8 Passive mental process clauses

question is 'What was her reaction?', or, with Phenomenon as Subject, 'What effect did it have on her?'. There are some cases, however, where these questions are also not appropriate, which leads us to identify three sub-categories of mental processes: **affection**, or reaction (the type illustrated in Figures 5.7 and 5.8); **cognition** (processes of deciding, knowing, understanding, etc.); and **perception** (seeing, hearing, etc.). Figures 5.9 and 5.10 give examples of these two last sub-categories. Note that 'discover' in Figure 5.9 means 'find out': if it was used to mean 'find' (e.g. 'Columbus discovered America') it would be a material process.

You	can imagine	his reaction.
No one	would choose	such a colour.
She	never discovered	the exact address.
Senser	**Process: Mental (cognition)**	**Phenomenon**

Fig 5.9 Mental processes: cognition

He	could not see	anything.
He	heard	a faint sound.
Cordelia	felt	her face burning.
Senser	**Process: Mental (perception)**	**Phenomenon**

Fig 5.10 Mental processes: perception

As the examples suggest, these tend to be less easily reversible than affection/ reaction processes – they most naturally occur in active clauses with Senser as Subject; but it is possible to reverse them in some cases, though often only by using wordings that are to some extent metaphorical (usually encoding the mental process as if it were a material process; see Figure 5.11).

One feature of mental processes that you may have noticed in looking at the examples is that they all involve two participants. This is in fact a further

An awful thought A flash of colour	has just struck caught	me. her eye.
Phenomenon	**Process: Mental**	**Senser**

Fig 5.11 Cognition and perception processes with Phenomenon as Subject

difference between them and material processes: whereas a number of material processes have no Goal (they are genuinely 'intransitive' in the traditional use of the term), with mental processes there are always two participants involved. This is not to say that the clause always has two participants expressed; but both are understood. It is particularly the Phenomenon that may be omitted: omission of the Senser tends to occur in more restricted contexts. In Figure 5.12, the kind of participant that is understood is added in brackets.

Can	you She	see was delighted	[the blackboard]? [by his attentiveness].
Process:-	**Senser**	**-Mental**	**[Phenomenon]**

My elbow These amazing tricks	doesn't half hurt will delight and intrigue	[me]. [people]!
Phenomenon	**Process: Mental**	**[Senser]**

Fig 5.12 Mental processes with one participant expressed

5.2.3 RELATIONAL PROCESSES

None of what we have said so far about different categories of processes applies easily to examples like the following:

> This bread is stale.

Here a relationship is set up between two concepts, in this case an object ('bread') and a quality ('stale'), and the function of the Predicator ('is') is simply to signal the existence of the relationship. Strictly speaking, neither of the basic experiential terms, 'process' and 'participant', is completely appropriate for this category. There is no process in the normal sense of 'something happening'; and, although there are always two concepts – one on each side of the relationship – there is only one participant in the real world: the attribute 'stale' is hardly a prototypical participant at all, while even in an example like the following, the two concepts are presented as different ways of referring to the same entity:

His immediate objective was *the church.*

However, no grammatical term will cover equally well all the phenomena to which we need to apply it, so we will continue to talk about process and participants.

The discussion of the examples given above has informally indicated two different types of **relational process**: in the first 'this bread' has been ascribed the attribute 'stale', while in the other a relationship of identity has been set up between 'his immediate objective' and 'the church'. It is useful to show the difference through the labels we give each of these, not least because, as we shall see, there is at least one crucial grammatical difference between them. The first type is called an **attributive** relational process; and the two participants are the **Carrier** (the entity which 'carries' the attribute) and the **Attribute**. Figure 5.13 shows the analysis of the example above, and adds some other examples.

This bread	is	stale.
He	's not	a very good painter.
She	was	an art student.
He	felt	uneasy.
The weather	has turned	quite nasty.
Carrier	**Process**	**Attribute**

Fig 5.13 Attributive relational process

The second type is called an **identifying** relational process. The function of this kind of process is to identify one entity in terms of another. In the example above, 'his immediate objective' is identified as 'the church'. The participants are therefore labelled the **Identified** and the **Identifier**. Figure 5.14 shows the analysis and again adds other examples.

His immediate objective	was	the church.
My name	is	Edward.
This	used to be	our dining room.
Pat	is	her brother.
Identified	**Process**	**Identifier**

Fig 5.14 Identifying relational process

The Predicator in identifying processes is equivalent in a way to an equals sign '='; and it is therefore not surprising that these processes are reversible (if x = y, then y = x). Thus the examples above could all be reworded as follows:

> The church was his immediate objective.

> Edward is my name.

> Our dining room used to be this [room].

> Her brother is Pat.

However, some of these rewordings, though grammatically correct, do not seem to express quite the same experiential meaning as the original versions. In order to explore why, it is worth expanding the context in which the sentences were or might be used. For example, the last of the sentences in Figure 5.14 was said to someone who had heard the name 'Pat' and had mistakenly assumed that this was a woman:

> So you met Florence's sister?   No, Pat's her **brother**.

(The bold type face shows which word had the main stress.) The reworded version, on the other hand, would be more likely in the following kind of context:

> What are the rest of Florence's family called?   Her brother's **Pat**.

What has happened here is that 'Pat' is now the Identifier: the questioner knows that Florence has a brother, and the answerer identifies him as being called 'Pat'. As a simple rule of thumb, we can say that the main stress in an identifying clause typically falls on the Identifier. Since the main stress indicates the new information in a clause, the Identified is typically a participant that has already been mentioned or whose existence is assumed, whereas the Identifier is typically mentioned for the first time.

   This implies that, if the stress pattern changes, the roles of Identifier and Identified also change; and this is in fact what happens. We can, with a bit of ingenuity, think of contexts in which either of these versions could be spoken with the stress on the first participant:

> So her sister's Pat and ...   No, I've already told you: her **brother's** Pat.

This does not mean the same as the original, but we still have 'Pat' as something that has just been mentioned – i.e. the Identified – and 'brother' as information that the speaker treats as new (since the other person clearly did not hear or understand it the first time) – i.e. the Identifier.

> So Nicky's her brother?   No, **Pat's** her brother.

Here 'brother' has just been mentioned, and it is the name 'Pat' which has to be (re)introduced as the Identifier. The reason why ingenuity is needed to construct contexts where these last two versions sound acceptable is that there is a general tendency in English for the main stress to fall at or near the end of an information unit (which, in order to avoid introducing even more complications, we can take to be the same as the clause). In writing, this tendency is even stronger, since stress is rarely indicated graphologically. Thus the more usual order is Identified ˆ Identifier.

It is important to note that attributive relational processes are not reversible in this way. In certain contexts, the Attribute may come first, but this is relatively rare in most types of text, and the Attribute cannot switch roles with the Carrier in the way that, for example, 'Pat' switches from Identified to Identifier in the rewordings above. The most common case where Attribute comes first is when it is a circumstantial Attribute (see below). Examples are shown in Figure 5.15. This structure is also discussed, from the point of view of Theme, in 6.3.1.

Beyond the roundabout	is	the site of the new Gulf University.
Opposite Pier Head	stands	the Liver Building.
Attribute	Process: Relational	Carrier

Fig 5.15 Circumstantial attribute in first position

I have said above that both Identified and Identifier refer to the same real-world entity: 'Pat' and 'her brother' are the same person. We have also seen that the context determines which role is filled by each of these two ways of referring to the same entity: the form which is already 'on the table' fills the role of the Identified, while the newly (re)introduced form fills that of the Identifier. But how do we actually identify something for our hearer? How is it that we can say 'Pat [= her brother] is her brother [= Pat]' and still make sense? Essentially, identification is a matter of relating a specific realisation and a more generalisable category. It may be easier to grasp this admittedly difficult concept if we look at another example:

> Marlowe was the greatest dramatic writer in the sixteenth century apart from Shakespeare.

The writer has been summarising Marlowe's work, and here he moves to 'place' the dramatist in a wider perspective. He does this by identifying Marlowe as the specific holder of a more general role (the role of 'greatest dramatic writer' could in principle be assigned to other individual dramatists). We could paraphrase the sentence (rather clumsily) as:

> Marlowe filled the role of/represented the greatest dramatic writer in the sixteenth century apart from Shakespeare.

We can contrast this with another sentence where the identification proceeds in the opposite direction:

>The strongest shape is the triangle.

Here the writer has been describing an experiment in which she tested which of several shapes stood up to pressure best. She has therefore already established that she is interested in the general category of the strongest shape. In this concluding sentence, she identifies this in terms of the specific entity which realises or embodies it. This sentence could therefore be paraphrased as:

>The role of the strongest shape is filled by the triangle./The strongest shape is represented by the triangle.

The more general category is called the **Value**, while the specific embodiment is the **Token**. The direction of identification – from general to specific or from specific to general – depends on which entity is 'on the table': if the general category has already been established, then it will be identified in terms of its specific embodiment, and vice versa. The analysis of the examples is shown in Figure 5.16.

Marlowe	was	the greatest dramatic writer in the sixteenth century apart from Shakespeare.
Token	**Process**	**Value**

The strongest shape	is	the triangle.
Value	**Process**	**Token**

Fig 5.16 Value and Token in identifying relational clauses

As the paraphrases above indicate, one simple way of deciding which is Value and which Token in any particular clause is to use the verb 'represent': if the passive form provides a better paraphrase, it is the Value which is the Subject ('a general value *is represented* by its specific token'); if the active form sounds better, it is the Token which is the Subject ('a specific token *represents* a general value').

This is an extremely tricky concept to get one's head around, but it is, I hope, clear that the roles of Value and Token are different in nature from those of Identified and Identifier. Identified and Identifier depend on the unfolding language event: whichever of the two ways of referring to the entity has already been used is the Identified, and the new way of referring to it is the Identifier. Value and Token, on the other hand, depend on the pre-existing external semantic properties of the two ways of referring to the entity: whichever of the two ways is potentially the more generalisable is the Value, while the more specific embodiment is the Token. We therefore need to take account of both in examining the meaning of an identifying clause in context; see Figure 5.17.

Marlowe	was	the greatest dramatic writer in the sixteenth century apart from Shakespeare.
Token/Identified	**Process**	**Value/Identifier**

The strongest shape	is	the triangle.
Value/Identified	**Process**	**Token/Identifier**

Fig 5.17 Value/Token and Identified/Identifier

The Identified/Identifier analysis will help us to see how the particular text is unfolding, while the Value/Token analysis, perhaps more interestingly, will often guide us towards the broader concerns and values of the writer. Essentially, the Value reveals what values the writer (and ultimately the culture that s/he is part of) uses to measure the Tokens that s/he deals with. In some cases, these will be constrained by the demands of the particular task s/he has in hand, e.g. deciding on the strongest shape amongst several possible candidates, and tell us little of the writer's own view of what is important in the world. But in other cases, they suggest wider ideological beliefs, e.g. that dramatic writers can and should be ranked in competition with each other, that 'league tables' have a valid place in literary appreciation. Halliday (1994: 126) mentions particularly 'scientific, commercial, political and bureaucratic discourse' as areas where an investigation of ideological values can be rewardingly based on an analysis of the experiential Values used in identifying clauses (see also 4.5 on evaluation).

Figure 5.18 gives a number of other examples, showing both orderings of Value and Token (to keep this a little simpler, I have only given examples with Identified in first position). The examples show other verbs apart from 'be'; these all have an underlying 'equative' meaning, although you may sometimes find it hard to decide definitely whether a verb is equative in meaning (Halliday, 1994: 123) gives a useful list of these verbs; but remember that some of the verbs in the list, such as 'indicate' and 'realise', are more commonly found in other, non-equative, uses). Figure 5.18 also illustrates the very common phenomenon of a 'to'-infinitive or 'that' projected clause (see Chapter 10) as Token, usually in clauses with Value^Token ordering. You can confirm that these are all identify-

ing clauses by checking that they can be reversed (you will need to change the
form of the verb if it is not 'be').

Planned scarcity	was (and is)	the key to the profitability of diamonds.
Meaning-focused activity	constitutes	a condition for language acquisition.
These writings	represent	the official views of Victorian society.
Einstein's predictions	matched	what was observed.
Allometry	is defined as	'the study of proportion changes correlated with variation in size'.
What	was	the origin of these density fluctuations?
Token/Identified	**Process**	**Value/Identifier**

The first goal of colonialism	was	wealth.
The optional courses	include	Stylistics and Phonetics.
The point	is not	to present knowledge to the students to be absorbed.
The explanation	is	that it is forbidden by the second law of thermodynamics.
The aim of this book	is	to try to understand the different ways in which people talk about reading and writing.
Value/Identified	**Process**	**Token/Identifier**

Fig 5.18 Further examples of Value and Token

So far, I have been implying that it is relatively easy to distinguish the two
basic types of relational process, identifying and attributive; and, in many cases,
this is in fact so. The key test is reversibility, but each type also has other typical
features which help to distinguish them. For example, if the second participant is
an adjective ('stale', 'uneasy', etc.), it must be an Attribute and the process must
be attributive rather than identifying. If the second participant is a nominal
group, you can often decide according to definiteness: an Attribute is typically
indefinite (i.e. the noun is a common noun, with no article or an indefinite article
such as 'a' or 'some'), whereas an Identifier is typically definite (i.e. there is a
definite article such as 'the' or 'this'; or a possessive determiner such as 'my' or
'John's'; or the noun is a proper noun, such as a name). In many cases, the two
types of process can be probed by asking different questions: 'What is x (the

Carrier) like?' probes attributive processes, whereas 'What/Which is x (the Identified)?' probes identifying processes. However, there are cases where it may be more difficult to distinguish the two types: in isolation one of the tests mentioned above may not be enough to decide on a definite analysis, so it is always best to try them all (bearing in mind that there will be a few indeterminate cases which could equally well be analysed as either type). Is the following example identifying or attributive?

> This little pattern is a common building block of spoken interaction.

By now, you will probably be feeling that the outline of relational processes has become quite complex enough. Part of the problem is that the kinds of issues that we have been dealing with are relatively unfamiliar: traditional accounts have tended to simplify, or even ignore, them. However, there is still one further aspect that we need to explore before moving on. This concerns the specific types of relationships that are reflected in the language. Cutting across the basic distinction between attributive and identifying processes, it is in fact possible to identify three main types of relationships: **intensive, circumstantial**, and **possessive**.

The differences between these are easiest to grasp in attributive clauses. The intensive relationship is most familiar: this is where the Carrier has an attribute or quality ascribed to it. Most of the examples of attributive relational processes given in this section so far have been of this type. The Predicator need not be 'be', though (as with all relational clauses) in most cases it is possible to paraphrase the process as 'be' plus some extra specification. In the examples in Figure 5.19, 'seem' expresses, roughly, 'be' plus 'opinion', 'turn' expresses 'be' plus 'change of state', and so on.

The room	was	sunless and cold.
The office	seemed	even more sordid than before.
The weather	's turned	pretty nasty.
He	went	as white as a sheet.
The castle	looks	amazing.
Our car	's	a Corolla.
Carrier	**Process: Relational**	**Attribute**

Fig 5.19 Intensive attributive processes

The circumstantial relationship is similar to the intensive, but, as the label suggests, it involves concepts like location, time, etc. Rather than saying what the Carrier is like, the speaker says, for instance, where or when it is:

> The kitchen was *at the back of the house.*

> Dinner will be *in about twenty minutes.*

These examples show the easiest type to recognise, where the circumstantial element is explicitly encoded in the prepositional phrase. However, we can also have this element encoded as part of the meaning of the verb, which can therefore again be paraphrased as 'be' plus some extra specification. In this case, the extra specification can often be expressed as a preposition: for example, 'concern' is 'be' plus 'about', while 'last' is 'be' plus 'for (a period of time)'. See Figure 5.20.

Carrier	Process: Relational	Attribute
The kitchen	was	at the back of the house.
Dinner	will be	in about twenty minutes.
Hope Street	runs	between the two cathedrals.
The story	concerns	his attempts to marry the rich Lady Clare.
'The Trojans'	lasts	a very long time.
The drink	must have cost	a bomb.

Fig 5.20 Circumstantial attributive processes

The possessive relationship is that of ownership. This might at first seem an odd category to include as a relational process; but something possessed can be seen as a kind of attribute. This is clearest when the thing possessed is an inherent part of the possessor:

> She's got *long, dark hair.*

From here it is only a short step to seeing other kinds of possession as differing not in essence but only in terms of how temporary the possession is:

> Do you have *any bigger ones?*

> I've got *a splitting headache.*

> She had *terrible things to say.*

In these examples, the relationship is encoded from the point of view of the possessor; this is the more usual way, since it is natural to think of the possessor as the Carrier of the Attribute. However, it is also possible to encode it from the point of view of the thing possessed, by using the verb 'belong to': 'being possessed' is in fact as much an attribute as 'possessing'. Figure 5.21 shows both possibilities.

All the different attributive clauses illustrated in Figures 5.19 to 5.21 share the common feature that they are not reversible. This is the main way in which they can be differentiated from the corresponding identifying clauses in each of the three categories. Intensive identifying processes have already been fully illustrated and discussed, so at this point we merely need to look briefly at those which fall into the circumstantial and possessive categories.

She	's got	long, dark hair.
I	've got	a splitting headache.
She	had	terrible things to say.
Carrier: possessor	**Process: Relational**	**Attribute: possessed**

| This inkstand | used to belong to | Nelson. |
| **Carrier: possessed** | **Process: Relational** | **Attribute: possessor** |

Fig 5.21 Possessive attributive processes

Some circumstantial identifying clauses are easy to recognise: like circumstantial attributive clauses, one of the participants is a prepositional phrase; but the clause is reversible.

The best place for it would be *behind the chest of drawers.*

[Behind the chest of drawers would be the best place for it.]

However, Halliday (1994: 132) also includes certain verbs which encode a circumstantial element: in the examples below, 'follow' is 'be' plus 'after', and 'occupy' is 'be' plus 'for (a period of time)':

The speech was followed by polite applause.

Looking after the cats occupies all my time.

These are categorised as identifying clauses because they have passive forms and are thus reversible. I must admit that I have not yet managed to convince any group of students that this categorisation is viable: they generally prefer to analyse these as material processes (used metaphorically). Fortunately, they do not often occur in texts and the problem of analysis rarely arises. Figure 5.22 shows what the analysis is if they are seen as identifying clauses.

The final category, of possessive identifying clauses, also tends to be problematic in my experience. Halliday (1994: 133) points out that one type of clause in this category may be either attributive or identifying:

The gun must be mine.

That jacket is yours.   [Yours is that jacket./Your jacket is that one.]

On the reversibility test, only the second of these examples may be identifying (in a context where there are several jackets and they are each being assigned to different owners). As with possessive attributive processes ('belong to'), the element of possession may be encoded as part of the meaning of the verb. Some

The best place for it	would be	behind the chest of drawers.
The speech	was followed	by polite applause.
Identified/Value	Process	Identifier/Token

| Looking after the cats | occupies | all my time. |
| Identified/Token | Process | Identifier/Value |

Fig 5.22 Circumstantial identifying processes

of these verbs have a fairly clear equative meaning: 'include', 'contain', 'comprise', 'consist of' (although 'consist of' does not have a passive form, so it is not in fact reversible). With other verbs it takes a little more effort to discern why they are included as identifying processes: 'own' (it helps to see this as encoding 'be the owner of', which is clearly identifying); 'deserve' ('possess' plus modulation 'ought to'); 'owe' ('possess' plus 'someone else's possession'). The Value/Token labelling is tricky in these cases. Figure 5.23 gives the analysis of a few examples of this category as a guide.

The course	comprises	two years of full-time study.
The Yearbook	contains	a separate chapter for each of these institutions.
He	owns	half of Cheshire.
The character	deserves	contempt.
Ptolemy's model	provided	a reasonably accurate system for predicting the positions of heavenly bodies in the sky.
Identified/Token	Process	Identifier/Value

Fig 5.23 Possessive identifying processes

Incidentally, I would (tentatively) categorise the 'little pattern' example earlier as identifying rather than attributive, even though the Identifier is indefinite.

5.2.4 OTHER TYPES OF PROCESS

In addition to material, mental and relational processes, there are three less central types which can be distinguished on the basis of the usual combination of semantic and grammatical criteria. Each of these shares some of the characteristics of the major types.

The most important of them is **verbal processes** – verbs of 'saying'. In one way these are intermediate between mental and material processes: saying something is a physical action which reflects mental operations. At one extreme, a verbal process can be represented as fitting easily into a series of material processes:

He kicked, bit, *screamed abuse*, and finally collapsed in a furious heap.

At the other, a verbal message can be represented as being formulated entirely in the mind:

Why can't people be both flexible and efficient, *thought Evelyn*.

Various aspects of the physical action or the mental purpose may be encoded in the verb: for example, 'scream' indicates something about the speaker's volume, while 'promise' indicates something about the speaker's intention. The central verbal processes, however, are fairly easily recognised, in that they all relate to the transfer of messages through language.

There is one participant that is involved in any verbal process: this is the **Sayer**. Typically, of course, the Sayer is human, but messages can be represented as conveyed by other types of Sayer as well:

One report says a man was seen running from the house soon after the shooting.

The Sayer need not be explicitly mentioned in the clause:

I was reproached for not noticing anything.

However, we can always in principle ask for the identity of the Sayer ('Who reproached you?'), indicating that this role is inherently present in the meaning.

Another participant that may be involved, and that is also typically human, is the **Receiver**: this is the participant to whom the saying is addressed. With some verbs, the Receiver is nearly always mentioned:

'You're very sure of yourself,' she *admonished him*, gently.

With others, the Receiver is not normally mentioned:

'And I'm leaving tomorrow,' he *added*.

With others, the speaker can decide whether or not to mention the Receiver. The decision may be bound up with other choices such as the kind of structure following the verb:

The station commander had *threatened to arrest me*.

They *threatened the patients with injections of painful drugs*.

The Receiver is an 'oblique' participant (see 5.2.5), and often appears in a prepositional phrase:

I explained *to her* what it meant.

A soldier shouted *at them* to stop.

In certain cases, the verbal process may be directed at, rather than addressed to, another participant. This participant is called the **Target**. The Target can be distinguished from the Receiver in two main ways. First, it need not be human:

> The report sharply criticizes *Lilly's quality-control procedures.*

Related to this is the fact that the person to whom the message is addressed (the Receiver) may be different from the entity at which it is directed (the Target). In this example, 'me' is the Target and 'the other people in the office' is the Receiver:

> She keeps rubbishing me to the other people in the office.

With the Target, we are moving towards the other kind of participant that may appear in a verbal process apart from the people talking: the message itself. There is a wide variety of structures which can convey the message, but they can be grouped into two main types. The message may be reported in a separate projected clause or it may be summarised within the same clause. If a projected clause is used, this is not analysed as a participant in the verbal process: the process and participants in the projected clause are analysed separately, see Figure 5.24. The projected clause may be a quote or a report (see 10.4 on projection).

She He I She	answered: reiterated swore told		'Don't ask, just go.' that he had made no private deals. to uphold the constitution of the United States. that she didn't mind being recognised.
		one interviewer	
Sayer	Process: Verbal	Receiver	
Projecting			Projected

Fig 5.24 Verbal processes with separate projected clauses

If, on the other hand, the message is summarised in the same clause, it is treated as a participant in the process, and is called the **Verbiage** (the label is not intended to be derogatory). The Verbiage may consist of a label for the language itself:

> He repeated *the warning.*

> The owner made *a public apology.*

Alternatively it may summarise the content of what was said:

> Many people claimed *cures* as a result of her intercession.

> Someone asked *his name.*

Closely related to the Verbiage is a category of Circumstance called **Matter** (see 5.2.6 below). This is used to label a summary of the message when it is given in a prepositional phrase:

> He thanked her *for the tea.*

> Local residents have long complained *about oil storage.*

Figure 5.25 gives illustrative analyses of some of the examples of verbal processes used above, excluding those with projected clauses. Remember that, as Figure 5.24 above shows, Verbiage is not used to label a separate projected clause.

He	repeated	the warning.
Sayer	Process: Verbal	Verbiage

I	explained	to her	what it meant.
Sayer	Process: Verbal	Receiver	Verbiage

They	threatened	the patients	with injections of painful drugs.
Sayer	Process: Verbal	Receiver	Circumstance: Matter

I	was reproached	for not noticing anything.
Receiver	Process: Verbal	Circumstance: Matter

The report	sharply	criticises	Lilly's quality-control procedures.
Sayer	Circumstance	Process: Verbal	Target

Fig 5.25 Verbal processes

Another group of processes is also intermediate between mental and material processes. These are **behavioural processes**. Unlike verbal processes, they have few distinctive grammatical features, and are largely identified on semantic grounds. They relate to specifically human physiological processes. One of the main reasons for setting up this category is that they allow us to distinguish between purely mental processes and the outward physical signs of those processes. For example, many mental perception processes have paired processes which express a conscious physical act involved in perception: 'see' (mental) and 'watch', 'look', 'stare', etc. (behavioural); 'hear' (mental) and 'listen' (behavioural); and so on. Halliday (1994: 139) also includes, for example, verbs referring to actions which reflect mental states: 'laugh', 'cry', 'gasp', 'grimace', etc.

Typically, behavioural processes have only one participant: the human **Behaver**:

> *He* stared in amazement as she leapt through the window.

> *We all* laughed.

In some clauses there may be another apparent participant (typically functioning as Complement): this is the **Range**, which is not a real participant but merely adds specification to the process (see 5.2.5). This is especially clear in examples like the following:

> She gave *a faint sigh.*

> The boy laughed *a high, embarrassed laugh.*

Here, the 'sigh' and the 'laugh' do not encode separate participants: in semantic terms, these nominal groups form part of the way in which the process is expressed, rather than a separate participant at which the process is directed (we cannot ask, for example, 'What did she do to the sigh?'). This also applies in less obvious cases like the following:

> She waved *her hands* helplessly.

The analyses of the examples are given in Figure 5.26.

He	stared		in amazement.
We all	laughed.		
She	gave	a faint sigh.	
The boy	laughed	an embarrassed laugh.	
She	waved	her hands	helplessly.
Behaver	**Process: Behavioural**	**Range**	**Circumstance**

Fig 5.26 Behavioural processes

Behavioural processes form a rather indistinct category in the grammar, and you may well find that you hesitate particularly over the more 'action-oriented' verbs that Halliday includes, such as 'dance'. I find it most useful to look on the category as one of the process 'blends' that I have mentioned above: the difference is that behavioural processes form a large enough group in the lexicon to be worth giving a separate label to.

The final process type is one that can almost be defined in negative terms: essentially it expresses the mere existence of an entity without predicating anything else of it. These are **existential processes**, and they are normally recognisable because the Subject is 'there':

> There was *a ramp* leading down.

> Maybe there's *some other darker pattern*.

There is only one participant in such clauses: the **Existent** (in italics in the examples). The word 'there' is needed as Subject (see 4.3.2), but it has no experiential meaning: in a sense, its function is to avoid the need for, or the possibility of, a second participant in the clause.

What is happening with existential processes is that the speaker is renouncing the opportunity to represent the participant (the Existent) as involved in any 'goings-on'; and the distinctive structural pattern provides an explicit signal of this renunciation. Other details concerning the Existent can be given, but only in circumstantial elements, which, as noted earlier, are less central to the meaning of the clause. Existential processes are clearly related to relational processes, but they also have links with material processes of the 'happen' type. It is useful to compare an existential process with a possible rewording using the verb 'exist':

> Maybe some other darker pattern exists.

The verb 'exist' itself is best analysed as a material process: the rewording reflects at least partly a choice to represent the entity ('pattern') as involved in a 'going-on' (which happens to be that of existing). The analyses of the two clauses are given in Figure 5.27 for comparison. ('Maybe' is, of course, left unlabelled since it has no experiential meaning.)

Maybe	there	's	some other darker pattern.
		Process: Existential	Existent

Maybe	some other darker pattern	exists.
	Actor	Process: Material

Fig 5.27 Existential and material process compared

This link (or, more accurately, this contrast) with material processes can also be seen in the relatively infrequent cases when more 'active' verbs than 'be' are used in existential clauses.

> Then there arose one of those odd situations that no–one ever predicts.

Here the writer could have written 'one of those odd situations arose'; but this would to some extent weaken the 'presentational' meaning of the original. The writer is explicitly signalling that he is going on to give more detail about the 'odd situation': the function of the existential clause is simply to announce the existence of the situation, as a first step in talking about it. We can thus see its function in terms of the writer staging the flow of information in the text.

We have now completed this survey of process types in English and the participant roles associated with each. Figure 5.28 (slightly adapted from Halliday, 1994: 143) summarises the categories that have been set up, together with an informal indication of their core meaning and a list of the participants uniquely associated with each type.

Process type	Core meaning	Participants
material	'doing', 'happening'	Actor, Goal
mental:	'sensing':	Senser, Phenomenon
perception	'perceiving'	
cognition	'thinking'	
affection	'feeling'	
relational:	'being':	
attributive	'attributing'	Carrier, Attribute
identifying	'identifying'	Identified, Identifier/ Value, Token
verbal	'saying'	Sayer, Receiver, Verbiage, Target
behavioural	'behaving'	Behaver
existential	'existing'	Existent

Fig 5.28 Overview of process types

5.2.5 OTHER PARTICIPANT ROLES

In discussing the role of Receiver in verbal processes earlier, I mentioned that it was an 'oblique' participant which frequently appears in a prepositional phrase. The central participants in a process are those which relate directly to the verb (Subject and Complement, in terms of the Mood/Residue analysis), while circumstances, which give background information, are often realised by nominal groups which are only indirectly linked into the clause by means of a preposition. Oblique participants tend to vary between these two possibilities, which suggests that they have an intermediate status in terms of their closeness to the central experiential meanings of the clause.

There is one general group of oblique participants of which the Receiver forms a particular sub-category: the **Beneficiary**. The Beneficiary is equivalent to the 'indirect object' in traditional terms, and is defined as 'the one to or for whom the process is said to take place' (Halliday, 1994: 144). It can appear with all process types except existential processes, though not with all verbs within each type. It is possible to give different labels according to the process type (as we have already done with the Receiver for verbal processes), but in many cases it will be sufficient just to label it as Beneficiary.

With verbal processes, the question of whether the Beneficiary (Receiver) appears with or without a preposition depends primarily on the particular verb used to express the process – compare 'said *to me*' and 'told *me*', or 'promised *me*' and 'swore *to me*'. With material processes, either possibility is normally available for any verb that includes the Beneficiary as one of the possible participants:

> I'm just giving *the kids* money this year. [I'm just giving money *to the kids* this year.]

> I bought *them* computer games last year. [I bought computer games *for them* last year.]

There will be factors that influence whether the Beneficiary in such cases is mentioned as a direct participant or in a prepositional phrase; but they will vary from context to context and are beyond the scope of the present outline. It is worth noting that the different prepositions which are used in the rewordings of the two examples here allow us, if it is useful, to distinguish between two slightly different types of Beneficiary in material processes: **Recipient** (with 'to') and **Client** (with 'for'). In a few cases, we also find a Beneficiary role in relational (attributive) processes:

> That has just cost *me* thirty quid.

As this example shows, the label 'Beneficiary' should not be taken as necessarily indicating that the participant actually benefits in the usual sense of the word.

The final participant that we need to take account of has been mentioned in passing in the discussion of behavioural processes: this is the Range. The Range covers a variety of disparate-seeming cases, and is often difficult to identify with certainty. What the cases all have in common is that they are, in informal terms, Objects that do not seem very Object-like. Halliday (1994: 146) provides a more formal definition of Range as 'the element that specifies the range or scope of the process'. Strictly speaking, the Range is not a participant: it is more like a circumstantial element (i.e. specifying an aspect of the process, like an adverbial) disguised as a participant. There are certain kinds of examples which show this very clearly, particularly with material processes of movement, where the 'Object' encodes the distance or the location of the movement.

> We must have walked *three miles*.

> They crossed *the Channel* by ferry.

The next step is to see that certain 'Objects' are an extension of the verb: either they are derived from the verb itself, or they form a semantic unit with the verb:

> The boy was singing *a wordless song*.

> I do *the work of a servant* in this house.

> She was having *a taste of real family life*.

> She's given *birth* to twins.

> He lost *his temper*.

We can therefore see the Range basically as the label given to a nominal group which works together with the verb to express the process. The difference emerges most strongly in material processes when we compare it with the Goal, where we can see a clear referential 'space' between the process and the entity at which the process is directed:

> She's given him *a briefcase* for his birthday.

> He always loses *his umbrellas*.

Note that the status of Range as 'not a real participant' does not prevent it from having the potential of becoming Subject in a passive clause:

> *The Channel* was first swum by a woman in what year?

> *Tempers* were lost, and insults flew.

However, this is part of a wider tendency which allows any nominal group in a clause in principle to become Subject – even those which are dependent on a preposition:

> *The lock's* definitely been tampered with. ['Someone has definitely tampered *with the lock*.']

Range is a rather slippery category; but, as a simple rule of thumb, where you feel that the concept of Goal is inappropriate in clauses with material or behavioural processes, you may well decide that you have a Range.

5.2.6 CIRCUMSTANCES

As has been mentioned at several points, **circumstances** (realised by circumstantial Adjuncts) essentially encode the background against which the process takes place. There are a few well-established categories of circumstance which correspond to our intuitions about the kinds of background conditions that recur: time, place, manner. However, beyond that, there is a very wide range of possible conditions that may be referred to, and there is no generally agreed set of categories. In addition, circumstances frequently seem to combine two different types of meaning (though by now this should not come as a surprise). For example, time sequence and cause are often blended:

> I unscrewed the top. *Then* I was able to reach the lever. [= after that + because of that]

Similarly, manner and reason may both be present:

> She was fidgeting *with impatience* [= in an impatient way + because she was impatient]

A further predictable complication comes from the frequent use of circumstances in metaphorical meanings:

> She shook herself *out of her lethargy*. [location: place]

> Someone had called *with a casual message*. [accompaniment]

Whichever set of categories you rely on, you are likely to find that they will not easily account for all the examples of circumstances that you come across in texts.

One way into exploring the possible categories is by looking at the different questions to which the circumstances provide answers. Partly on this basis, Halliday (1994: 151) proposes nine main types of circumstantial elements.

1. Location
2. Extent
3. Manner
4. Cause
5. Contingency
6. Accompaniment
7. Role
8. Matter
9. Angle

He begins by re-orienting the familiar categories of place and time in terms of points or lines: **location**, or point, in time ('When?') and space ('Where?'); and **extent**, or line, again in time (duration – 'How long/often?') and space (distance – 'How far?'). Simple examples of each of these four types in turn are given below:

> He was killed *in 1937*.

> We had a dinner party *at Trumpington*.

> *From time to time* she dropped the weeds into her basket.

> She drove on *for another few miles*.

Halliday accepts **manner** – the 'How?' category, in which most '-ly' adverbs come – but extends it to include **means** ('With what?/By what means?') and **comparison** ('What ... like?'):

> He wrapped the parcel *expertly* and tied it *with string.*

> It's OK, she went out *like a light.*

The category of **cause** can also be divided into three sub-categories: **reason** ('Why?'/As a result of what?'), **purpose** ('What for?') and **behalf** ('Who for?'):

> I went *out of curiosity.*

> Do you fancy coming *for a drink?*

> We had a bribe *for her.*

Contingency includes concession circumstantials with 'despite' and 'in spite of'.

> *Despite his exhaustion*, he hauled himself over the wall.

These are less easy to probe with a particular type of question. They are obviously closely related to clauses with 'although' – just as cause circumstantials are closely related to clauses with 'because' and 'to'-infinitive clauses of purpose (see Figure 5.29 below for more on this link between prepositional circumstances and clauses).

Accompaniment circumstantials answer the question 'Who/what with?'.

> She's sitting on the grass over there *with her brother.*

Role circumstantials basically answer the question 'What as?', although they include a small sub-category of **product** circumstantials answering the question 'What into?':

> I asked him for the name of his tutor *as a referee.*

> They've turned the drill hall *into a fitness centre.*

There are two final groups, both of which have particular links with verbal processes. The first, **matter** ('What about?'), has already been mentioned in 5.2.4 above. It can also appear with mental processes, as in the example below. The other group is **angle** ('From what point of view?'), realised especially by 'according to' or just 'to'.

> Please don't worry *about me*!

> *To Miss Lewisham*, this had been a great relief.

In a way, many circumstantials, particularly those realised by prepositional groups, can be seen as clauses that did not quite make it to full clausehood, and have been sucked into a minor supporting role in another clause. Halliday (1994: 158) in fact describes prepositions as '**minor processes**', a kind of 'mini-verb'. There are many cases where a cline can be drawn up with a message being expressed either as a separate independent clause, or as a dependent clause in a clause complex, or as a circumstance inside a clause. Figure 5.29 gives three examples of such clines. In each case, it is the circumstantial realisation which is the original version, and the other versions have been written to illustrate the point.

Despite the companionship of her father, Katie missed children of her own age to play with.

Although she had her father as companion, Katie missed children of her own age to play with.

Katie had her father as companion. Yet she missed children of her own age to play with.

After the first shock of the discovery, he gradually accepted the situation.

After he had recovered from the shock of the discovery, he gradually accepted the situation.

At first the discovery was a shock. But he gradually accepted the situation.

Because of the lack of space, this topic will be dealt with only briefly.

Because there is not enough space, this topic will be dealt with only briefly.

There is not enough space. Therefore, this topic will be dealt with only briefly.

Fig 5.29 From circumstance to clause

Having the cline set out like this underlines not only the connections but also the important differences between each version. There is no space here to explore the reasons why one version might be chosen in a particular context, though we will come back to this issue in Chapters 8 and 10 from slightly different perspectives. One problem in looking at circumstantial elements in text is that as yet we have no principled way of analysing their effect: we can often comment on individual cases but, whereas it is fairly standard practice in discourse analysis for, say, patterns in the choice of process types throughout a text to be examined to see how they contribute to the overall meanings (see below), circumstantial elements have tended to be overlooked or treated in an *ad hoc* way. This is partly because of the complexity of the issues involved; but it must be admitted that as yet this area has not had the attention which it deserves.

§   Refer to Exercise 5.1.

5.2.7 TRANSITIVITY IN TEXT

At this point it will be useful to look at what a transitivity analysis in the terms set out above can tell us about how texts work. To do this, we can return to the advertisement that was analysed in Chapter 4 (p. 70). Space does not allow a presentation of the analysis of the whole text, though you might like to try it for yourself. What I would like to do is to focus on one short section of the text.

Do the financial rewards match the emotional ones?

Emotionally, nursing is one of the most satisfying of professions.

Imagine how rewarding it is to nurse a stroke victim towards independence. Or to watch a critically ill patient go into intensive care and come out of it in a stable condition. Or being recognised and thanked by former patients.

Of course these sorts of experiences are worth a great deal. But you can't live off experiences any more than you can live off fresh air. So what sort of money can you expect as a nurse?

Before carrying out the analysis, we need to consider the question of levels. Most of the examples used above have, for the sake of simplicity, consisted of single clauses. If we want to explore the experiential meanings in a text, however, we may well need to include an analysis of all the clauses, even if they are embedded. In doing this, though, we cannot simply go through clause by clause, since embedded clauses not only have their own transitivity structure but also function as elements in the transitivity structure of the clause in which they are embedded. This means that we may need to show several **levels of analysis**. As an example, we can take the following sentence from the advertisement:

In other words, it's no longer necessary for a nurse to leave the patient's bedside in order to earn a higher salary.

Here, at the first level, we have an attributive relational clause ('x is no longer necessary'), in which the Carrier is the delayed Subject clause 'for a nurse to leave ...' (see 4.3.2). That clause itself has a material process ('leave') with 'a nurse' as the Actor. We can show this as in Figure 5.30 (the analysis has been split into two, to make it more manageable).

Note that the final clause of purpose ('in order to earn a higher salary') has been analysed first as a circumstance of purpose. This actually runs contrary to Halliday's practice (see, for example, his analysis in Halliday, 1994: 143, Figure 5.23). Halliday analyses all ranking (non-embedded) clauses in a clause complex separately, see Chapter 10. I find it more revealing in practice, however, to treat what are traditionally called adverbial clauses as circumstances: they stand in the same experiential relation to the process in the dominant clause as circumstances realised by Adjuncts (the purpose clause in the example could be paraphrased as 'for a higher salary'). The decision to treat such clauses separately or as circumstances depends on whether you wish to emphasise the formal differences or the functional similarities.

In other words,	it	's no longer	necessary	for a nurse ... salary
	Ca-	Pr: Relational	Attribute	-rrier

a nurse	to leave	the patient's bedside	in order to earn	a higher salary.
... Carrier ...				
Actor	Pr: Material	Range	Circ: Purpose	
			Pr: Material	Range

Fig 5.30 Levels of transitivity analysis

Having seen this glimpse of transitivity analysis in action, you might like to try it out on the extract above, before looking at my version, given in Figure 5.31. (NB: 'Imagine' is followed by a separate projected clause, which is therefore not labelled as Phenomenon – cf. 5.2.4 on verbal processes; and see 10.4 on mental projections.)

The analysis inevitably makes the text look fairly complex – particularly the three 'sentences' which are projected by 'Imagine'. However, the complexity is in fact there in the meaning (although we are so skilled at handling such messages that we hardly notice). What, though, is the meaning that is being conveyed? The question which opens the advertisement sets up the question of a potential relationship of identity between financial and emotional rewards, and as we saw in the Mood analysis, the text as a whole provides an answer. I have coded 'the financial rewards' as Identified and 'the emotional ones' as Identifier, but in fact the coding could be either way. This reflects the fact that we have, as it were, come in on the middle of a conversation; this question could hardly function as an opening move in a 'real' exchange. We do not actually know what has gone before (the interactants might have been talking about the money or the emotional aspects); but we do know that one of these must already be 'on the table'. It is the ambiguity which helps create the impression that we are in the middle of a conversation. Interestingly, this ambiguity is not matched by ambiguity in the Value/Token coding: the financial rewards are definitely being measured against the emotional ones. This assumes that the emotional rewards exist and are accepted (by the writer and the reader) as valid measuring rods. We have already seen that there is no modality in the parts of the text relating to the

Do	the financial rewards	match	the emotional ones?
	Identified/Token	**Pr: Rel**	**Identifier/Value**

Emotionally,	nursing	is	one of the most satisfying of professions
	Identified/Token	**Pr: Rel**	**Identifier/Value**

Imagine	how rewarding	it	is
Pr: Mental	**Attribute**	**Carrier =**	**Pr: Rel**

to nurse	a stroke victim	towards independence
= Carrier 1 ...		
Pr: Material	**Goal**	**Circumstance**

Or to watch	a critically ill patient	go	into intensive care
= Carrier 2 ...			
Pr: Behavioural	**Range ...**		
	Actor	**Pr: Material**	**Circumstance**

and come	out of it	in a stable condition
... Carrier 2 ...		
... Range ...		
Pr: Material	**Circumstance**	**Circumstance**

Or being recognised	and thanked	by former patients
= Carrier 3 ...		
Pr: Mental	**Pr: Verbal**	**Senser/Sayer**

Of course	these sorts of experiences	are	worth a great deal
	Carrier	**Pr: Rel**	**Attribute**

But	you	can't live	off experiences	any more than you can live off fresh air
	Behaver	**Pr: Behavioural**	**Circ: Means**	**Circ: Comparison**

So	what sort of money	can	you	expect	as a nurse?
	Phenomenon	**Pr:-**	**Senser**	**-Mental**	**Circ: Role**

Fig 5.31 Transitivity in a text

emotional aspects: these are treated as fixed, accepted values. The writer then reinforces the assumption in the question by stating it explicitly in the first sentence of the body of the text.

With 'Imagine', we move into a further reinforcement of this assumption. The three 'sentences' (which are in fact all grammatically part of the same clause complex) can be seen in almost filmic terms, as a sequence of scenes from the life of a nurse. The scenes are set within a double frame (this is where the complexity slips in): 'Imagine' asks the reader to become Senser, the viewer of the scenes; and 'how rewarding' assumes an evaluative frame, by the Senser, which is not easily open to challenge because of its grammatical location within the Phenomenon (in Mood terms, the clause is not 'about' whether nursing is rewarding, it is 'about' the reader accepting the command to 'imagine'). We can also note that in the middle scene of the three we have a further depth of framing, since the nurse in the scene is watching the patient's movements. The frames in fact correspond very exactly to the levels in the analysis.

I mentioned in the Mood analysis that throughout this stretch there is a missing participant which is most easily realised, at some level of consciousness, by 'you'.

We can examine the participant roles that the putative 'you' is invited to fill. First, as noted above, 'you' is Senser – this reinforces the projected image of the reader as a caring, sympathetic person who accepts the emotional appeal of nursing. After that, 'you' can be carried over successively into the roles of Actor ('to nurse'), Behaver ('to watch'), and Phenomenon ('being recognised') and Receiver ('being thanked'). Simultaneously, the other participant, 'a stroke victim' moves from Goal to Actor (though only as part of the range of your watching) to Senser and Sayer. The transitivity thus reflects a switch from 'done to' patient and 'doer' 'you' to 'senser/sayer' patient and 'sensed/beneficiary' 'you'. 'Your' job as nurse is portrayed as being to help patients recover their normal transitivity roles (their normal functions as human beings), while withdrawing modestly into a support-ing role; 'you' lets the patients take back control of their lives.

We then switch markedly back to a single level for an evaluative relational clause in which the Carrier ('these sorts of experiences') encapsulates what has gone before. 'You' now appears explicitly, no longer as involved in the world of the mind as Senser, but in the real world as Behaver; and the 'experiences' are moved into the background as a circumstance for the process of living. In that context 'you' then starts thinking about a new kind of Phenomenon: 'money'. This forms one of the central participants for the rest of the text.

There are other aspects revealed by the transitivity analysis which could be followed up; but I hope that enough has been drawn from the text to convince you that the transitivity analysis is a useful way into exploring the meanings. It should also indicate some of the technical skill that has been put into the writing of the text. A final issue that I will leave unresolved at this stage is: how far do these insights correspond to how 'normal' readers see the meaning of the text?

§   Refer to Exercise 5.2.

5.3 Ergativity

The transitivity approach to material processes differentiates sharply between 'doer' (Actor) and 'done to' (Goal). It is also possible to look at these processes from another perspective, one which focuses on the fact that the process may happen by itself or be caused to happen. In Functional Grammar, this is called the **ergative** perspective (you should be aware, though, that the term 'ergative' is used in a different way by many linguists to describe languages which have particular ways of marking whether a noun is Subject or Object in its clause; many of these linguists would not accept the application of the term to English).

The stimulus for adopting this perspective comes from the recognition that there is a very large class of verbs in English which show a curious but systematic **alternation** between two patterns of use. Consider the following pair of examples:

We increased our profits over the year.

Our profits increased over the year.

If we do a transitivity analysis of these clauses, the result is as shown in Figure 5.32.

We	increased	our profits	over the year.
Our profits	increased		over the year.
Actor	Pr: Material	Goal	Circ: Extent

Fig 5.32 Transitivity analysis of an ergative pair

What this analysis obscures, of course, is the fact that in both cases the increase happened to the profits. We have seen that the Goal can be Subject in a passive clause (e.g. 'Our profits were increased'); but it remains Goal. In the second sentence in Figure 5.32, however, the Goal has not only changed its Mood function to become Subject but has also changed its transitivity function to become Actor.

We could overlook this as a mere oddity in the use of 'increase' if it were not that, once we start looking for them, we find similar pairs cropping up all over the place – and, Halliday (1994: 163) claims, the number of verbs which allow this alternation has increased in modern English. Figure 5.33 gives some idea of the variety (the examples are invented, to keep them simple).

the colour altered	we altered the colour	his eyes narrowed	he narrowed his eyes
the top caramelised	I caramelised the top	the fruit ripened	sun ripened the fruit
the door closed	he closed the door	it short-circuited	he short-circuited it
the sky darkened	clouds darkened the sky	I slimmed down	it slimmed me down
the ball deflated	he deflated the ball	we slowed down	it slowed us down
the peas defrosted	he defrosted the peas	the boat steadied	she steadied the boat
the car drove away	she drove the car away	the bell rang	they rang the bell
the ice melted	the heat melted the ice	I worried	it worried me

Fig 5.33 Ergative pairs

The last example in Figure 5.33, with 'worry', in fact indicates that for mental process verbs we have already built in one kind of reversibility: the Senser remains the Senser whether it appears as Subject or Complement. However, we have taken one of the distinguishing features of material processes to be their non-reversibility; and it would clearly not make sense, in the terms in which the labels have been defined, to say that 'our profits' is Actor in both the clauses in Figure 5.32 (for one thing, we would then not have a label for 'We').

If we return to mental processes, we can see that we identify the Senser by identifying the mind in which the process takes place; and one description of the Phenomenon which has been given is that it is the stimulus which triggers the process in the sensing mind. If we translate this into more general terms, we can say that one participant is the 'host' of the process – without a mind there can be no mental process – while the other is the cause of the process. These general terms can then be applied to the material processes that we are looking at: the 'host' of the process of increasing is the profits in both clauses in Figure 5.32, while one of the clauses also identifies a second participant, whose role is to cause the process to happen. Halliday (1994: 163) suggests the terms **Medium** for the 'entity through the medium of which the process comes into existence', and **Agent** for the 'participant functioning as an external cause'. Thus we can reanalyse the clauses in Figure 5.32 as shown in Figure 5.34.

We	increased	our profits	over the year.
Agent	**Process**	**Medium**	**Circ: Extent**

Our profits	increased	over the year.
Medium	**Process**	**Circ: Extent**

Fig 5.34 Ergativity analysis of an ergative pair

From this perspective, we are interested in whether the process is encoded as happening by itself or as being caused to happen: the process remains recognisably the same (reflected in the fact that the same verb is used in both cases), but the structure varies to reflect the presence or absence of causation. Ergativity is very close to the concept of causation (it means something like 'work-doing'): and thus the clause with Agent + Medium expressed is an ergative clause, while the clause with only Medium expressed is a non-ergative clause. In a sense, the two perspectives on material processes look at the clause from opposite ends. From the transitivity perspective, the Actor does something, which may or may not affect another participant, the Goal. From the ergativity perspective, on the other hand, the Medium 'hosts' a process, which may or may not be caused by another participant, the Agent. Note that the examples in Figure 5.33 suggest that ergativity is typically associated with some kind of change of state – it is natural to think of changes as self-engendered or caused by external forces.

The exact relationship between ergativity and transitivity in the description of English is still controversial: Halliday (1994: 165) argues that all processes of any type can be usefully analysed from either perspective, but other functional grammarians (e.g. Davidse, 1992) argue that the two perspectives are mutually exclusive – any clause encodes either a transitive or an ergative view of the world, but not both. In practice, I find that the most useful approach in text analysis is a compromise position: the ergativity analysis can be restricted to material process verbs in which change, self-engendered or externally caused, is an important element, and can be brought in especially where the verb itself is reversible like those in Figure 5.33; but the transitivity analysis can also be shown in these cases, particularly since it allows us to capture the difference between the two functional configurations of Medium/Subject/Actor (non-ergative) and Medium/Subject/Goal (ergative, passive); see Figure 5.35. We do not need to use the ergative analysis for mental processes since the 'Senser' label already allows reversibility.

We He She	increased deflated drove	our profits the ball. the car	over the year. away.
Agent/Actor	**Process**	**Medium/Goal**	**Circumstance**

Our profits The ball The car	increased deflated. drove	over the year. away.
Medium/Actor	**Process**	**Circumstance**

Our profits The ball The car	were increased was deflated. was driven	over the year. away.
Medium/Goal	**Process**	**Circumstance**

Fig 5.35 Combined analysis of ergative/non-ergative verbs

§   Refer to Exercise 5.3.

EXERCISE 5.1

The following six sentences all express more or less the same 'meaning', but in different experiential terms. Analyse each one in terms of process, participants and circumstances. If possible, decide which category the circumstantial elements come into – but don't expect to be able to do this easily in all cases!

1   She bought the car from him for £3000.
2   He sold her the car for £3000.
3   She paid him £3000 for the car.

 4   He got £3000 for the car.
 5   The car cost her £3000.
 6   The car was sold to her for £3000.

Now analyse each of the following clauses in the same way. Note that 16 has two slightly different readings.

 7   The cat's eaten all the fish.
 8   All our pasta is made daily.
 9   This decision was the most difficult of her life.
 10 A car backfired outside in the street.
 11 They finally announced their engagement to the press.
 12 The house stands beside the River Weaver.
 13 I worry about her health.
 14 Her illness worries me.
 15 It was snowing heavily outside.
 16 Most children like jelly with ice-cream.

EXERCISE 5.2

Look back at the letter and response from a medical advice column that you analysed in Exercise 2.1 (p. 24). Analyse it in transitivity terms.

EXERCISE 5.3

The following is an extract from a meeting at which three university lecturers are discussing a proposal to get funding from the European Community for academic exchanges. I have taken out hesitation noises, and have added a minimum of punctuation to indicate the chunking of clauses shown by the intonation. Don't expect the transitivity analysis to be straightforward. Use ergativity labels as well where you think they are useful. (NB: An 'ecu' is a European Currency Unit.)

> Now however to get onto that programme which starts in 1995 you have to bid for a preliminary programme referred to by the initials JEP and that was 50 thousand ecus which is about 30 grand. Now this has come from Gareth whose of course general view is if there is money there get it you know and then worry about it later on which has caused him a few hiccups from time to time, but I feel there is probably something in this. He called Linda and Dennis to see him and said, 'Look, I think you should put a bid together under this general heading just in principle' – Linda obviously because it's Russian-related and Dennis because it talks about the economic things. They kindly then deputed me to make it happen.

> (Recorded by Johanna Jakabovicova)

6

Organising the message: the textual metafunction: Theme

6.1 Introduction

Having looked at the clause from the perspective of what interaction is being carried out and what is being talked about, we will now turn to examining aspects which can only be properly understood by looking at the clause in its context in the rest of the language around it.

When we look at language from the point of view of the textual metafunction, we are trying to see how speakers construct their messages in a way which makes them fit smoothly into the unfolding language event (which may be a conversation, or a newspaper article, for example). As well as interacting with their listeners and saying something to them about the world, speakers constantly signal to them how the present part of their message fits in with other parts. To get an idea of this, look at the following example from a letter appealing for money for an organisation which tries to prevent cruelty to animals:

> You probably haven't heard of the SOU before. That's because we fight cruelty undercover.

There are a number of signals in the second sentence here that it functions as a coherent continuation of the first: 'that' encapsulates the whole of the information given in the first sentence; while 'because' signals the logical relationship between the new information in the second sentence and the information in the first. Less obviously, perhaps, the placing of 'that' in initial position makes the second sentence fit more smoothly (try changing the order of the constituents around and see the effect, e.g. 'The fact that we fight cruelty undercover is the reason for that'). What we have identified here are three of the main ways in which textual meanings are constructed in a text: **repetition, conjunction** and **thematisation**.

Repetition, as I am using the term, clearly includes repetition of the same word or a synonym; in the letter from which the example is taken, 'the SOU' is repeated three times in the first four paragraphs. This is usually called '**lexical** repetition'. However, it also includes more '**grammatical**' kinds of repetition of *meaning*, which may not be expressed by the same or similar wording – in the example, 'that' brings into its sentence the meaning of the whole previous sentence. The function of repetition is typically to show that parts of a text (not necessarily adjacent to each other) are related in some way. By repeating a wording or a meaning speakers signal that they are keeping to the same topic, whereas an absence of repetition might make it difficult for the hearers to understand that they are.

While repetition typically signals *that* parts of a text are related, it is the function of conjunction to show *how* they are related. This is clearest when a conjunction such as 'because' is used to relate two clauses:

> You probably haven't heard of the SOU before, because we fight cruelty undercover.

Conjunctive Adjuncts such as 'therefore', and certain unspecific nouns (see Winter, 1982) such as 'the reason' can also perform the same kind of function, though in different ways.

Conjunction obviously works primarily between two or more clauses. So, too, does repetition, since it occurs when a speaker chooses to express certain elements of one clause in a way which recalls the elements of earlier clauses. Thematisation is different in that it relates not to the way that individual components are expressed but to the structuring of the clause itself – the order in which elements appear in the clause. The Theme of a clause is simply the first constituent of the clause. In choosing the starting-point for a clause – the constituent which appears in first position – co-operative speakers select something which will make it easier for their hearers to 'hook' this clause onto the earlier clauses, to see immediately how the information that will come in the remainder of the clause is likely to fit in with what has already been said.

The discussion on textual meanings is split over two chapters, to make it less daunting. In this first part, Chapter 6, we will be dealing with Theme. In the next chapter, Chapter 7, I will give an outline of grammatical kinds of repetition. We will not be looking in detail at lexical repetition, since that would take us beyond what is traditionally accepted as grammar. I will also discuss the general phenomenon of conjunction, a topic that we will return to, from the particular perspective of its role in combining clauses into clause complexes, in Chapter 10.

6.2 Theme

The following example is the first sentence of a newspaper report of an exhibition on industrial history:

> *For centuries*, yellow canaries have been used to 'test' the air in mining.

The first clause constituent in this case (which is in italics) is an Adjunct. Without changing the wording too much, we can re-order the components of this sentence in a number of different ways:

> *Yellow canaries* have been used to 'test' the air in mining for centuries.

> *Miners* have used yellow canaries to 'test' the air for centuries.

In mining, yellow canaries have been used to 'test' the air for centuries.

To 'test' the air in mining, yellow canaries have been used for centuries.

The air has been 'tested' in mining for centuries by using yellow canaries.

What we have done in each case is to start the message from a different point, that is, to choose a different **Theme** for the clause. As mentioned above, the Theme is the first constituent of the clause. All the rest of the clause is simply labelled the **Rheme**. You might like to think about what the effects of changing the starting-points are, and in what context each might be appropriate.

The original sentence starts from the historical perspective – 'For centuries' – which makes sense since the theme of the exhibition is industrial history and this is the opening sentence of the article. Both 'Yellow canaries' and 'Miners' could work in the context, but they might be read as indicating that canaries or miners will be the main topic of the article rather than just an example of the interesting things dealt with in the exhibition. 'In mining' suggests even more strongly a restricted starting-point, from which it would be a little more awkward to shift to the general theme of the exhibition. The final two Themes ('To "test" the air in mining' and 'The air') are both very restricted as starting-points in this context, and would be more likely to occur later in the article rather than at the beginning. The comparison of the different versions underlines the fact that, although each refers to the same state of affairs in the world, they are by no means interchangeable. That is, the different choice of Theme (amongst other changes) has contributed to a different meaning.

You may feel, in reading this analysis, that it is tempting to say that the Theme is 'what the clause is about' and indeed Halliday (1985a: 39) originally suggested that this was the meaning of Theme. However, this can lead to problems. It certainly seems a good way of capturing the difference between the second and third versions above to say that one is 'about' yellow canaries, while the other is 'about' miners; but the original version also seems intuitively to be 'about' yellow canaries, since that is the Subject of the clause. In other words, this way of expressing the meaning of Theme makes it hard to distinguish it from Subject. That is why it is better to keep to the idea of Theme as the 'starting-point for the message' or 'the ground from which the clause is taking off' (Halliday, 1994: 38). The idea of 'starting-point' will probably still seem rather vague, but the analyses later in this chapter of Theme in a whole text should help to make it clearer.

6.3 Identifying Theme

6.3.1 THEME IN DECLARATIVE CLAUSES

The kind of clause in which Theme is usually most straightforward to identify is a simple declarative (a statement). In the majority of cases, with this kind of clause Theme and Subject are the same (they are said to be 'conflated'). Subject is the 'normal' Theme choice: it is the constituent which is chosen as Theme unless there are good reasons for choosing something else. It is therefore said to be the **unmarked** Theme choice, see Figure 6.1.

You	probably haven't heard of the SOU before.
Yellow canaries	have been used to 'test' the air in mining for centuries.
The Queen	yesterday opened her heart to the nation.
This large sixth form college	is one of only two offering boarding accommodation.
Theme	Rheme

Fig 6.1 Subject as Theme

As was mentioned in 4.3.2, the Subject may be fairly extensive, if, for example, the nominal group acting as Subject includes a long Postmodifier. In these cases, it is the whole nominal group which is Theme. The Subject may also be a nominal group complex, where, for example, two coordinated nominal groups function together as Subject: again, the whole group complex is a single clause constituent and thus functions as Theme (see the second example in Figure 6.2).

The languages that the Eskimo people speak around the top of the world, in places as far apart as Siberia, Alaska, Canada, and Greenland,	differ quite a lot in details of vocabulary.
A keen interest in the environment, familiarity with the workings of Government and/or the town and country planning systems	would be a strong advantage.
Theme	Rheme

Fig 6.2 'Heavy' Subject as Theme

The other kind of constituent which is relatively often chosen as Theme in declarative clauses is an Adjunct. Unlike Subject and Complement, which typically occur in a relatively fixed order in relation to the Predicator ('Subject–Verb–Object' in traditional terms), the position of Adjuncts is fairly flexible, and they can be placed in Theme without this seeming particularly unusual or marked compared to the choice of Subject as Theme.

As with Subject Themes, the Adjunct may be quite long, as in the last example in Figure 6.3.

Last night	a man was helping police inquiries.
In our classical collection	you will find many well-loved masterpieces.
Out of Britain's 37 most senior judges	only one is a woman.
As a tax-payer,	I object to paying for the restoration of Windsor Castle.
In common with almost every art movement born in the early part of this century,	it considered itself revolutionary.
Theme	Rheme

Fig 6.3 Adjunct as Theme

It is possible to have a constituent other than Subject or Adjunct as Theme in a declarative clause, but this is not very common, and usually needs a particular kind of context, such as where the constituent in Theme position is being contrasted with something else in the text. In the first example in Figure 6.4, the travel agency who have issued the advertisement have listed all the (pleasant) tasks that the client will do on holiday, such as exploring the beaches or learning the local dances; now they are about to list all the tiresome tasks which they will undertake for the client, such as making the travel arrangements.

All the rest	we'll do for you.
Friends like that	I can do without.
Theme	Rheme

Fig 6.4 Complement as Theme

Clauses like those in Figure 6.4 are said to have **marked** Theme, because they are unusual enough to draw attention to themselves, and because they only occur when contextual reasons overrule the unmarked choice of Subject as Theme. I mentioned earlier that it is easy to confuse Theme and Subject since we can say that, in some sense, the clause is 'about' both. But looked at from the speaker's point of view, it makes sense to start the clause with the constituent which combines both these types of 'aboutness'. This is why Subject is the natural choice as Theme. What is slightly odd about the sentences in Figure 6.4 is that the Theme slot is filled by the Complement, an entity which, as mentioned in 4.3.5, could have been Subject as well (e.g. 'All the rest will be done for you',

'Friends like that aren't any use to me'). In other words, Theme and Subject have been separated when they need not have been.

Adjuncts, on the other hand, could usually not move so easily into the Subject role. In addition, as mentioned above, their position in the clause is typically flexible. Therefore, when an Adjunct is used as Theme, as in Figure 6.3, it is somewhere in the middle on the scale of markedness (though for simplicity they are labelled as marked Theme, see Halliday, 1994: 44). As we shall see, Adjunct Themes tend to serve a particular function in signalling textual organisation.

It is worth mentioning one case which is intermediate in markedness between Complement (very marked) and Adjunct (less marked) as Theme. This is where a circumstantial attributive Complement is Theme. In certain contexts we find that Theme choices like those shown in Figure 6.5 are relatively common and feel less marked than other thematic Complements. Indeed, in some cases (see the last example) they are the normal Theme.

Next door	is the Liverpool Museum.
Towards the northwest end of the Corniche	lies the Qatar National Theatre.
There	's the tin-opener.
Theme	**Rheme**

Fig 6.5 Circumstantial attributive Complement as Theme

6.3.2 THEME IN NON-DECLARATIVE CLAUSES

The other main type of clause is interrogative (a question). To understand the unmarked Theme choice in these clauses, we need to think about the communicative function of questions. The basic reason for asking a question is to find out some 'missing' information (of course, questions may be used to serve many other purposes, e.g. to invite someone to do something, but that basic function remains present in all cases). As mentioned in 4.3.4, with **WH-interrogatives**, the WH-word or group itself represents the missing information that the other person is being asked to provide. In questions the natural starting-point is the thing that the questioner wants to know about, and therefore it is the WH-word or group that almost invariably appears in Theme position. Indeed, the clause structure of WH-questions has evolved as different from that of declaratives precisely in order to allow the thematisation of the WH-element.

As the examples in Figure 6.6 show, the missing information may be any part of the message – Subject in the first example, Complement in the second, Complement of a preposition in the third, Adjunct in the fourth, and so on: unlike Theme in declarative clauses, the type of clause constituent does not affect markedness. A marked Theme choice in a WH-question is when the WH-word or group does not come in first position. However, since the structure of

Theme	Rheme
What	happened to her?
What	do you want to know?
Which platform	does it leave from?
How	did you come to employ him?
What use	is a second?
How often	are you supposed to take them?

Fig 6.6 Theme in WH-questions

interrogative clauses is specifically designed to bring the WH-element to first position, marked Theme choices are relatively rare with questions; see Figure 6.7.

Theme	Rheme
After the party,	where did you go?

Fig 6.7 Marked Theme in WH-questions

As well as WH-interrogatives, we also need to consider **yes/no interrogatives**. As pointed out in 4.3.4, the missing information in these cases is polarity ('yes' or 'no'). We can see a question like 'Has he gone?' as the speaker inviting the other person to clarify which of the two possibilities is correct: 'He has/ hasn't gone'. It is, of course, the finite verbal operator which expresses polarity: 'has' vs. 'hasn't'. Thus again it is natural for this to be in Theme position. However, for reasons which will be discussed in section 6.6.4 below, the Theme in these cases also includes the Subject; see Figure 6.8. As with WH-questions, marked Theme is rare.

Theme	Rheme
Have you	finished your meal, sir?
Did he	tell you where I was?
Hasn't he	changed his name?

Fig 6.8 Theme in yes/no questions

A further type of non-declarative clause is **imperative**. Once again, the unmarked Theme choice can be understood by considering the communicative purpose. This is normally to get the other person to carry out the action, and the natural starting-point is therefore the Predicator, which expresses the action. In the case of a negative imperative, the Predicator is still included along with 'don't' (for essentially the same reason as in the case of the Subject in yes/no questions, see section 6.6.4). With most imperatives, it is the addressee that is understood as the person who will carry out the action. However, there is a sub-category of imperatives in which both the addressee and the speaker are involved: this is the form of imperative with 'let's'. As noted in 4.3.4, 'let's' expresses, albeit in an idiomatic way, the Subject, and is therefore analysed as Theme; see Figure 6.9.

Leave	the lamp here.
Don't cry	about it.
Do have	some cheese.
Let's	go for a walk, shall we?
Theme	**Rheme**

Fig 6.9 Theme in imperative clauses

Marked Theme is rather more common with imperative clauses than with the other non-declarative types. As mentioned above, the understood doer of the action in an imperative clause is normally the addressee; and it is in fact possible to make this explicit by using 'you' as a marked Theme choice. In addition, an imperative clause may start from an Adjunct, which often gives an explanation of why the command should be carried out. Figure 6.10 gives examples of some possibilities.

You	just shut up, will you?
On arrival in Liverpool	take a taxi to the University.
For a sharper taste	squeeze some lime over it.
Theme	**Rheme**

Fig 6.10 Marked Theme in imperative clauses

A final small group of clauses are **exclamative**: clauses which are very similar to WH-interrogatives, and which are analysed in the same way, with the WH-element as the natural Theme. See Figure 6.11.

Exclamative clauses bring us to the question of **minor clauses**: clauses which do not have a Predicator. These include: exclamations like 'How interesting!' and 'Congratulations!'; greetings and vocatives like 'Hallo' and 'Sue!'; and certain

What a nice plant How absolutely lovely	you've got! she looks tonight!
Theme	**Rheme**

Fig 6.11 Theme in exclamative clauses

idiomatic expressions such as 'What about the other two?'. Generally, only major clauses (those which have a Predicator) have thematic structure, and thus minor clauses are not analysed for Theme/Rheme.

To conclude the discussion of different Theme choices in the basic clause types, it is worth mentioning that either the Theme or Rheme may be missing from a clause. This happens with **elliptical** clauses, where part of the message may be 'carried over' from an earlier message (e.g. in the answer to a question), or may be understood from the general context. A few examples of the possibilities are given in Figure 6.12, with the elliptical elements given in brackets to show how the decision is made to assign the elements which are present to Theme or Rheme.

Who (I Why ever (That (Are you)	(would you most like to meet)? 'd most like to meet) Your real father. (will you) not (come)? 's an) Amazing discovery! Not sure what a special delivery is?
Theme	**Rheme**

Fig 6.12 Theme in elliptical clauses

§   Refer to Exercise 6.1.

6.4 Thematising structures

Having established the basic types of Theme, in the following three sections we will look at certain aspects in more detail. We begin by examining ways in which the speaker can manipulate the structure of her message in order to establish specific kinds of starting-points.

6.4.1 THEMATIC EQUATIVES

So far, all the Themes that we have examined have consisted of a single clause constituent. However, there is a textual resource in English by means of which the speaker can group together more than one element of the message as a single constituent, and then use that 'multi-element constituent' as Theme (and Subject). This is the structure illustrated in Figure 6.13, which is traditionally called a 'pseudo-cleft', but which Halliday (1994: 40) prefers to call a '**thematic equative**'.

What you need to do	is to write me an official letter asking for an extension.
What really got up my nose	was the way she excepted me to organise it.
What I want to talk about	is the nature of certain kinds of evidence used in the courts.
What one will not learn here	is anything about the Enlightenment.
What happened	was that Benjamin Lee Whorf picked up Boas' example and used it.
Theme	**Rheme**

Fig 6.13 Thematic equatives

Halliday uses the term 'thematic equative' because the Theme-Rheme structure here is expressed in the form 'Theme = Rheme', with the '=' expressed by the Predicator 'be' (this formulation is a reminder of the fact that these are actually a type of identifying clause, in which the embedded WH-clause always acts as the Value, see 5.2.3). Most of these examples could be re-written to distribute the components of the message in their 'normal' positions. For example:

You need to write me an official letter asking for an extension.

Note that a re-writing of the final example does not in fact use any of the words from the Theme, since none of the specific components of the message are placed in Theme: the writer's starting-point is simply 'something happened'.

Benjamin Lee Whorf picked up Boas' example and used it.

Re-writes like these show that more or less any combination of the meaning components can be grouped in the single constituent functioning as Theme.

It is revealing to compare WH-clauses as Themes with WH-interrogative clauses. In both, the WH-element represents a 'gap' which is about to be filled in: with questions, it is the addressee who is expected to fill the gap, whereas in thematic equatives it is the speaker who completes his or her own message by filling the gap. This link with questions helps us to understand why a speaker might use a thematic equative. In a sense, the starting-point in a thematic equative is often a question which the speaker imagines the hearer might want to ask at this stage in the text. It helps us to see this if we look at the context of the examples. For instance, the sentence

What one will not learn here is anything about the Enlightenment

comes at a transition point in a book review. The reviewer has begun by making it clear that he does not like the book as a whole. He then, however, lists a number of good aspects, things that can be learnt from the book. The example sentence signals the return to the more critical comments which his opening has led us to expect. It is as if the reviewer is imagining his reader thinking: 'Why has he said that the book is bad if I can learn useful information from it? What won't I learn here?'

In other cases, particularly in speech, the thematic equative seems to serve more as a way of 'staging' the message: splitting it into two chunks that the hearer will find easier to process. The Theme as starting-point is divided off from the Rheme in a way that is more obvious than in the corresponding non-equative version, which allows the hearer to process each part separately. This applies, say, to the third example in Figure 6.13, from the opening of a lecture. Theme choice in general serves to orient the listener or reader; and thematic equatives are particularly clear examples of this. Both the functions mentioned – asking the reader's or listener's question and staging the information – make explicit the interactive consideration of the audience.

As well as having the WH-clause as Theme, it is possible to start from the other end, and to put the WH-clause in Rheme. This is shown in Figure 6.14. Such clauses are, in fact, the marked version of thematic equatives. These marked thematic equatives often occur with pronouns (e.g. 'that') in Theme, which refer back to what has been said in the immediately preceding message. Even when the Theme position is not taken by a pronoun, the component of the message in Theme normally relates back to a meaning which has already been set up.

Theme	Rheme
That	's not what I meant.
That	's why he has finally resigned.
Making the Party feel good about itself	is, after all, what he does best.
And nothing	is precisely what we got.

Fig 6.14 Marked thematic equatives

6.4.2 PREDICATED THEME

One key feature of thematic equatives is that they group more than one element of the message into a single clause constituent which can then function as Theme (or, in marked cases, as Rheme). There is another thematising structure which allows the speaker to pick out a single element and give it emphatic thematic status. This is the structure exemplified in Figure 6.15, which is traditionally called a 'cleft sentence', but which Halliday (1994: 58) prefers to call 'predicated Theme'.

It's not the technology	which is wrong.
It is we	who have not learned how to use it.
It is not his painting, but politics,	which has once again brought him into the public eye.
It is the second of these points	that I shall be concentrating on in the rest of this talk.
It wasn't until 1986	that we finally came back to work in the UK.
Theme	**Rheme**

Fig 6.15 Predicated Theme

As the examples in Figure 6.15 show, the clause constituent which occurs in predicated Theme may be Subject (examples 1–3), Complement (example 4) or Adjunct (example 5). We can understand the function of predicated Theme if we focus first on Subject as Theme. As mentioned earlier, Subject is the natural choice for Theme, so it might seem unnecessary to use a specialised structure to place it in Theme position. But notice what happens if we re-write the first two examples (which follow each other in the original text) to remove the predicated Theme:

> The technology is not wrong. We have not learned how to use it.

What we have lost here is the clear signal of contrast between the two Subjects. In speech, it would be possible to signal the contrast by intonation, amongst other things by stressing 'technology' and 'we'; but in writing this resource is not available, and the tendency would be for the reader to assume that the emphasis was on the last lexical item of each clause ('wrong' and 'use'), which is the unmarked pattern in English. Predicated Theme here serves to guide the reader towards a particular pattern of emphasis which is not the most natural one. The same applies when the constituent in predicated Theme is not Subject: to see this, we can compare example 4 above with a possible rewording.

> The second of these points I shall be concentrating on in the rest of this talk.

This has the same constituent in Theme, but the most natural reading would put the main emphasis on 'rest'. This would fit most easily into a context where the speaker had just said something like: 'The first point I shall deal with immediately', in other words, where a double contrast was being established between the elements at each end of the clause 'first–immediately' and 'second–rest of talk'. The original version, on the other hand, implies 'I shall not concentrate on the first point at all'; in other words, there is only a contrast between 'first' and 'second'.

6.4.3 THEMATISED COMMENT

Another structure which in some ways resembles predicated Theme is used to allow speakers to thematise their own comment on the value or validity of what they are about to say. Figure 6.16 gives a few of the wide range of possibilities.

It is true	that it took five years to do so.
It may be	that the news reporters are manipulating the truth for reasons of strikingness.
It's interesting	that you should say that.
It is difficult	to know exactly how to characterise what we have just noticed.
It is regretted	that the University is unable to provide continuous nursing or domestic care.
Theme	**Rheme**

Fig 6.16 Thematised comment

The main similarity with predicated Theme is that in both cases the 'it' acts as a place-holder for the Subject of the Predicator 'be' in the first clause: the real Subject is the second clause. The main difference is that, with thematised comment, the comment in the 'it'-clause is not a meaning component of the second clause, and it is not possible to re-write them in the form of a single clause as we were able to do with the examples of predicated Theme.

> It's not the technology which is wrong. = The technology is not wrong.

> It's interesting that you should say that. = ?

However, this still involves a grammatical operation (the use of 'it' as a place-holder) which serves to set up as the starting-point of the message the speaker's own comment. One's own attitude is a natural starting-point, and thematised comment is extremely common in many kinds of discourse. The alternative (where Theme and true Subject, i.e. the embedded clause, are conflated) is possible, but it is very much the marked one of the pair:

> *To remark of* Brooksmith *that 'the scaffolding of this tale rests upon the existence of a class-stratified society'* is silly.

I should point out that Halliday (1994: 60) explicitly argues that this structure is not a thematic device, and that the Theme in all the examples in Figure 6.16 is 'It' alone. However, my own experience in analysing texts suggests strongly that it makes more sense to include the comment: in many cases, thematised comment occurs at key transition points in the text and it obscures the method of development of the text if one simply labels 'It' as Theme.

6.4.4 PREPOSED THEME

One final thematising structure, which occurs almost exclusively in impromptu speech or in writing which imitates speech, is **preposed Theme**. In such cases, the speakers announce their Theme as a separate constituent, and then substitute a pronoun in the appropriate place in the following clause.

People like us, in the middle,	we have to be careful about the children we have.
Happiness,	that's what life is about.
That bloke who rang last night,	what was he on about?
Your Mum,	does she know you're here?
Theme	**Rheme**

Fig 6.17 Preposed Theme

As the examples in Figure 6.17 show, the preposed Theme is normally a nominal element; and it is most commonly Subject. Most pre-position in authentic speech occurs with declaratives, but the last two examples show that such Themes may also occur with interrogatives.

6.4.5 PASSIVE CLAUSES AND THEME

Before leaving the topic of thematising devices, we should mention one structural resource which has a number of functions including that of moving a particular constituent into Theme. This is **passivisation**. In most cases, there will be a complex web of reasons for choosing passive rather than active; but there are some cases where the influence of Theme choice is relatively dominant. This is clearest where the Agent (the 'doer' of the action) is explicitly mentioned in a prepositional phrase with 'by', since in these cases both potential Subjects are present. As an example, here is a slightly simplified extract from a narrative.

> They'd managed to get themselves on the wrong coach at Exeter. They were rescued by a soldier who spotted them both crying. He took them back to Exeter on another bus.

One reason for the passive form in the second sentence is that it enables the writer to maintain the starting-point 'They' which is carried over from the previous sentence. The other character, 'a soldier', is introduced in the Rheme of the second sentence, and is then available as a natural starting-point for the third sentence. This 'chaining' is weakened by switching the active and passive forms:

> They'd managed to get themselves on the wrong coach at Exeter. A soldier who spotted them both crying rescued them. They were taken back to Exeter by him on another bus.

This version is not incoherent, but it certainly sounds less natural.

§   Refer to Exercise 6.2.

6.5 Theme in clause complexes

So far we have concentrated on Theme in single clauses. But what happens when we have a **clause complex** consisting of more than one clause? When a dependent clause in a clause complex precedes the clause on which it depends, there appear to be good practical reasons for analysing the dependent clause as the Theme for the whole clause complex. We can take the following as an example:

> As the universe expanded, the temperature of the radiation decreased.

If we follow strictly the basic assumption that every clause has a Theme, we will analyse this sentence as in Figure 6.18.

As the universe	expanded,	the temperature of the radiation	decreased.
Theme^1	**Rheme^1**	**Theme^2**	**Rheme^2**

Fig 6.18 Theme in dependent and dominant clauses

However, if we compare this sentence with the one immediately following it in the text from which it is taken, the dependent clause seems to be functioning in a very similar way to the Adjunct in the second sentence:

> One second after the big bang, it would have fallen to about ten thousand million degrees.

In both cases, the component before the comma serves to set the following information in a sequenced time frame; and in fact, in the sentences around these, there is an alternation between dependent clauses and Adjuncts signalling the successive steps in the origin of the universe. This suggests that it may be equally valid to analyse both sentences in similar ways, as shown in Figure 6.19.

As the universe expanded, One second after the big bang,	the temperature of the radiation decreased. it would have fallen to about ten thousand million degrees.
Theme	Rheme

Fig 6.19 Dependent clause vs Adjunct as Theme

The different analyses of the dependent clause in Figures 6.18 and 6.19 capture different aspects of what is going on. We can show both together, as in Figure 6.20.

As the universe	expanded,	the temperature of the radiation	decreased.
Theme[1]		Rheme[1]	
Theme[2]	Rheme[2]	Theme[3]	Rheme[3]

Fig 6.20 Theme in the clause-complex

But for practical purposes you rarely need to show so much detail. In analysing a text, as we shall see, the way in which the Themes work to signal the 'method of development' (Fries, 1981) of the text emerges more clearly if dependent clauses in initial position are taken as the point of departure for the whole clause complex; i.e. the analysis shown in Figure 6.19 is generally preferable. This applies both to finite and non-finite clauses. Figure 6.21 gives a range of examples.

After the police arrived Since he's already paid the bill Although they are aware of its existence,	I brought them to this cottage. there's not much point in arguing. none of these linguists discusses the Problem–Solution structure in any detail.
If he was in the house, Having worked on the Who's rock opera *Tommy*, Without replying	would he keep out of sight? I later found myself at the front of a tribute band called Who Two. he put his head under the blankets.
Theme	Rheme

Fig 6.21 Dependent clause as Theme

There are two practical points about analysing Theme in this way which need to be borne in mind. The first is that a dependent clause following the clause on which it depends normally does not need to have its Theme separately identified. In the analyses in Figure 6.21 we have assumed that the dependent clause represents in itself the starting-point for the whole clause complex: we are thus to some extent treating it as equivalent to a constituent of the dominant clause. The corollary of this is that when the dominant clause comes first, the Theme of that clause functions as Theme for the whole clause complex, including the dependent clause. In Figure 6.22, the dependent clauses in Rheme are in italic.

My dad	died *when I was five.*
I	do it *because it's an addiction.*
Down	she ran to the kitchen, *where there were voices.*
Theme	Rheme

Fig 6.22 Dependent clause in Rheme

The second point is the question of what happens when there is more than one dominant clause. In such cases more than one Theme may need to be identified in a sentence. Fries (1994) argues that the most useful unit for analysing Theme in a text is the **T-unit**: that is, an independent clause together with all the clauses that are dependent on it. Thus, if a sentence has more than one independent (or main) clause there will be two T-units, each with its own Theme. In the following sentences, the T-units are separated by the slashed lines, and the Themes are in italic. (For more on clause complexes and T-units, see 10.1.)

> *When we talked* I was thinking of myself, ‖ *and you* may have thought me very selfish.

> *Then, as the universe expanded and cooled,* the antiquarks would annihilate with the quarks, ‖ *but since there would be more quarks than antiquarks,* a small excess of quarks would remain.

§   Refer to Exercise 6.3.

6.6 Multiple Theme

So far, I have deliberately tried to keep to examples where it is reasonably easy to identify the boundary between the Theme and the Rheme. However, in looking at dependent clauses in the preceding section, I have passed over without comment the fact that conjunctions like 'and', 'but' and 'as' are included in Theme but do not fill the Theme position by themselves. These and certain other elements have a special status in the thematic structure of the clause.

6.6.1 CONJUNCTIONS IN THEME

With **conjunctions**, this status is reflected by the fact that, if present, they must come in first position. Their function is to signal that the coming clause forms part of a larger structural unit, the clause complex, and also to signal how it relates to the other clause(s) in the complex. Therefore, they constitute a natural point of departure, helping the hearer to fit this clause in its appropriate context. However, since they must come first they do not 'exhaust the thematic potential of the clause' (Halliday, 1994: 52): the speaker still has the main thematic options open. For example Figure 6.23 shows different thematic choices following the conjunction 'but'.

but all rooms	look out onto the secluded garden.
but by the morning	the snow had all melted.
but it was never easy	to find a restaurant that was open.
But if she missed those in Hyde Park in 1838,	she made up for it in the following year.
Theme	**Rheme**

Fig 6.23 Conjunctions as part of Theme

What may be a little trickier to grasp is that there are two classes of Adjunct which also have special thematic status. It is to these that we now turn.

6.6.2 CONJUNCTIVE AND MODAL ADJUNCTS IN THEME

We have seen a number of examples where Adjunct has been chosen as Theme; but I have deliberately restricted these to circumstantial Adjuncts which contribute to the experiential meaning of the clause, as in the following example:

> *After about five minutes* she came out of the door.

There are, however, two other kinds of Adjunct which serve a different purpose, which contribute a different kind of meaning to the message.

Conjunctive Adjuncts, such as 'however', 'alternatively' and 'as a result', signal how the clause as a whole fits in with the preceding text. They are obviously similar to conjunctions in the kinds of semantic relationships that they signal, but, unlike conjunctions, they do not link the clause into a larger structural unit (in over-simple terms, they show how two sentences relate to each other, whereas conjunctions join two clauses into one sentence).

Modal Adjuncts, such as 'probably', 'surprisingly' and 'frankly', convey the speakers' judgement of the relevance or truth value of their message (see 4.3.6). They may be seen as a comment on the 'content' of the message rather than part of the content itself (just as conjunctive adjuncts may be seen as linking the content of the clause to that of other clauses without forming part of the content). Thus they orient the hearer to the message by signalling a standpoint from which to view the information in the clause.

Figure 6.24 gives examples of a range of these two kinds of Adjuncts in Theme. The first four examples show conjunctive adjuncts, while the last three show modal adjuncts. (For a detailed list of Adjuncts which fall into these two categories, see Halliday, 1994: 49.)

Thus disorder	will tend to increase with time.
Nevertheless, we	can reflect on our own activities.
However, when ice crystals form,	they will have definite positions.
Then we	haven't met before, have we?
Certainly his wife June	was a very odd woman.
Admittedly, he	took the trouble to destroy all the papers in the cottage.
Please may I	leave the table?
Theme	Rheme

Fig 6.24 Conjunctive and modal Adjuncts in Theme

From the account of their functions above, it should be clear that both conjunctive and modal Adjuncts are natural starting-points, just as conjunctions are. However, unlike conjunctions, they do not have to be thematic: the speaker can choose whether or not to put them in Theme. They frequently occur in second position in the clause, immediately after the Subject or whatever other constituent has been chosen as Theme; and they may appear even later in the Rheme, see Figure 6.25.

The little station,	*however*, had not changed at all.
In North America,	*for example*, there is a grade system for measuring reading.
Then	they would *certainly* have to send you home.
It	doesn't last, *naturally*.
Theme	Rheme

Fig 6.25 Conjunctive and modal Adjuncts in Rheme

The fact that there is a choice involved in placing these Adjuncts in Theme raises the question of why we then need to include other elements in Theme. To answer this, we need to broaden the scope of the discussion a little and to establish a more specific definition of Theme.

6.6.3 TEXTUAL, INTERPERSONAL AND EXPERIENTIAL ELEMENTS IN THEME

We have already established that the clause expresses experiential, textual and interpersonal meanings. Lexical elements, such as conjunctive and modal Adjuncts, which express primarily textual and interpersonal meanings have the function of 'placing' the content, of signalling how it fits coherently with the content around it. They therefore naturally tend to gravitate towards the beginning of the clause, which is the structural slot (the Theme) where 'fitting-in work' is done.

However, the textual and interpersonal elements signal *how* the fitting-in is going to work; they do not signal *what* is going to be fitted in. In a sense, they indicate the location of the starting-point in the text's semantic space without in themselves constituting the starting-point. In order to see what is going to be fitted in, what the actual starting-point is, we need to have an element from the experiential content of the clause. This is not an easy concept to grasp, and I find that sometimes it is useful to think simply in terms of getting your hearer settled in before launching into what you want to tell them. Older British readers may still have imprinted on their memories the words with which 'Listen with Mother', a radio programme for children, always started the stories that were told: 'Are you sitting comfortably? Then I'll begin. Once upon a time ...'. On a small scale, Theme can be seen as performing the same function.

This means that Theme must always include a constituent that plays a role in transitivity: a participant, process or circumstance. Halliday labels the thematic experiential constituent the 'topical Theme', arguing that it corresponds closely to what is called 'topic' in topic-comment analysis. However, 'topic' is a notoriously shifty concept, and, like many people working in the Hallidayan approach, I prefer to avoid it in this context; so I will simply keep to the label **'experiential Theme'**.

If anything precedes the experiential element in Theme – textual and/or interpersonal elements – it is also part of Theme. This is then called a **'multiple Theme'**. There is a restricted range of elements that may precede experiential Theme in multiple Themes. As textual elements, we have already mentioned conjunctions and conjunctive Adjuncts; and to these we can add 'continuatives': a small set of what are sometimes called discourse markers ('yes', 'no', 'well', 'oh', 'now', etc.) which signal the beginning of a new move in the exchange. If more than one textual element is present, they occur in the order: continuative, conjunction, conjunctive ('Well, but on the other hand ...'). As interpersonal elements we have mentioned modal Adjuncts; to these we can add Vocatives (e.g. names or other forms of direct address such as 'darling').

Examples of multiple Themes, showing various combinations of elements preceding the experiential element, are given in Figure 6.26.

As Figure 6.26 suggests, the typical ordering of elements in multiple Theme is textual^interpersonal^experiential. But when a conjunctive and modal Adjunct

Well,	certainly,	sanity	is a precarious state.
	My God, Harriet	we	've been dealt a bad hand!
But	surely	the course	doesn't start till next week.
And,	oddly,	he	was right.
textual	interpersonal	experiential	
Theme			

Fig 6.26 Multiple Themes

appear together in Theme, the modal Adjunct normally precedes the conjunctive one; and the order of elements is interpersonal^textual^experiential; see Figure 6.27.

Unfortunately,	however,	the 'Un-artist'	proliferated within the art institutions as well.
Not surprisingly,	then,	its operations	were viewed with admiration.
interpersonal	textual	experiential	
Theme			

Fig 6.27 Alternative ordering of elements in multiple Themes

6.6.4 INTERROGATIVES AS MULTIPLE THEMES

In section 6.3.2 above, I mentioned that the unmarked Theme of yes/no interrogatives included the Subject as well as the initial verbal operator. With the concept of multiple Theme established, we can now come back to the question of why Subject needs to be included. As discussed earlier (see 4.3.5), it is the Predicator not the Finite which expresses the process in transitivity. Thus, in line with the rule that the Theme of a clause goes up to and includes the first experiential constituent, it becomes clear that we must include Subject. Yes/no interrogatives are in fact simply a kind of multiple Theme, with the Finite as an interpersonal element. Similarly, imperative clauses in which the negative or emphatic operator ('don't' or 'do') is present have a multiple Theme with the operator constituting an interpersonal thematic element; see Figure 6.28.

This does not apply to WH-interrogatives, since, as we have seen, the WH-element always plays a role in the transitivity of the clause – it stands in for a participant or circumstance – and therefore it expresses an experiential meaning.

	Had	she	missed her Mum?
Well,	Mrs Lovatt, would	you	say it is untrue?
	Do	have	one of these eclairs.
	Please don't	make	me out as some kind of hysterical idiot.
textual	interpersonal	experiential	
Theme			Rheme

Fig 6.28 Yes/no interrogatives and imperatives as multiple Themes

§   Refer to Exercise 6.4.

6.7 Some problems in Theme analysis

In any analysis of real text, you will almost certainly find that you run up against problems, some more serious than others, in deciding exactly what to label as Theme in some cases. The following sections look briefly at some of the difficulties that have come up in my experience, and suggest possible ways of handling them.

6.7.1 EXISTENTIAL 'THERE' AS THEME

The problem with existential 'there' is that it is Subject (see 4.3.2) and therefore ought to be Theme, but in experiential terms it has 'no representational function' (Halliday, 1994: 142) and therefore does not fulfil the thematic criterion of expressing experiential meaning. As I argued in 5.2.4, existential clauses typically take as their starting-point the simple fact that some entity exists (and, in the present clause at least, does nothing else). The existence is signalled not just by 'there' but by 'there' plus the existential process (typically realised by the verb 'be'). Thus it seems to make sense to include the process in Theme, and, in addition, this means that the Theme includes experiential content. Figure 6.29 exemplifies the analysis suggested here. Note that this runs counter to Halliday (1994: 44), who argues that 'there' alone is Theme.

There was	no question of Kate's marrying Ted.
There is	something special about this situation.
Theme	Rheme

Fig 6.29 Existential 'there'-Theme

6.7.2 THEME IN REPORTED CLAUSES

One recurring difficulty in analysing Theme is how to treat reported clauses. As we shall see in Chapter 10, reporting – or projection, as we shall call it – involves a different kind of relationship between clauses than other types of clause complex; and this is reflected in the uncertain status of projected Themes in text. In the case of quotes, the analysis is usually straightforward: the reporter makes a Theme choice in the projecting (reporting) clause and also re-cycles the original speaker's Theme choice in the quote. Both Themes typically seem to be important in the development of the text, and they are best shown separately, as in Figure 6.30 (for convenience, when drawing up a separate list just of the Themes in a text – see e.g. Figure 6.34 below – a Theme in a quote can be marked with double inverted commas: "Some people").

He	said:	"Some people	won't like it."
"What deters them	is the likelihood of being caught,"	he	said.
Theme	Rheme	Theme	Rheme

Fig 6.30 Theme in quotes

With indirect speech, on the other hand, it is difficult to decide whether to treat the projected (reported) clause as forming a T-unit with its projecting clause, in which case the Theme need not be shown separately; or as a separate message on a different 'level', in which case the Theme should appear separately. (If the Theme is shown separately, a single inverted comma can be used in a list of Themes to mark it as projected: see e.g. Theme 3a in Figure 6.34 below.) On the whole, I prefer to treat the projected clause as a separate message, as shown in Figure 6.31, but I must admit that this is an unresolved issue.

He	also says	he	wants to be a writer.
Having reviewed the relevant research	Heath argues	that these six genres	are the crucial ones for success in literacy.
It	was just luck,	she	claims.
Theme	Rheme	Theme	Rheme

Fig 6.31 A possible analysis of Theme in projected clauses

6.7.3 INTERPOLATIONS IN THEME

Interpolation is a little analysed but very common linguistic phenomenon, in which the speaker suspends his/her clause at a point where it is clearly not complete in order to comment on it, add extra details, etc. before returning to complete the original clause. The interpolations in the following examples are in italics:

> Maureen Freely's piece, *which is pure personal invective*, I will not dignify with a response.

> Karr, *40*, is a testimony to survival.

> It was a philosopher – *was it Sartre or Ken Dodd?* – who proposed that happiness was just a story we tell about the past.

In a sense, interpolations are not part of the clause which they interrupt (this is signalled in writing by the paired commas, dashes or brackets which separate them off): they are a separate message. They can therefore often be analysed as having a separate thematic structure. However, they are tethered to the host clause by the fact that the speaker has chosen to bring them in as interruptions rather than as structurally independent messages; and when the peg to which they are tethered is the constituent in Theme, it is more practical simply to include them as part of Theme, as in Figure 6.32.

Karr, 40,	is a testimony to survival.
Maureen Freely's piece, which is pure personal invective,	I will not dignify with a response.
It was a philosopher – was it Sartre or Ken Dodd? –	who proposed that happiness was just a story we tell about the past.
Theme	**Rheme**

Fig 6.32 Interpolations in Theme

6.7.4 PREPOSED ATTRIBUTIVES

In certain texts, you will come across a distinctive structure often associated with tourism and advertising genres. This is where an attribute of the Subject, rather than following it as with the interpolated non-defining relative clauses illustrated above, is placed in front. The preposed attributives in the following examples are in italics.

> *One of the most imposing buildings in Liverpool*, St George's Hall was designed by Lonsdale Elmes, who was only 24 when the foundation stone was laid in 1838.

> *Always ready the instant you need it*, the torch needs no battery or mains recharging.

> *Standing in extensive gardens*, the house has been carefully maintained to a high standard.

Priced from under £200 to around £20,000, our choice of rings is seemingly endless.

The preposed attributive clearly has thematic prominence and experiential content, and could therefore be taken as Theme. Like interpolation, however, it is expressed as structurally dependent, tethered to the following nominal group, and therefore the nominal group can be taken as forming the real starting-point of the clause: the preposed attributive, in this view, merely smuggles in a bit more information before the writer gets down to his/her real message. The suggested Theme analysis for some of the examples is given in Figure 6.33.

Theme	Rheme
Always ready the instant you need it, the torch	needs no battery or mains recharging.
Standing in extensive gardens, the house	has been carefully maintained to a high standard.

Fig 6.33 Preposed attributives in Theme

6.8 Theme in text

In the discussions of how to identify Theme above, mention has been made at various points of different reasons for choosing certain constituents as Theme and for choosing certain structures to express Theme choices. These reasons are typically those which hold at the level of individual clauses: what, in the context, helps to explain why this Theme choice has been made for this clause? Now I want to look at Theme in a slightly broader perspective, and to explore how Theme choices work together through a text to signal its underlying coherence. In very broad terms, it is possible to identify four main, related functions:

1. Signalling the **maintenance** or **progression** of 'what the text is about' at that point. This is especially done through the choice of Subject as unmarked Theme: maintenance is done by keeping to the same Theme as the preceding clause, progression often by selecting a constituent from the preceding Rheme (see also the discussion of encapsulation by nominalisation in 8.2).

2. Specifying or changing the **framework** for the interpretation of the following clause (or clauses) – the wording here is taken from Fries (1995). This is mostly done by the choice of marked Theme, especially Adjunct, or a thematic equative or predicated Theme. A 'heavy' Subject Theme, giving a large amount of information, can also be used for this purpose.

3. Signalling the **boundaries** of sections in the text. This is often done by changing from one type of Theme choice to another. In many cases, there may be a number of successive Themes (typically three) of different types: for example, a summative Theme (e.g. 'All this'), followed by an evaluative one, followed by a framework-changing Theme.

4. Signalling what the speaker thinks is a **viable/useful/important starting-point**. This is done by repeatedly choosing the same element to appear in Theme (a particular participant, the speaker's evaluation, elements which signal interaction with the hearer, etc.).

In order to see these functions in action, let us look at the Themes from a complete short text, the advertisement about nursing that we have been analysing in the two preceding chapters. Before checking my list of the Themes in Figure 6.34 below, look at the text on p. 70 and try to identify them for yourself.

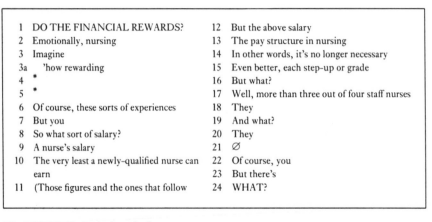

1	DO THE FINANCIAL REWARDS?	12	But the above salary
2	Emotionally, nursing	13	The pay structure in nursing
3	Imagine	14	In other words, it's no longer necessary
3a	'how rewarding	15	Even better, each step-up or grade
4	*	16	But what?
5	*	17	Well, more than three out of four staff nurses
6	Of course, these sorts of experiences	18	They
7	But you	19	And what?
8	So what sort of salary?	20	They
9	A nurse's salary	21	Ø
10	The very least a newly-qualified nurse can earn	22	Of course, you
11	(Those figures and the ones that follow	23	But there's
		24	WHAT?

Fig 6.34 Theme in the 'nursing' text

Notes: Capital letters and brackets are from the original text, but the following special symbols have been used:

? Shows that the clause is interrogative in form; this is normally clear from the Theme itself, but the symbol makes them easier to identify

* means that the Theme is carried over from the preceding one

Ø means that the clause is elliptical, and Theme has been omitted

Most of the Themes are straightforward to analyse, but I should comment on (2) and (15). In both, I have analysed the first element ('emotionally', 'even better') as modal Adjuncts, i.e. interpersonal rather than experiential elements. In (2), the Adjunct expresses the standpoint from which the information in the clause is valid ('emotionally speaking' could be an alternative). In (15), the Adjunct is similar to clearly modal Adjuncts such as 'fortunately' or 'luckily'.

Before looking at the commentary below, you may find it interesting to see what you can understand by working just from the Themes as far as possible. Then look at the commentary; and only then look back at the whole text.

Two things perhaps stand out from the list of Themes: the text starts and ends with a typographically highlighted question (note that it is natural to start with a question, but odder to end with one); and there is a chunk in the middle where the topics of nurses and salaries are maintained, but otherwise the Themes seem fairly diverse.

If we look in more detail, we notice that all the questions apart from the final one seem to relate to the first: (8) clearly concerns 'financial rewards', while (16) and (19) fall within the nurses/salary text chunk and seem most likely to be about money. We also notice that the first Theme in the body of the text, (2), not only introduces the content area ('nursing') but also sets up what could be an opposition to 'financial' in 'emotionally'. Given our cultural expectations, a contrast between money and emotion, between hard reality and imagination, is easily accepted. Thus we can see 'emotion' as picked up again in 'Imagine', 'rewarding' and 'experiences' (an 'experience', by definition, is an event that affects our feelings). The two 'carried-over' Themes in (4) and (5) indicate topic maintenance; but with (6), (7) and (8) we move into a transition stage: a summary Theme looking back ('these sorts of'), followed by the first explicit mention of a human participant ('you') followed by an interrogative bringing in a different entity ('salary'). We also have a shift in the non-experiential elements; 'of course' (= we both know this); 'but' (= something problematic about what we both know); 'so' (= a possible solution?). I have mentioned that 'you' is the first mention in Theme; but it is worth noting that there is an underlying 'you' in the imperative, and that the imperative itself is interactive – it is addressed to the reader.

Sentences (9) to (20) can then be seen as a single section, mostly maintaining Subject as Theme, but with a transition between sub-sections in the middle: (9)–(13) maintain the focus on nurses' salaries, whereas (17)–(20) focus on the nurses themselves. The transition is again marked by three 'irregular' Themes (irregular in terms of the small-scale thematic patterns that are set up in (9)–(13) and (17)–(20)). In (14) it is the textual element ('in other words') which introduces a summative note, while the experiential element thematises the writer's comment. In (15), the evaluation moves into the interpersonal element ('Even better'), while the salary re-emerges in the experiential element. In (16), we have another interrogative, the first since (8) which signalled the start of the section dealing with salaries. It is perhaps significant that this section has no 'you' in it: the human participants (nurses) are 'they'.

This section is brought to an end quite abruptly by a 'missing' Theme in (21). Note that I have not coded it as carrying over understood elements from the preceding clause: what is missing is something that can be recovered by the reader from the more general context of interaction with the writer (what Halliday, 1994: 63, calls 'exophoric ellipsis'; see 7.2.2 below). The interactive aspect is reinforced by the return to the 'you' and 'of course' from the first transition in (6)–(8); note that 'of course' is interactive since it signals that the writer assumes agreement from the reader. Then we have an existential Theme, which in a transition stage might be expected to set up the topic for a new section, but instead we simply get another question and the text ends.

Thus the Themes alone indicate that we have a text about nursing which works on the basis of an opposition between money and emotion. Having set up the money pole as a question, it moves to emotion, associating this with 'you' and interaction; then, at greater length, it moves back to the question of money, with a minor shift inside this section from the money to the humans (though the humans are 'they'). Then there is a further shift back to interaction with the reader, which is left hanging – the final question has no answer.

This is the point at which we need to turn back to the text, to map this progression onto the full text. However, although the Theme analysis could obviously be developed further – we have not taken any account of what appears in Rheme, for example – I will leave the discussion here, since many of the points have already been developed in the analyses of the text from the interpersonal and experiential perspectives.

EXERCISE 6.1

Identify the Theme in the following sentences. Decide which kind of clause is involved: declarative, WH-interrogative, yes/no interrogative, imperative, exclamative, minor or elliptical. Also decide whether the Theme is marked or unmarked (label Adjunct as marked Theme in declarative clauses as well as in other clause types).

1   This was Bono's first interview in two years.
2   In this same year, he also met Chester Kallman.
3   What are you currently reading?
4   Don't you feel more relaxed already?
5   Print your name and address on a piece of paper.
6   More heads at independent schools are considering testing their pupils for drugs.
7   Ever wondered where your favourite pop star is?
8   How many times a week do you buy the *Guardian*?
9   Actions which are inconsistent with an individual's usual behaviour and which give rise to some concern may be an indication of psychological distress.
10   For enquiries relating to this offer please phone 0227 773111.
11   Don't forget to look out for new winning numbers every day!
12   With a CharityCard tax-free giving is easier than ever!

13 Out of the pub came a small, intent-looking woman with a helmet of dun-coloured hair.
14 What sort of car are you thinking of buying?
15 A £2 million, two-hour adaptation of *Emma*, Austen's fourth novel, planned for ITV's autumn 1996 season, will coincide with the release of a big budget Hollywood version in British cinemas.

EXERCISE 6.2

Identify the Theme in the following sentences. Decide which kind of thematising structure is involved: thematic equatives, predicated Theme, thematised comment or preposed Theme. Identify any marked alternatives.

1 What often happens is that a new theory is devised that is really an extension of the previous theory.
2 It is vital to keep up the high standards of an élite music station.
3 It's not only our engine that's refined.
4 These mass parties, they lose touch with the people.
5 This is what I have attempted to do in this book.
6 All I want is a room somewhere.
7 What we didn't realise was that he'd already left.
8 That book you were talking about, is it the one that came out last year?
9 It was with an infinite feeling of tolerance she allowed that other people had need of these struts and supports.
10 Eating at home was what they would have to learn to do.

EXERCISE 6.3

Identify the T-unit Themes in the following sentences.

1 If she were to survive, all her energy must be harnessed for the next painful inch.
2 The workmen waved, and she waved back, conspicuous on her high ridge.
3 While drinking it, she read the paper.
4 He was killed in 1937, fighting in Spain for the Republican cause.
5 When talking about people in industrialised countries with problems in reading or writing, it is important to stress that they are ordinary people.
6 As long as the Chancellor funds tax cuts by cutting spending he could assuage the City's fears while making it even more difficult for Labour to match the Conservatives cut for cut.
7 To find out more about this unique, new way of giving and how you can make the most of your generosity, just call free or use the coupon provided.

8   Eventually, when the region got small enough, it would be spinning fast enough to balance the attraction of gravity, and in this way disklike rotating galaxies were born.

EXERCISE 6.4

Identify the Themes in the following sentences. If any are multiple Themes, label the thematic elements as interpersonal, textual or experiential.

1   Now at first sight this might seem to be contradictory.
2   However, I was held up on my way to the airport by heavy rain.
3   Surprisingly, however, this tendency has declined in the mid-1970s.
4   And no doubt he'll deny everything.
5   Well, perhaps he simply isn't interested in the same kind of things.
6   The first three letters, of course, were his mother's initials.
7   Oh, Alice, you are all right, aren't you?
8   The coming of print in Europe at this point in history, then, appears to have played a very dynamic role in the way people think about and read texts.

7

Organising the message: the textual metafunction: cohesion

7.1 Cohesion and coherence

At the start of Chapter 6, I discussed the idea that the speaker attempts, more or less consciously, more or less expertly, and more or less successfully, to help the listener to perceive the coherence of the text by organising the way in which the meanings are expressed. We have been concentrating on one of the main ways of doing this, Theme choice, which directly affects the structure of the clause itself. Before leaving the description of the textual metafunction, however, I also want to look more briefly at some of the other resources for creating 'texture', i.e. the quality of being recognisably a text rather than a collection of unconnected words or clauses. These are generally grouped together under the label of 'cohesion' (see Halliday, 1994: Chapter 9; Halliday & Hasan, 1976).

I have used both 'cohesion' and 'coherence' in talking about texts, and the terms may seem almost interchangeable. However, there is an important difference between them. Cohesion refers to the linguistic devices by which the speaker can signal the experiential and interpersonal coherence of the text, and is thus a textual phenomenon: we can point to features of the text which serve a cohesive function. Coherence, on the other hand, is in the mind of the writer and reader: it is a mental phenomenon and cannot be identified or quantified in the same way as cohesion. The two are in most cases linked, in that a text which exploits the cohesive resources of the language effectively should normally be perceived as coherent. However, all language users are generally predisposed to construct coherence even from language with few recognisable cohesive signals, if they have reason to believe that it is intended to be coherent. The following pair of sentences have only one cohesive link ('Hugo' – 'He'), but they make sense together, that is, they are coherent (although you might like to consider what cultural knowledge the reader needs in order to reconstruct the coherence):

> Hugo spent all of his legacy laying down wine. He was ensuring a happy middle age.

Nevertheless, cohesion is a crucial linguistic resource in the expression of coherent meanings; and the analyst may gain equally important insights into how it works from cases where a lack of cohesive devices in a text does not lead to the interactants perceiving it as incoherent.

7.2 Reference and ellipsis

As mentioned earlier, one of the main cohesive resources can be broadly described as repetition – as long as the term is understood to include repetition of meaning not just of words, and to include grammatical as well as lexical repetition. Grammatical repetition consists of two main types: reference and ellipsis. **Reference** is the set of grammatical resources which allow the speaker to indicate whether something is being repeated from somewhere else in the text (i.e. we have already been told about it), or whether it has not yet appeared in the text (i.e. it is new to us). In the following sentences, 'it' refers to the same entity as 'their bedroom', whereas 'a' in 'a large bed' signals that this is something not mentioned so far.

> They came again into their bedroom. A large bed had been left in it.

Ellipsis is the set of resources by which full repetition of a clause or clause element can be avoided, and by which it can be signalled to readers that they should repeat the wording from a previous clause (or, in some cases, from their own knowledge). There are two basic ways of doing this. In **ellipsis proper**, the element is simply missed out; in the example below, the reply presupposes the wording 'he is … old':

> 'How old is he?' 'Two months.'

In **substitution,** on the other hand, a linguistic token is put in the place of the wording to be repeated from elsewhere; in the example below, 'so' stands in the place of 'large for five months':

> It's large for five months, but not abnormally so.

Both reference and ellipsis can operate within the clause or clause complex (as in the last example), or across clause complexes (and even utterances by different people, as in 'Two months' above). Since we are looking at the way the message fits in with other messages, we will concentrate on cohesion between rather than within clause complexes, though it should be borne in mind that the resources are essentially the same for both.

7.2.1 REFERENCE

Some uses of reference do not in fact count as repetition, but it is only the cases of reference that are linked with repetition of meaning which function as cohesive devices. The differences emerge when we look at cases where the reference is 'outwards': that is, it does not point to a meaning earlier (or sometimes later) in the text, but out into the world. Compare the function of 'he' in these two examples:

> Who's *he*? [speaker pointing at photograph]

> She appealed to Philip. *He* turned the main tap.

In the first, the hearer interprets the meaning of 'he' by relating it to something outside language – the photograph of a man. In the second, on the other hand, 'he' is understood as referring back to 'Philip' in the previous sentence. Both uses of 'he' rely on the basic meaning 'male human being that I assume both of us know about'; but it is only in the second that the 'knownness' is dependent on the previous mention in the text. Therefore it is only the second which contributes to the texture of the text.

The first kind of reference is known as **exophoric** ('pointing outwards'), whereas the second is **endophoric** ('pointing inwards'). As the examples show, a pronoun like 'he' can be used in either way. Halliday (1994: 312) argues that the exophoric use is probably the original one; and with the first and second person pronouns ('I', 'me, 'you', etc.) this has remained the central use ('I' means 'the person who is speaking now in the real world' rather than 'the person just referred to in the text'). The other pronouns have developed both kinds of use and can often serve both functions simultaneously (e.g. if two people are talking about a man they are watching, 'he' could be seen as referring outwards to the man or backwards to the earlier mentions of 'him' in their conversation).

Both uses of reference serve the broad function of showing how the message fits into its context; but exophoric reference links the language to the external context, while endophoric reference signals how the message fits specifically into its textual context (the 'co-text'). It is the latter – reference as cohesion – that we will focus on. Most cohesive, endophoric, reference is **anaphoric** ('pointing backwards'): the meaning that is being repeated has already been mentioned earlier in the text. Less often, reference may be **cataphoric** ('pointing forwards'): this signals that the meaning of the reference item will not be specified until further on in the text. The following example comes just before a full quotation of the 'different idea' as set out in Pat's answer paper – 'here' points forwards to that quotation ('different' also has a cohesive function, see 'comparative reference' below):

> But Pat and another kid had a different idea. Here is Pat's paper.

In the following outline, the examples are of anaphoric reference, since that is more common; but all the types discussed may also be used for cataphoric reference.

There are three main types of cohesive reference. The first includes the **third-person personal pronouns**:

> Parnell was generally not a hater. *He* spoke tolerantly of his foes.

> Cholera first struck England in 1832. *It* came from the East.

The second includes the **demonstratives**: 'this', 'that', 'these', 'those'. Note that 'here' and 'there' and 'now' and 'then' also come into this group.

> The British Council also arranges refresher courses for teachers of English in the summer vacation. *These* courses are often organised in conjunction with a university.

> He merely laughed and said that she was imagining things. *This* typical male reaction resulted in a row.

> All *this* time he was running up debts.

> He later made the unusual switch to the army. *There* he had a brilliant career.

> They seem to have been idyllically happy. *Then* they had their first quarrel.

One use of 'this' is worth mentioning separately, since it has such an important role in organising texts, particularly in more formal registers. 'This' (and to a lesser extent 'these') is often used to refer back to a whole stretch of text. Sometimes it is used on its own but it also frequently appears with a noun encapsulating the content of what has been said:

> *This* brings to mind something that happened when I was in prep school.

> *This approach* can provide an idea of the range of literacy practices in a community.

For a fuller discussion of this kind of textual 'labelling', see Francis (1994).

The most 'neutral' item amongst the demonstratives is 'the'. Whereas, for example, 'this' as a cohesive signal means 'the one I have just mentioned', and 'there' means 'the place I have just mentioned', 'the' has a wider scope. It essentially means something like 'you know which I mean, either because I have already mentioned it, or because I am about to mention it, or because you are familiar with it from your own knowledge and experience'. Of these three basic meanings, the third is basically exophoric: if, for example, I ask my wife 'Are you taking *the* car?' we both understand it as meaning our car. It is therefore not cohesive in the sense of repeating a meaning from a previous message. The second is also of less relevance to us here, because it typically operates not only within the clause but within the nominal group – it points forward to the Postmodifier (see 9.1.1). For example, in the group 'the arrest of Parnell', the function of 'the' can be informally paraphrased as 'I am about to specify which arrest I mean: it is that of Parnell'. It is the first meaning which is anaphoric and is central as a cohesive resource. Sometimes, the repetition underlying 'the' is explicitly reinforced by the repetition or near-repetition of the noun – this is called the 'second-mention use':

> Bungling ram raiders tried to smash their way into *a* furniture shop –
> using *a* stolen Mini.

> But *the* tiny motor just bounced off *the* store's plate-glass window.

Equally, or perhaps more, often, however, the presence of 'the' signals that the
meaning at this point is being repeated from earlier in the text even though there
may be no clear lexical repetition. In many of these cases, the anaphoric use of
'the' overlaps with the exophoric use. In the following example, the writer is
talking about a theatre show on Broadway:

> To make sure of it, he and *the* box office manager secretly hired a
> carpenter to build an extra row of seats which were quietly removed at
> the end of the show's two-year run. *The* theatre management never
> knew of the existence of row AA.

The uses of 'the' in italics in the example can be seen as both relating out to the
reader's knowledge of the world and relating back to meanings brought implicitly
into the text by the mention of theatre: since all theatres have a box office manager
and a management, the use of 'the' when they are first explicitly mentioned
indicates that the writer is in retrospect treating his mention of a 'theatre show' as
carrying with it the meanings of 'box office manager' and 'management'.

The third type of cohesive reference is **comparative**. Any comparison of
course includes two things that are being compared; and any comparative
attached to one entity or concept thus implies the existence of the other entity or
concept. As with the other types of reference, the comparison can be with
something in the outside world rather than in the text:

> Do you want some *more* wrapping paper? [= I can see that you already
> have some paper.]

However, it can also have a cohesive role by bringing back into the text the
meaning of a previously mentioned entity or concept that is now being compared
with something else. Note that comparison needs to be seen in a fairly wide
sense, not just as including comparative forms of adjectives: items like 'another',
'different', 'the same' and 'similarly' can all contribute to cohesion:

> There are many *other* stories about her staunch individuality.

> Otherwise his story is *the same as* Katharine's.

> If children worry *so much* about failure, might it not be because they
> rate success too highly?

We can also include ordinal numbers in this group, since, for example, 'the second'
only makes sense as being compared with the previously mentioned 'first':

> The *third* type of cohesive anaphoric reference is comparative.

In concluding this brief outline of reference, it might be useful to have a reminder of the set of 'phoric' terms that have been introduced, since they are easy to confuse until you are used to them. Figure 7.1 summarises them with examples.

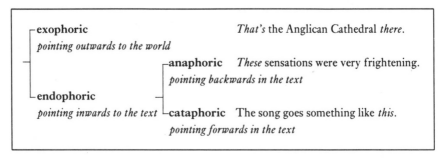

Fig 7.1 Phoric categories of reference

7.2.2 ELLIPSIS

As mentioned above, there are two basic types of ellipsis: ellipsis proper, where a gap is left to be filled by 'carrying over' elements from a previous message; and substitution, where a substitute form marks the place where the earlier elements need to be brought in. As some of the examples above have shown, reference can operate over fairly long stretches of text, and the meaning that is being repeated need not be in the immediately preceding message. Ellipsis, on the other hand, typically operates between adjacent clauses. This is at least partly because the message with ellipsis is formally incomplete: the hearer or reader is required to recall (or adequately reconstruct) the actual words needed to fill out the clause; and psychological research has shown clearly that we typically remember the meanings of what is said to us far better than the wordings. Ellipsis tends to be more fully exploited in speech than in writing: it reflects the negotiation and cooperation that are an explicit feature of face-to-face interaction. (See also the examples of elliptical clauses consisting of Mood in 4.3.1.)

The exophoric/endophoric distinction that we have discussed in relation to reference can also be applied, though in a slightly different way, to ellipsis. It was mentioned above (6.3.2) that in elliptical Themes or Rhemes the missing element may be understood from the situation (i.e. it is supplied from 'outside' the text) or it may be carried over from the preceding message. As with reference, it is only the second of these that is properly speaking cohesive. The following slightly shortened extract, from Iris Murdoch's novel *The Philosopher's Pupil*, shows missing elements replaceable both from the context and from the co-text; and it also shows both ellipsis proper and substitution:

'You've got a black eye.'
'Yes.'
'So have I, at least it's swollen, can't think how I got it.'...
'Gabriel got here early.'

'Yes.'
'What did she say to you?'
'Nothing.'...
'I can't remember much about last night.'
'I'm glad you can't, neither can I.'
'If you can't remember, why are you glad I can't?'
'It was a horrid accident, better to forget it.'
'We do a lot of forgetting. How long will you be in here?'
'I don't know. You could ask matron.'
'Do you want anything, flowers or books or anything?'
'No, thanks.'
'I feel awfully tired.'
'You're suffering from shock.'
'Yes, that's it, I suppose I am.'
'Better go home and rest.'

Before reading the summary below of the resources by which ellipsis is realised, you might like to try to identify all the 'missing' elements in this conversation.

The contextually-determined ellipsis, which will not be discussed below, occurs in:

'[I] can't think how I got it.'
'[it's] better to forget it.'
'[You'd] Better go home and rest.'

Note that in each case it is the Subject that is ellipsed, usually but not always with the Finite.

As the conversation shows, one context in which cohesive ellipsis is particularly common is in answers and responses. 'Yes' and 'No' answers presuppose the wording from the preceding question or statement.

'You've got a black eye.'
'Yes [I've got a black eye].'
'Do you want anything, flowers or books or anything?'
'No, [I don't want anything] thanks.'

In response to a WH-question, it is often just the missing element called for by the WH-word (see 4.3.4) that is supplied in the answer, with everything else presupposed from the question:

'What did she say to you?'
'[She said] Nothing [to me].'

If the answer cannot be supplied, the whole question is typically ellipsed:

'How long will you be in here?'
'I don't know [how long I will be in here]. You could ask matron [how long I will be in here].'

WH-questions themselves can also be elliptical. This happens when they are used to demand that the original speaker supply additional information to what he has just said. The wording of his clause is then presupposed in the question (and very often in the following answer). In the following extract from *The Philosopher's Pupil* the first speaker wrongly assumes that the other person can supply the missing Subject from the context:

'Rum jerk,' said Bobbie.
'Who [is a rum jerk]?'
'The parson [is a rum jerk].'

So far we have looked at cases of ellipsis proper. There are two cases of substitution in the long extract above:

'You've got a black eye.'
'So [= also got a black eye] have I.'
'I can't remember much about last night.'
'neither [= also not remember much about last night] can I.'

Here, a 'counter' ('so', 'neither') is put into the elliptical clause to represent the missing wording. As the paraphrase in brackets makes clear, the resulting clause is not simply the non-elliptical clause with a substitute form in the same place as the missing wording – the substitute form has developed its own grammar. Note that it would be possible to keep the grammar of the elliptical clause parallel to that of the non-elliptical one, but in this case we would have ellipsis proper rather than substitution:

'I have [got a black eye] too.'
'I can't [remember much about last night] either.'

This possibility of alternating between ellipsis proper and substitution is not accidental: in principle, wherever in the structure of the clause you can have one you can also have the other (although contextual factors will influence or determine which occurs in any particular case).

One way of grouping substitute forms is according to what they substitute for. 'So', 'neither' and 'nor' can substitute for the **Residue** (as in the examples above, where the Mood is explicit). In addition, they can substitute for a whole projected (reported) clause following a verbal or mental process verb – 'not' can also function in this way:

'Are you there, Luce?'
'I've just said so [= that I'm there].'
'It was the rest of the people who made him a monster really, wasn't it?'
'I suppose so [= that it was the rest of the people who made him a monster really], sir.'
'Do you think it's possible?'
'I hope not [= that it is (not) possible].'

Compare this with the examples above of reported WH-questions where the whole projected clause is ellipsed ('I don't know. You could ask matron.')

Within the verbal group, **Predicators** can, under certain circumstances, be substituted by 'do':

'Has he gone?'

'He might have done [= gone].'

In other cases, 'do' by itself stands in for the whole Residue, not just the Predicator:

'I haven't even met Mrs McCaffrey. I suppose I ought to have done [= met Mrs McCaffrey]?'

Note that 'do' also appears in elliptical clauses as Finite rather than as a substitute form. In this case, we have ellipsis proper, since the filled-out clause would preserve 'do' in most cases:

'I don't care about the scandal –'

'Well, you ought to [care about the scandal] and I do [care about the scandal].'

This can be confusing if you are trying to identify exactly what grammatical structure is involved; and in some cases it is not possible to decide. In the following example, 'do' in the response could equally well be seen as the emphatically positive Finite (i.e. with elliptical Residue) or as the substitute form:

'Strong probabilities amount to proof.'

'Perhaps they *do* in philosophy, but I prefer to believe what I see clearly.'

Fortunately, in practice the distinction is rarely crucial.

In the nominal group, the substitute form 'one(s)' can replace the head noun or the nominal group as a whole:

'And you'll meet lots of nice men there, gentlemen, not like the ones [= men] I knew.'

'I'm looking for an Indian man with a beard, have you seen one [= an Indian man with a beard]?'

The negative substitute form in these cases is 'none'. The following example combines the use of this substitute form with ellipsis in response to a WH-question (see above):

'What wonderful things have you told her about me?'

'[I have told her] None [= no wonderful things].'

Possessive pronouns also act as substitute forms for nominal groups:

> Lady Emma was considered a saint by all who knew her, but even saints have their faults.
> Hers [= her fault] seems to have been a habit of making favourites among her children.

> 'What about our images of ourselves?'
> 'You have none [= no images of yourself]. Yours [= your images of yourself] are illusions.'

The use of these substitute forms can be compared with the fairly common type of ellipsis in the nominal group where only the determiner is kept:

> 'Whisky? I'll get some [whisky].'

> 'I didn't know you'd written a novel. I hope you'll write another [novel]?'

As with the ambiguous cases of 'do' mentioned above, ellipsis and substitute forms are very close to each other here: in functional terms they are doing essentially the same job.

This has, of necessity, been only a very brief summary of ellipsis. This area of the grammar is complex and comprises a highly developed set of resources; but in terms of text analysis the details are less important than the general role of ellipsis in the co-operative negotiation of meaning between speakers. In certain texts ellipsis can contribute to a distinctive 'tone': one reason for selecting the majority of the examples in this section from *The Philosopher's Pupil* is that Murdoch is a writer who frequently makes conscious use of rapid dialogue, with ellipsis creating a constant chain of tight links from one utterance to the next (one of the characters in the novel in fact characterises the conversations as 'patball').

7.3 Conjunction

In Chapter 10, we will be looking at the ways in which clauses may be combined in clause complexes. However, the resource of conjunction is wider than that; and this section will give a very brief overview to indicate some of the important features of the role of conjunction in creating coherence.

Conjunction refers broadly to the combining of any two textual elements into a potentially coherent complex semantic unit. There are basically two ways of approaching the investigation of conjunction. On the one hand, we can start from the clause constituents which we have already identified as serving a textual function: in particular, conjunctions such as 'but' and 'because', and conjunctive Adjuncts such as 'nevertheless' and 'therefore'. The outline of circumstantial elements in 5.2.6 suggests that we might also want to include prepositions as textual linkers within the clause. We thus have three basic levels at which conjunction can be investigated: within the clause (prepositions), between clauses (conjunctions), and between clause complexes/sentences (conjunctive Adjuncts). These levels have in fact been introduced in Figure 5.29 above. Of these, of course, only the last contributes to cohesion as we have defined it here (between clause complexes). Once we have the list of constituents which function in this way, we can proceed to classify the different kinds of conjunctive relations which are signalled by them.

On the other hand, we can go from the assumption that in normal language use any clause will be interpreted as being in a coherent relation with the clause or clauses preceding it (and will therefore, of course, provide the context in which the following clause(s) can be interpreted coherently). We can then identify as far as possible the general kinds of relations that are set up between clauses in texts; and finally we can look for any cohesive features in the text that signal the relation in each case. This approach will lead us to identify a set of cohesive signals that include some which are not traditionally counted as conjunctive items. Here are a few examples:

> The Prince alienated the aristocracy because he did not visit. This was probably not *a question of* snubbing them or of snobbery but of a certain rectitude.

> After 10 years of standardisation, there should be a healthy UK market for used models. *Curiously*, there seems to be only one big second-hand PC dealer in London.

> Thus heroines, with but few exceptions, tend to be so deadly dull as to appear almost half-witted. *Not dull* is the *heroine* of Charlotte Brontë's *Jane Eyre* (1847).

The signals are: in the first example, the textual label 'question' (functioning as a kind of alternative to 'because of'); in the second, the comment Adjunct (functioning as an interpersonal equivalent of 'however'); and in the third, the lexical repetition reinforced by marked thematisation (signalling contrast).

The two approaches to conjunction result in rather different perspectives, although, as one might expect, there is a good deal of overlap. Hoey (1983) is the most fully developed account of the second approach, which, amongst other things, serves the essential function of ensuring that we do not restrict our view of conjunction in text too narrowly (see also Winter, 1994). Halliday (1994) relies primarily on the first approach, but he indicates (p. 327) that a wider view is needed to account for all the manifestations of cohesion. He also makes the useful point that different types of discourse resort to different amounts of explicit conjunction and to different types of signal; we will see a particularly clear example of this in 7.4 below.

I have already related conjunction to circumstantial elements in the clause; and the similarities also hold in the difficulty that linguists have in agreeing on a list of types of conjunction. As with circumstantial elements, there are certain types which are clearly important, as is reflected in the frequency with which certain labels recur in grammatical descriptions: cause and effect (signalled at the three levels by, for example, 'because of', 'because', 'therefore'); condition (e.g. 'assuming', 'if', 'in that case'); concession (e.g. 'despite', 'although', 'nevertheless'); comparison and contrast (e.g. 'like', 'whereas', 'similarly'); time (e.g. 'during', 'after', 'meanwhile'); and so on. However, each list tends to contain categories that are less familiar and less generally agreed on: for example, Halliday (1994: 324) includes the categories of distractive ('by the way') and resumptive ('as I was saying'), while Hoey (1983) includes Instrument-Achievement (the relation in the 'laying down wine' example earlier). Hoey also goes beyond relations between clauses to examine larger textual patterns that help the creation of coherence in a text, of which the most fully discussed is Problem-Solution.

Rather than attempt to set out a detailed classification here, which would almost inevitably suggest an illusory definitiveness, I prefer to leave the question at the general level. In Chapter 10, we will be looking at Halliday's system for the grammatical categorisation of relations within the clause complex; but in text analysis it is probably a good enough basis to start simply from the recognition of conjunction as a crucial element in cohesion and coherence, and to explore how it operates in individual texts, particularly in terms of the very diverse range of resources that are called on to signal different types of conjunction, and how they work together with other cohesive devices like reference.

7.4 Cohesion in text

To gain some idea of how such an analysis can be undertaken, we can look at a short extract from a textbook (*Evolution*, Prentice Hall Science, 1994), which has been chosen because the cohesive signals are unusually dense and explicit in some ways but not in others. Before reading the analysis below, try identifying as many features as possible that contribute to the cohesion (the sentences are numbered for ease of reference).

(1) Today, scientists know that chromosomes play an essential role in heredity. (2) Chromosomes control all the traits of an organism. (3) How do they perform this complex task? (4) The main function of chromosomes is to control the production of substances called proteins. (5) All organisms are made up primarily of proteins. (6) Proteins determine the size, shape, and other physical characteristics of an organism. (7) In other words, proteins determine the traits of an organism. (8) The kind and number of proteins in an organism determine the traits of that organism. (9a) So by controlling the kind and number of proteins produced in an organism, (9b) chromosomes are able to determine the traits of that organism.

Probably the most striking feature of the text is its lexical explicitness. This comes out especially in the reliance on lexical repetition rather than reference items such as pronouns. Apart from 'they' in (3), the main participants (chromosomes, proteins, organisms) are always referred to by full nominal groups; and there is also obvious repetition of the near-synonyms for the main process, 'control' and 'determine'. Related to this is the way in which each sentence builds on the preceding one by repeating nearly all the elements and simply changing one. This is most evident in (6), (7) and (8), where 'the size, shape, and other physical characteristics' becomes 'the traits', and then 'The kind and number (of proteins)' is added; but there is a similar relationship between (2) and (9b) and between (4) and (9a).

Interestingly, despite such a high degree of repetition, there is very little cohesive use of demonstratives: 'the' is always used to point forward to a postmodifying prepositional phrase within the same nominal group, not to signal anaphorically that a participant has already been mentioned; and 'that' in (8) and (9) refers back to a participant mentioned in the same sentence, not in an earlier sentence. There is also relatively little signalling of conjunction. We do have 'In other words' in (7), just in case the reader misses the relationship between 'the size, shape, and other physical characteristics' and 'the traits'; and 'So' in (9) – we will come back to this in a moment. But there is, for example, no signal of the relation between (1) and (2): to construct the coherence, the reader here needs to see that (2) specifies what the 'essential role' mentioned in (1) is.

The main exception to this relative lack of cohesive signals apart from repetition comes in (3), a sentence which plays a key role in organising the text. Here we have the demonstrative 'this' which, together with the general noun 'task', refers back to the message in (2). Sentence (3) is also a question: since the rest of the extract provides the answer, the interrogative Mood choice in fact plays a cohesive role. It is in relation to (3) that we can explain 'So' in (9): it is used in a way which is more typical of informal speech than of formal writing, and signals roughly 'Here comes a summary of the most important information which answers the question above'. Thus (4) to (8) are bracketed off as preparation for the main answer in (9).

The overall effect of the text might be characterised as myopic: the impression is given of a reader who can only just about manage to handle one sentence at a time and cannot really cope with reconstructing logical connections between messages for himself, except at the most basic level of question and answer. The writer, we feel, does not trust the reader to do much of the coherence-construction. Given that, as you can probably guess, the extract is from a school textbook for relatively young children, this is understandable: the intended reader almost certainly does not have the ability to make much sense of a fairly complex topic without help. I leave it to you to decide whether or not you feel that the writer has given help in the most appropriate way.

To conclude this overview of cohesion, we can return once again to the nursing advertisement (p. 70). Try analysing the text in terms of cohesive signals, watching out especially for ellipsis, and for demonstratives that summarise longer stretches of text. Only a few of the points that you might pick up on are discussed below: as with all the analyses, the discussion is not intended to be exhaustive, but merely to indicate lines that you might follow up in greater detail.

We have already noted, in the transitivity analysis, that the initial question ('Do the financial rewards match the emotional ones?') gives the impression that we are coming in on the middle of a conversation. One thing that reinforces this impression is the use of 'the', which assumes that we already know which financial and emotional rewards the speaker (whoever s/he is) is talking about. In a small way, the question presents us with a puzzle: we are treated as knowing what is being talked about when in fact we don't. This does not cause problems, since, as readers, we are used to such deliberate indeterminacies. Many short stories exploit very much the same technique, though for different purposes. To take James Joyce's 'Clay' as an example again, the first sentence begins:

> *The* matron had given *her* leave to go out as soon as *the* women's tea was over

The reference to the matron, the women and, even more, 'her' in a way which implies that we already know who they are means, as we soon realise, that we are seeing them from Maria's point of view: *she* knows who they are, and we are merely eavesdroppers. Familiarity with the technique makes us skilled at suspending the resolution of such puzzles – we know that things will become clearer as we read on. Nevertheless, we do need to read on to make things clearer, which is exactly what the writer of the advert hopes we will do. It would be very easy for the writer to include a postmodifying prepositional phrase ('the financial rewards *of nursing*') to make the use of 'the' more 'normal'; but this would water down the effect.

A little further on, the transition point from emotion to finance is marked by a nominal group with an anaphoric demonstrative, summarising what has been said so far: 'these sorts of experiences'. This is in a way balanced by the transition near the end back to interaction with the reader. As noted in the Theme analysis, this transition is marked by ellipsis: 'Not as bad as you thought, is it?' The ellipsis reinforces the conversational tone, but note that what is ellipsed is most likely to be a pronoun or demonstrative referring back to everything that has been said about money ('[It's/All this is] Not as bad as you thought, is it?'). Again we can see this as a small-scale puzzle that allows the writer to exploit our natural communicative co-operativeness: to fill out the ellipsis, we need, however subliminally, to think back to what might be the missing Subject (since it is not simply a nominal group in the preceding clause); and in doing that we are in fact reviewing the information about salaries that we have just read.

One small last point about conjunction in the text (I leave you to examine the organisational role of the four instances of sentence-initial 'But' for yourself; and it is also interesting to compare the function of the sentence-initial 'So' in the advert with its function in the textbook extract above). We saw in the textbook extract the conjunctive Adjunct 'in other words' used to introduce an unfamiliar term to the reader: 'traits' re-phrases 'size, shape, and other physical characteristics'. The same Adjunct is used in the advert, but with very different intentions: 'In other words, it's no longer necessary for a nurse to leave the patient's bedside in order to earn a higher salary.' This is not so much a re-phrasing of the preceding sentence as a re-interpretation of it: a re-interpretation which relates higher salaries in nursing directly to the unchallengeable emotional rewards (not leaving the patient's bedside). It is probably not coincidental that this is also the only point where modulation (in an explicit, objective formulation: 'it's no longer necessary') appears in the section on salaries: 'in other words' financial rewards and moral obligation need not be seen as incompatible (and, as we noted in the interpersonal analysis in Chapter 4, this link is repeated explicitly at the end: 'there's no reason in the world why you shouldn't be'). The 'other words' here are, in fact, a translation of the money situation into terms that the assumed reader will understand and approve of. Whereas the movement in the textbook extract is from familiar to unfamiliar (known non-technical terms translated into an unknown technical term), in the advert it is from unfamiliar to familiar. This movement reflects the underlying message of the advert: that, contrary to the reader's assumed beliefs, the financial rewards of nursing do match the emotional ones, in moral as well as practical terms.

We could even see this difference between the two texts as mirroring on a very small scale larger ideological differences in the functions of educational and advertising text: the former aiming to enlarge our horizons by providing new ways of classifying and labelling the world, and the latter hoping (in many cases at least) to lull us into compliance by encouraging us to accept the unfamiliar as essentially familiar (and what we always in fact wanted). You may feel that this is pushing the conclusions a little too far from such a small base; and we would, of course, need to find other evidence elsewhere in the text and in a range of similar texts if we want to justify such claims. But the important point, which relates to the fundamental aim of a functional approach to language analysis, is that we can in principle use even individual lexico-grammatical choices in context to understand something of the way in which language, and thus language users, construe the world – that we can see the world in a linguistic grain of sand.

§   Refer to Exercise 7.1.

EXERCISE 7.1

Look back at the letter and response in Exercise 2.1 (p. 24) and the doctor's consultation in Exercise 4.3 (p. 74). Identify the Themes, and consider any insights that the analysis gives you into the way the texts develop. Also identify any cohesive signals: reference, ellipsis and conjunction. The second text will be discussed in Chapter 11. That discussion will suggest points that you can explore in relation to the textual meanings in the first text.

8

Grammatical metaphor

8.1 Introduction

In some of the analyses in the three preceding chapters, especially of transitivity, we have run up against problems in deciding how best to code certain wordings. These problems have arisen for a number of reasons; but one of the most common sources of difficulty is metaphor. Metaphor is a familiar concept, and it is generally taken to be easy to recognise. In the following sentence, for example, it is clear that 'crippled' and 'burden' are being used metaphorically:

> The north is crippled with the burden of the industrial revolution to an extent that the south hardly begins to understand.

A typical analysis of the metaphors will point out that 'crippled' has a literal meaning of 'lame', while 'burden' literally means 'something heavy'. In this view, metaphor is seen as relating to the way a particular word is used, and the term metaphorical is used as the opposite of literal, to describe the meaning of the word. We can show this as in Figure 8.1, with the wording in italics and the meaning in quotation marks.

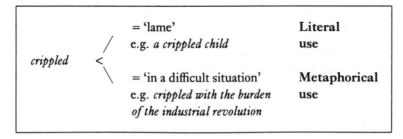

Fig 8.1 Literal and metaphorical meanings of a wording

However, it is also possible to look at metaphor from the perspective of the meaning being expressed. For example, a 'translation' of the example above (overlooking the personification in 'the north' and 'the south') into less metaphorical language might be:

> The north is in a difficult situation because of the effects of the industrial revolution to an extent that the south hardly begins to understand.

If we compare this translation with the original, we are no longer comparing different meanings of the same words ('crippled' and 'burden'); instead, we are comparing different ways of expressing the 'same' meaning. If we want to talk about metaphor from this perspective, Halliday (1994: 342) suggests that it is less confusing to use slightly different terminology. We can still say that the original expresses the meaning in a **metaphorical** way; but we can use the term **congruent** to describe the way in which the reworded version expresses the meaning. We can show this as in Figure 8.2.

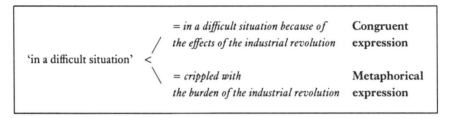

Fig 8.2 Congruent and metaphorical wordings of a meaning

The rationale for introducing this alternative perspective becomes clearer when we look at examples like the following (from the same article as the example above):

> The north emerges from every statistical comparison that can be made as significantly poorer than the south.

Here it is difficult to talk in terms of a literal meaning for 'comparison' which differs from its metaphorical meaning. But if we think in terms of the meaning being expressed, we can see that, just as with the first example, we can 'translate' it into something like:

> Whenever people compare statistics about the north and the south, they find that the north is significantly poorer than the south.

This way of expressing the meaning is intuitively closer to the events in the external world: instead of representing the process of 'comparing' as a thing from which something else can 'emerge' of its own volition, it represents it as an event involving human participants which results in those participants understanding a phenomenon. Using the terms introduced above, we can say that the 'translation' is more congruent – in other words, the term congruent can be informally glossed as 'closer to the state of affairs in the external world'. In simple terms, nouns congruently encode things, and verbs congruently encode happenings. The original wording above is metaphorical because there a noun ('comparison') encodes a happening, and a verb ('emerges') encodes a complex meaning which involves amongst other things the logical relation of cause and effect ('as a result of comparing, people find out').

We can therefore give a provisional definition of **grammatical metaphor** as: the expression of a meaning through a lexico-grammatical form which originally evolved to express a different kind of meaning. The expression of the meaning is metaphorical in relation to a different way of expressing the 'same' meaning which would be more congruent. Note that this formulation is designed to cover lexical metaphor as well: there is no essential difference between the two kinds, and lexical metaphor can be seen as a sub-category of grammatical metaphor. The formulation also indicates the fact that metaphor is simply a natural extension of the in-built flexibility and multi-functionality of language. A language element (a word, a grammatical structure, etc.) initially evolves to serve a particular function; but once it exists as part of the language, it is available for other recognisably related uses: the use of the word 'leg' can be extended to cover part of a table, or the grammatical class of nouns can be extended to cover actions, events and states (e.g. 'comparison').

Before exploring the concept of grammatical metaphor in more detail, there are three general points which it is worth stressing. First, strictly speaking we should not talk as if a particular way of expressing a meaning were either metaphorical or congruent in absolute terms: it is always a matter of degree, and we should talk of a wording being more or less metaphorical or congruent in relation to a different way of expressing the meaning. For convenience I will in fact describe certain wordings as metaphorical; but it should be borne in mind that this is shorthand for 'more metaphorical than another wording that I could suggest'.

Second, I have talked about metaphorical and congruent ways of expressing the 'same' meaning; but one of the fundamental assumptions of a functional approach is that it is not possible to separate expression and meaning in this simple way. The expression *is* the meaning; and the choice of a more metaphorical wording construes a different meaning from the choice of a more congruent wording. Let us return to the example given above:

> The north emerges from every statistical comparison that can be made as significantly poorer than the south.

The wording here construes an objective world in which facts 'emerge' unmediated by human consciousness and in which 'comparison' is a fixed, countable entity rather than a dynamic process. Although the more congruent wording suggested above refers to recognisably the same state of affairs in the external world, it clearly construes a very different meaning about that state of affairs. Congruent rewordings can be useful in exploring metaphorical wordings; but it is important not to see them as in some sense expressing the 'real' meaning.

The third point is that more metaphorical wordings are inherently neither better nor worse than more congruent wordings: they are simply doing different jobs. There will be many factors influencing the extent to which metaphorical wordings of a particular kind might be preferred in particular contexts: in certain registers such as scientific writing the metaphorical 'objectivisation' illustrated in the example above tends to be highly valued, whereas in others such as oral narratives it is not. Conversely, in oral narratives certain kinds of interpersonal metaphors will be heavily relied on which will hardly appear in scientific writing. We will explore some of these correlations between discourse type and grammatical metaphor in the following sections.

8.2 Experiential and logical metaphors

In 8.1, I drew a distinction between the meaning of a message and the state of affairs referred to by the message. This distinction has already been implied in the discussion of transitivity; and in fact transitivity analysis provides one rule of thumb for the recognition of grammatical metaphor. If a transitivity analysis does not seem to reflect adequately the state of affairs being referred to, it is very likely that the meaning is being expressed metaphorically. In this case, it is usually possible to give a **parallel analysis** which does reflect the state of affairs more closely, in other words, more congruently. We can then see the meaning of the clause as being derived from the combination of the two readings reflected in the different analyses. This amounts to a claim that in understanding the clause we are in effect understanding both readings simultaneously. (As we shall see, this rule of thumb also works to a large extent for interpersonal and textual metaphors.) As an example of a relatively straightforward parallel analysis, see Figure 8.3.

The year the villa was completed	saw	the end of 20 years of war with France
Senser	Pr: Mental	Phenomenon

'in the year the villa was completed	20 years of war with France	ended'
Circ: Temporal	Actor	Pr: Material

Fig 8.3 Metaphorical and congruent readings combined

Deciding on a satisfactory congruent reading is not always so straightforward. Consider this headline from a newspaper:

Fears mount for ailing King

A simple transitivity analysis would show a material process with 'fears' as Actor. If we then '**unpack**' the experiential meanings of the clause, we could arrive at a more congruent reading such as the following:

People fear more strongly because the King is ailing

Figure 8.4 shows how we can present both of these readings together.

Fears		mount	for ailing King		
Actor		Pr: Material	Circ: Behalf		
'people	fear	more strongly	because	the King	is ailing'
Senser	Pr: Mental	Circ: Quality	Circ: Reason		
				Behaver	Pr: Behavioural

Fig 8.4 A double analysis of a less straightforward case

However, as well as being disturbingly clumsy, the more congruent reading leaves certain questions unanswered. In particular, it makes explicit the Senser of the process, but not the Phenomenon. We can guess that what people fear would be something like 'the idea that the King might die'; but it is difficult to decide whether we should include this as part of the meaning of the original clause.

Nevertheless, even if we cannot always decide how best to unpack metaphorical meanings, we can identify the main ways in which grammatical metaphor arises. One of the most important is **nominalisation**, i.e. the use of a nominal form to express a process meaning:

These ideas have been subject to widespread *criticism*.
[Many people *have criticised* these ideas.]

Nominalisation can also be used to express an attributive meaning – a relational process together with the Attribute:

This ambivalence towards literacy seems to be a strong element in contemporary culture.
[People *are ambivalent* towards literacy ...]

This type of grammatical metaphor plays a key role because it involves a realignment of all the other elements of the message. As we have seen, the process is central in the clause, and the other elements are defined by their relationship to it: they are participants in, or circumstances for, the process.

If the process is nominalised, it has an inevitable knock-on effect on these other elements. In simple terms, a verb has a Subject, for example, but a noun does not; on the other hand, a noun can have attributes. When a process is expressed as a 'thing' by nominalisation, the participants may be expressed as attributes of the 'thing'. The following examples show just a few of the possibilities:

> Select the printer settings recommended for enhanced *printer* performance.
>
> [*the printer* (= Actor) performs better]

> The coming *of writing* is associated with the development *of towns* ...
>
> [*Writing* (= Actor) comes at the same time as *towns* (= Actor) develop]

> The use *of the term* implies something more than development or change.
>
> [When people use *the term* (= Goal) ...]

> They ignored *his* suggestion that it was too late.
>
> [*He* (= Sayer) suggested that it was too late]

> Chkdsk: Checks the *structural* validity of the selected compressed drive.
>
> [checks whether *the structure* (= Carrier) of the selected compressed drive is valid]

These are cases where the participant is relatively easy to retrieve; but the congruent expression may need a little more filling out:

> Those ideas have been subject to *widespread* criticism.
>
> [*Many people* (= Sayer) have criticised these ideas.]

> Under the *no boundary* proposal one learns that ...
>
> [I have proposed that there is *no boundary* (= Existent) ...]

If a nominal group is used to express a process, what happens in the process slot in the clause? In many cases, the process is 'normal', with the nominalisation as an abstract metaphorical participant. Compare these two examples, where the Phenomenon is a nominalisation in the first case but not in the second:

> They ignored *his suggestion that it was too late*.

> They ignored *him*.

Frequently, however, the choice of a nominalisation is part of a more generally metaphorical way of representing the state of affairs which influences the whole clause. One fairly common feature of formal language is the use of the process slot at least partly to encode **logical relations** which would more congruently be expressed by conjunctive elements:

> This world-wide expansion of English *means* that it is now one of the most widely spoken languages in the world [= '*because* English has expanded world-wide ...']

> But the introduction of a capital gains tax *would permit* a reduction in the level of personal income tax [= '*if* they introduced a capital gains tax, they could reduce ...']

As these examples suggest, it is particularly logical relations in the area of cause and effect (including conditional relations) that are expressed by the process.

In other cases, the process contributes relatively little to the meaning of the clause. It may be a lexically empty verb which combines with the following nominalisation (functioning as Range) to express the process:

> It may also be that the analysis of fads and fashions could *make a substantial contribution* to a more rounded picture of the period.

Alternatively, it may be a neutral process meaning roughly just 'happen':

> Further encouragement for the existence of black holes *came* in 1967.

Another common use of the process is to establish a relation between a nominalisation and following evaluation in the Attribute slot:

> Consequently, faithfulness to propositional content *is also in danger*.

> Official recognition that the state school system of a country has not solved difficulties with literacy *is often reluctant*.

As we shall see in Chapter 10, one group of projected clauses, 'facts', are intermediate between independent clauses and full nominalisations. Evaluative examples like those above are therefore similar in function to cases of thematised comment (see 6.4.3), where what is evaluated is a projected fact:

> It is probable that we are moving towards the American position.

The result of all of these ways of exploiting nominalisation tends to be a wording that is extremely simple at the level of the clause complex – often just a single clause – but extremely complex at the level of the group. The following is a fairly typical (and relatively short) example:

> The unification of England under the West Saxon kings led to the recognition of the West Saxon dialect as a literary standard.

This type of wording is instantly recognisable as associated above all with formal written registers; and it is one of the main bases for Halliday's (1994, 1985b) claim that written English tends to be characterised by syntactic simplicity. A more 'spoken' rendering of the example would unpack the metaphors (i.e. be more congruent) and in the process would create greater syntactic complexity (more subordinate clauses):

> When/Because England became unified under the West Saxon kings, people began recognizing the West Saxon dialect as a literary standard.

This insight leads us towards the question of why grammatical metaphor of this experiential kind has evolved, and why it tends to be associated with formal uses of language (to the extent that someone aiming to sound appropriately formal may use metaphorical wordings whose oddity is striking until dulled by familiarity: an official being asked on radio about how many people use buses speaks of 'the amount of bus ridership'). There is no space here to do more than indicate briefly some of the functional reasons, and also some of the wider ideological implications; but I will suggest lines of enquiry that you might like to follow through for yourself.

One important function of nominalisation is **encapsulation**. Broadly speaking, co-operative text typically introduces new meanings in the form of clauses, since clauses are negotiable (see 4.3.3): they represent claims by the writer which the reader can, in principle, reject. Once a meaning has been introduced in this way and has been accepted (i.e. the reader has continued reading), it can then be used as a basis for the next step in the argument. Now, nominal groups have two qualities which are useful here. First, a noun typically refers to a 'thing', i.e. something which exists. By 'nouning' a process, the writer can reflect the fact that s/he has negotiated and established the meaning of the clause centred around the process – in other words, that meaning can now be treated as existing, as a kind of abstract 'thing'. Second, a nominalisation is itself available to function as a participant in another process. It can also, of course, function as Theme. We therefore find the fairly common pattern in formal discursive text where a meaning is brought in as a full clause, and is then encapsulated in a nominalisation which serves as the starting-point for the next clause. Here is an example from Lesley Milroy's book *Observing and Analysing Natural Language*:

> Because intra-speaker variation has been studied within frameworks associated with a number of different subject areas [...], it is practical to treat style-shifting and code-switching separately in this chapter. But *such a separation* has no theoretical justification.

This technique can be used in principle at each step in the argument.

The example also illustrates another important use of nominalisation. The **technical term** 'code-switching' is itself a nominalisation encapsulating a concept which has been established clausally a couple of sentences previously:

> ... some communities have access to linguistic repertoires which allow them to switch between codes which they (or others) perceive as different languages or different dialects of the same language.

Exactly the same is true of 'style-shifting'. The relationship between the technical terms and their clausal expression is reasonably easy to identify in these cases: we can see the technical term as a '**condensation**' of the clause. However, another nominalised technical term in the example works slightly differently: 'intra-speaker variation' has appeared earlier as 'variation in the language of a single speaker on different occasions'. This is also a nominalisation, though it is much less condensed and thus easier to translate into a more congruent wording ('a single speaker uses different language on different occasions'). This nominalisation itself relates back, not to a specific clause earlier in the text, but to the general concept of variation in language use which has been the subject of the whole book: this nominalisation expresses a new sub-category of a known phenomenon. Since they condense a clause down to a word or group, nominalised technical terms are clearly very economical; but equally clearly the reader needs to be able to identify the uncondensed wording that the nominalisation relates to. In a textbook like Milroy's, there will normally be an explicit uncondensed wording, since the writer assumes that the technical term is unfamiliar to the reader; but even here it may not be immediately obvious what the relevant uncondensed wording is. Once you deal with more specialist writing, there are many concepts which the writer assumes will be familiar and which are therefore introduced directly in their condensed form as technical terms. The uncondensed wording will have occurred in a different text entirely – the one in which the concept was introduced – and if you have not read that text there is a good chance that you will not fully understand the term. From this point of view, education at every level can be seen as largely a question of learning to handle condensed wordings.

As a final point, we can examine this concept of 'meaning condensation' (note the nominalised technical term derived from the paragraph above) from a slightly different angle. What is it that gets reduced or lost in the condensation? One key loss is often that of the doer of the process. One reason why nominalisation is in harmony with the ideology of science, and of academic, formal writing in general, is that it allows processes to be **objectified**, to be expressed without the human doer. This objectification, as noted above in the case of 'emerge', is often carried over into the verbs that express the process. Nominalised meanings may, for example, 'indicate' conclusions (to whom?):

> Here, a statistical analysis of the actual vote indicates that opposition was localised.

At the same time, nominalised processes are non-finite: they are not tied to any specific time in relation to the time of speaking. (Incidentally, this is yet another reflection of the functional unity of Mood: both Subject and Finite typically disappear when a process is nominalised.) Thus a nominalised process is detached from the here-and-now in a way that is not normally possible for a process expressed by a verb. It is therefore inherently generalised – again, in harmony with the aim of science to establish general truths not tied to specific conditions of time or observer.

If we go a step further, we can see that, by removing the option of a Mood, a nominalised process has been made **non-negotiable**. This is intimately connected with the fact that it is also 'thingified' by being expressed as a noun. Science aims to establish not only general truths, but unassailable, certain truths. Our current ideology of science is far happier with a view of the world as a series of fixed constants acting on each other in logically definable ways. In linguistic terms, this is reflected in, and reinforced by, the preference for nominalisations which represent '**fossilised**' processes and verbs whose primary function is to express not dynamic action but relationships between the nominals. In speech, the more obvious here–and–now interaction means that this tendency may be toned down: for example, talks on science will often deliberately 'humanise' and de–condense the topic to make it easier for the hearers to take in. Writing, on the other hand, is more susceptible for a range of reasons to the fossilisation of knowledge.

8.3 Interpersonal metaphors

The non–negotiability associated with nominalisation can clearly be a powerful weapon in cases where the speaker or writer wishes, for whatever reason, to avoid negotiation, with its possible outcome of rejection. In persuasive text, one common technique is to objectify opinion by nominalising it, so as to make it more difficult for the reader or hearer to disagree with it. Thus we can also identify metaphor in the expression of **modality** and **evaluation**.

The outline of modality in Chapter 4 – especially modal responsibility (4.4.4) – has already in fact drawn on metaphorical wordings, although the term itself was not used there. Explicit objective modality is essentially metaphorical. In the nursing advertisement, for example, the writer's modal point of view about the reader is expressed as if it were an objective description of an attribute of the reader:

> Of course, you're *unlikely* to be attracted to nursing because of the money.

As with other kinds of metaphor, we can give a double reading; see Figure 8.5.

you	're	unlikely to be attracted	to nursing	because of the money.
Carrier	Pr: Rel	Attribute		
'you	probably won't be attracted		to nursing	because of the money'
Senser	Pr: Mental		Phenomenon	Circ: Reason

Fig 8.5 Explicit objective modality as grammatical metaphor

We can also go further than this and express modality through a nominalisation:

> But *the possibility* always existed of giving it a second runway. [= 'people could always have given it ...']

As with other kinds of nominalisation, this can be simply a form of cohesive signal, with the modal nominal picking up on an earlier more congruent expression of modality:

> *We don't really know* what causes this inefficient nursing or the prompt waking. *One possibility* is that the babies' nervous system and digestive system are not yet working well enough ...

However, it can also serve as a means of both disguising the source of the modality and making it more difficult to query:

> *Doubts* remain whether BSE can infect man. [whose doubts?]

> *The likelihood* of a united Franco–German move to introduce a single currency makes it imperative to state our opposition clearly. [= it is a fact that it is likely]

Similarly, evaluation can be expressed through a nominalisation, which can make it appear more objective and factual:

> I wonder how many of your readers share my sense of disbelief in *the Government's indifference* to the present crisis. [= it is a fact that the Government is indifferent]

> *This failure to apply common sense* led to a nonsensical conclusion. [= it is a fact that people failed to apply common sense]

If we look at the other end of the modal responsibility cline, we can also see explicit subjective modality as a kind of metaphor. In this case, there is clearly no question of disguising responsibility; but the wording is metaphorical in that there is a tension between the grammatical dominance of the modal clause (which is the main clause in traditional terms) and the semantic dominance of the 'reported' clause (as we saw in 4.4.4, any tag question picks up the Mood of that clause rather than the Mood of the modal clause). We can once again show this with a double analysis (see Figure 8.6: the third analysis in the figure shows a related kind of metaphor in the area of evaluation rather than modality).

Note that, since we are dealing with interpersonal meanings metaphorically expressed as if they were experiential meanings, the main difference in the more congruent reading is that the former 'disappear' from the transitivity analysis. Because of this similarity between the two readings, in practice it is often simplest just to ignore the modal clause in the transitivity analysis, i.e. to analyse the clause as if it were expressed congruently. The modal and evaluative meanings can then be accounted for in the interpersonal analysis of the clause.

I	think	Mrs Taylor	would like	a drink.
Senser	Pr: Mental	Senser	Pr: Mental	Phenomenon
'probably		Mrs Taylor	would like	a drink'
		Senser	Pr: Mental	Phenomenon

I	doubt	if I	could help	anyway
Senser	Pr: Mental	Actor	Pr: Material	
'probably		I	could (not) help	anyway'
		Actor	Pr: Material	

I	'm	afraid	they	've left.
Carrier	Pr: Rel	Attribute	Actor	Pr: Material
'unfortunately			they	've left.'
			Actor	Pr: Material

Fig 8.6 Explicit subjective modality as grammatical metaphor

As well as metaphorical wordings of modal and evaluative meanings, we can also identify metaphor in the expression of **Mood** meanings. Again, this is essentially a matter of reinterpreting a phenomenon that we have already noticed: the fact that Mood choices and speech roles do not always coincide (see 4.2). Questions are most naturally (congruently) associated with interrogative Mood; but we can also ask questions with a declarative Mood choice:

'And he's been back with this girl since he's been with Gertrude?' 'Yes.'

(Here we cannot show the metaphor by a double transitivity analysis, because the metaphor operates completely within the interpersonal meanings.) This mismatch between Mood and speech roles is usually discussed under the label of indirect speech acts in studies of spoken discourse and pragmatics; but to see it as a kind of grammatical metaphor allows us to explain it in terms of a more general phenomenon. As with other cases of metaphor, it involves the use of one linguistic form to express a meaning that is not its most 'natural' function. Also, the meaning comes from the combination of both form and function. This is perhaps easiest to see when politeness is involved:

Could you get me a drink?

This functions as a demand for goods-&-services, but it is worded as a question about the other person's ability; the effect is therefore to soften the demand. Here are a few other examples: I leave you to identify the mismatch between wording and function, and the possible reasons for it.

Touch that and I'll thump you.

Would you like some tea?

We don't put those glasses in the dishwasher. [said to 'helpful' guest]

There's still some beer left.

What	you	need to do	is		to write	me		a letter
Identified/Value			Pr: Rel		Identifier/Token			
	'you	need to write				me	a letter'	
	Sayer	Pr: Verbal				Beneficiary	Verbiage	

What	one	will not learn	here	is	anything about the Enlightenment.
Identified/Value				Pr: Rel	Identifier/Token
	'one	will not learn	here		anything about the Enlightemnent'
	Senser	Pr: Mental	Circ		Phenomenon

What happened	was	that	Whorf	picked up	Boas' example
Id/Value	Pr: Rel	Identifier/Token			
		Actor	Pr: Material	Goal	

Fig 8.7 Double transitivity analysis of thematic equatives (see Section 8.4 overleaf)

8.4 Textual metaphor

It is debatable whether the label 'textual metaphor' is really justified (Halliday (1994) does not include this category in his survey of grammatical metaphor). I include it here because of the assumption that the presence of metaphor can be recognised by the need for a double transitivity analysis, one of the original wording and the other of a more congruent rewording; and there are in fact two types of thematic structure which also need a double analysis. These are thematic equatives and predicated Theme. They have been fully discussed in 6.4, so all that is needed here are some sample analyses: thematic equatives in Figure 8.7, and predicated Themes in Figure 8.8 (in some cases, the rewordings are so close to the original that the congruent analysis is simply given on the line below).

It	's not	the technology	which	is	wrong
Id-	Pr: Rel	Identifier/Token	-entified/Value		
		'the technology		isn't	wrong'
		Carrier		Pr: Rel	Attribute

It	is	we	who	have not learned	how to use it.
Id-	Pr: Rel	Identifier/Token	-entified/Value		
	Senser			Pr: Mental	Phenomenon

It	wasn't	until 1986	that we	came back	to the UK
Id-	Pr: Rel	Identifier/Token	-entified/Value		
Circ: Location (time)			Actor	Pr: Material	Circ: Location (place)

Fig 8.8 Double transitivity analysis of predicated Theme

8.5 A cautionary note

The examples in this chapter have shown that metaphorical wordings, amongst other things, allow a denseness of meaning that more congruent wordings typically dilute: I have often restricted the suggested rewordings to part of the original version because a complete rewording would result in a long, clumsy and frequently unsatisfactory version. In many cases, in fact, you will find that it is impossible to decide on a congruent reading which adequately reflects the meanings encoded in the metaphorical wording. One of the dangers of the concept of grammatical metaphor is that it opens a potentially bottomless pit of possible rewordings. It is difficult to decide at what point you are crossing from unpacking the meanings that are there to importing meanings that were not there before; it is also difficult to decide at what point you have arrived at a reading that is sufficiently congruent; and it is even difficult sometimes to decide whether a wording is actually metaphorical or not (for one thing, many wordings that were originally metaphorical have now become the normal wording, e.g. many mental processes of cognition are routinely expressed as material processes like 'grasp', 'take in', 'master', etc.). There is no answer to this dilemma: the concept is essential in explaining how the language works, but it is a dangerously powerful one. The only practical advice is to use it carefully and with caution.

§   Refer to Exercises 8.1, 8.2.

EXERCISE 8.1

Identify any grammatical metaphor in the following short text. Can you identify a common theme running through the metaphors which reinforces other aspects of the meaning of the text? (Think about the purpose of this kind of text.)

Providing magnificent views of the historic town of Frodsham, this split-level detached house has been carefully maintained and preserved. The ground floor boasts a large entrance hall, dining room, lounge, kitchen and bathroom. Upstairs are three more bedrooms. A fourth bedroom on the ground floor is available for conversion if required. The rear garden has a useful timber shed. Frodsham is well serviced with local shops; the M65 motorway is a few minutes drive away.

EXERCISE 8.2

Identify any cases of nominalisation in the following text, together with any associated features in the clause, such as verbs expressing logical relationships. Look particularly at the almost complete absence of people from the text: how is this done? The text will be discussed in Chapter 11.

'Frozen shoulder' is a clinical syndrome which can probably be produced by a variety of pathological processes in the shoulder joint. These can seldom be differentiated and treatment is empirical. It is a condition affecting the middle-aged, in whose shoulder cuffs degenerative changes are occurring. The outstanding feature is limitation of movements in the shoulder. This restriction is often severe, with virtually no gleno–humeral movements possible, but in the milder cases rotation, especially internal rotation, is primarily affected. Restriction of movements is accompanied in most cases by pain, which is often severe and may disturb sleep. There is frequently a history of minor trauma, which is usually presumed to produce some tearing of the degenerating shoulder cuff, thereby initiating the low-grade prolonged inflammatory changes responsible for the symptoms. Radiographs of the shoulder are almost always normal. In some cases the condition is initiated by a period of immobilisation of the arm, not uncommonly as the result of the inadvised prolonged use of a sling after a Colles' fracture. It is commoner on the left side, and in an appreciable number of cases there is a preceding episode of a silent or overt cardiac infarct. If untreated, pain subsides after many months, but there may be permanent restriction of movements. The main aim of treatment is to improve the final range of movements in the shoulder, and graduated shoulder exercises are the mainstay of treatment. In some cases where pain is a particular problem, hydrocortisone injections into the shoulder cuff may be helpful. In a few cases, once the acute stage is well past, manipulation of the shoulder under general anaesthesia may be helpful in restoring movements in a stiff joint.

(from R. McRae, *Clinical Orthopaedic Examination* (3rd edn) 1990, Edinburgh: Churchill Livingstone, p. 42)

9

Groups and phrases

9.1 Groups

The book so far has focused very much on clause-level choices, because clauses are the main way in which we express meanings. Nevertheless, clauses are clearly not the whole story. We have already had recourse to other, smaller grammatical units in identifying exactly how the three metafunctions work; and in this chapter we will look at in a more systematic way at the elements at the next rank down from clauses: groups and phrases (see 2.2 on ranks). Just as the clause has functional slots (e.g. Subject, Actor, Theme) which are filled by groups and phrases, so these elements themselves can be analysed in terms of the functional slots that they offer, the kinds of elements which can fill those slots, and the kinds of meanings that can thereby be contributed to the meaning of the clause as a whole.

9.1.1 NOMINAL GROUPS

Apart from the clause itself, the **nominal group** is the grammatical unit which allows the widest range of meanings to be expressed, not least because of the resource of **embedding**. Here is a fairly extreme, but by no means abnormal, example (the nominal group is marked by square brackets, and the noun which forms the central pivot, or '**Head**', of the group is in italics):

> This is [a different *example* of how the structure of languages is significant in understanding how the written language works].

Here the bulk of the nominal group follows the Head. This is a typical pattern; but it is also possible to fit in a fair amount of meaning, although rather less spectacularly extensive, before the Head. (In the following example, nominal groups inside embedded clauses and prepositional phrases – see 2.2 – are also enclosed in square brackets and their Heads are in italics.)

> Harry stared at [the big fox terrier *face*], [the cold pale blue *eyes* enlarged by [the thick donnish *glasses*]], [the neatly clipped *fringe* of [light grey *hair*]].

Although it may not at first sight appear so, it is the slots before the Head which show more functional diversity. The slot following the Head serves only one primary function, and is thus relatively simple in functional terms; but on the other hand it is structurally extremely complex and has a capacity for apparently infinite extension.

I have talked informally about the slots before and following the Head. We can formalise this by setting up a basic three-part functional structure for the nominal group: **Premodifier, Head, Postmodifier**. Of course, not all nominal groups have all three slots filled. The only obligatory slot is the Head. This is normally filled by a noun, though there are some exceptions: for example, in an elliptical nominal group the Head may be a determiner (or 'Deictic', see below). The following horoscope shows a sample of the range of possible structures; the analyses are given in Figure 9.1.

> There is a shift of planetary emphasis to the far away things of life whether these amount to events happening in the future or situations to do with overseas. With Mercury's move forward, you will soon be hearing the news for which you have been waiting. While you are poised for a significant development on the work and personal front you would be advised to separate fact from fiction.

Premodifier	Head	Postmodifier
a	shift	of planetary emphasis
the faraway	things	of life
	these	
	events	happening in the future
	situations	to do with overseas
Mercury's	move	forward
	you	
the	news	for which you have been waiting
a significant	development	on the work and personal front
	fact	
	fiction	

Fig 9.1 Different nominal group structures

In functional terms, we can analyse the nominal group according to the kinds of questions that are answered in each slot. The Head normally tells us the **Thing** that is being talked about. It may be expressed by a pronoun, a proper name or a common noun. Pronouns and proper names rarely need any further specification, since they refer to unique Things, and therefore usually appear with no pre- or postmodification – although this can happen in some cases:

It turns out he's *the same David Hays that we met in Hungary*.

Common nouns, on the other hand, refer to a class of Things, either concrete or abstract (e.g. 'eyes', 'situation', 'emphasis') and the communicative context frequently requires some kind of specification to be added. It is the function of the Pre- and Postmodifiers to provide the specification, in different ways.

Within the Premodifier, it is possible to identify four (or five) main functional slots, with a fixed ordering. The first of these is the **Deictic**. 'Deictic' (from a Greek word meaning 'showing/pointing') is the most 'grammatical' of the slots, and signals how the nominal group fits into the context of the text around it and/or of the wider context in which the language event is situated (there are therefore similarities with the first element in the verbal group, the Finite). There are a number of different ways in which this link with the context can be signalled, but they can be divided into two main groups: **specific** and **non-specific**.

Specific deixis may link the nominal group in by **identifiability** or **possession**:

That way you can steal a march on someone else.

Uranus and Neptune have yet to deliver *their* verdicts.

The identifiability signal can be paraphrased as 'the specific member of the type of Thing I am talking about is one that you, the hearer, are able to identify'. It is expressed by the demonstrative determiners, including 'the'. As mentioned in 7.2.1, the identification may come from the co-text (*'that* way' = 'the way I have just mentioned') or from the external context:

The home base is a priority for much of *the* day [= the day the horoscope is published]

Do you want *this* tea? [= the tea I am pointing to]

Possession represents a particular type of identifiability: the possession signal can be paraphrased as 'the specific member of the type of Thing I am talking about can be identified by the fact that it is possessed by the entity mentioned'. It can be realised in three ways: a possessive determiner (if the possessor is identifiable); an embedded specific nominal group with the genitive marker (if more information about the identifiable possessor is needed); or a non-specific genitive nominal group (if the possessor is not identifiable):

You'll feel that life has suddenly lost *its* buzz.

You will need to take *your partner's* feeling into account [identifiable possessor]

Refuse to be swayed by *other people's* opinions [non-identifiable possessor]

Very broadly, specific Deictics answer the question 'Which Thing?' (or 'Whose Thing?' in the case of possessives).

Non-specific deixis works in a different way: it signals that the hearer or reader is not assumed, or does not need, to be familiar with the specific identity of the Thing at that point. Since the Deictic slot is not needed for identification, it is used instead to indicate what quantity of the Thing is involved – all, some or none.

> There are still *some* tricky moments ahead.

> They tell you in *no* uncertain terms whether you are headed in the right direction.

Note that with non-specific deixis we may also have what is sometimes called 'zero article' (ϕ): that is, the Deictic function is carried out by the choice of nothing in the Deictic slot. This is only possible with plural and uncountable nouns, and is thus functionally equivalent to non-specific 'a' with singular countable nouns:

> There are ϕ moves underway.

> You would be advised to separate ϕ fact from ϕ fiction.

> The foundations of your ambitions are in *a* state of ϕ flux.

Most non-specific Deictics can be probed by asking the question 'How much/ many Thing?'. However, the zero article cannot be probed (there is nothing to answer with in the Deictic slot), and nor can 'a' (though its marked version 'one' can be).

In addition to the main Deictic, we often find a second Deictic element (the **Post-Deictic** or Deictic$_2$). The line between the Post-Deictic and the following Epithet (see below) is often indistinct, since both are typically realised by adjectives. Some of these items reinforce the meaning of the primary deictic: for example, in 'a certain project' 'a certain' means something like 'I am not specifying it here ['a'], but it is in principle specifiable ['certain']'; while 'own' in 'your own life' is clearly linked to the possessive meaning. Others serve a comparative function e.g. 'the *same* pattern', 'some *other* people' (in 7.2.1, we have already noted similarities in the functions of comparatives and demonstratives). It is also possible to include in this category certain adjectives related to the various types of modality ('possible', 'obvious', 'usual', 'necessary', etc., see Halliday 1994: 183), though these can equally well be categorised as attitudinal Epithets.

Overlapping with Deictics to a large extent is the category of **Numeratives**. These specify the number or quantity of the Thing, either in exact terms ('three', 'twenty') or inexact terms ('many', 'much'); or they specify order ('first', 'fifth'). Halliday (1994: 183) places these in a separate slot after Deictics in the nominal group, since they can follow specific Deictics (e.g. 'the two planets'); but it is also possible to see numeratives as a different type of non-specific Deictic, since they can precede Post-Deictics (e.g. 'ten more years') and cannot follow non-specific Deictics. If the latter analysis is accepted, ordinals – which normally follow specific Deictics ('the second') – can be analysed as Post-Deictics.

With the next slot, we move from primarily grammatical items to lexical items. This slot is the **Epithet**, which is normally filled by one or more adjectives and which can answer two main questions: 'What do you think of the Thing?' and 'What is the Thing like?' (typically in that order). In principle there can be any number of Epithets, though in practice it is rare to find more than two. There is no absolute line between attitudinal Epithets which express evaluation and modality (i.e. interpersonal meanings), and experiential Epithets which express properties of the Thing itself: often the Epithet expresses both at once (e.g. 'delicious'). Here are a few examples of the range of possibilities, with the Epithets in italics:

> There are still some *tricky* moments ahead.

> Tensions at work could undermine your *usual sunny* optimism.

> Harry stared at the *big* fox terrier face, the *cold pale blue* eyes enlarged by the *thick donnish* glasses, the *neatly clipped* fringe of *light grey* hair.

The final slot before the Head is the **Classifier**. This may be filled by an adjective or a noun, and broadly answers the question 'What kind of Thing?'. As the label suggests, the Classifier tells us which of the possible categories in a classificatory system the Thing belongs to. This classification may be 'natural': e.g. 'cooking' may be 'Chinese', 'Indian', 'French', etc. On the other hand, it may be established by that particular nominal group: in the last example above, the 'face' is classified as belonging to the 'fox terrier' class of faces. Whereas a noun in the Premodifier is almost certainly a Classifier, the same adjective may

Deictic	Deictic$_2$	Epithet	Classifier	Head
that				way
other people's				opinions
some		very tricky		moments
the		cold pale blue		eyes
the	other		lunar	influences
the			work and personal	front
			Chinese	cooking
the		big	fox terrier	face
a		nice collective	compromise	decision

Fig 9.2 Functional slots in the Premodifier

sometimes be used as a Classifier or Epithet: for example, 'green' is Epithet in 'green grass' but Classifier in 'a green salad'. Generally adjectival Classifiers can be distinguished from Epithets by the fact that they cannot be sub-modified: we can say, for example, 'some *very tricky* moments' or '*greener* grass', but we cannot do the same with 'Chinese cooking' or 'a green salad'.

Figure 9.2 on the preceding page shows the detailed analysis of the Premodifier in a sample of nominal groups (I have not taken the option of including a slot for the Numerative).

The Postmodifier is typically an embedded phrase or clause; and its primary function is to add specificity to the nominal group. The main question it answers is the same as the specific Deictic: 'Which Thing?'. Indeed, it frequently works together with the Deictic: as noted in 7.2.1, a specific determiner (especially 'the') can often be used to point forward to the Postmodifier, where the identifiability of the Thing will be established.

> ... you will soon be hearing *the* news *for which you have been waiting*.

> *The* decisions *made in your name* will not necessarily bring you thanks.

> So even if *the* results *of an endeavour* are satisfactory ...

> *The* foundations *of your ambitions* are in a state of flux.

This Deictic-Postmodifier link emerges very clearly in examples like the following:

> It is largely arms races that have injected *such* 'progressiveness' *as there is in evolution*.

Somewhat less frequently, the Postmodifier may appear in a nominal group with a non-specific Deictic. In this case, it typically answers the question 'What kind of Thing?', in other words, it is closer in function to the Classifier than the Deictic.

> Tensions *at work* could undermine your usual sunny optimism.

> You are dependent upon situations *beyond your control*.

> ... whether these amount to events *happening in the future* or situations *to do with overseas*

> The strange goings-on may give you a feeling *that you really don't know which end is up*.

Structurally, a postmodifying embedded clause may be **finite** or **non-finite**. If it is finite, it may be a defining relative clause ('the news for which ...') or a projected clause ('a feeling that ...' – see 10.4.1. on embedded projected clauses). If it is non-finite, it may be an '-ing' clause ('events happening ...'), or an '-en' clause (i.e. a clause with a part participle: 'decisions made ...'). These non-finite clauses can be expanded into finite ones, as relative clauses: this makes clear that the '-ing' clauses are basically active in voice ('events which will happen') whereas the '-en' clauses are passive ('decisions which have been made'). The embedded non-finite clause may also be a 'to'-infinitive clause, in which case it may correspond to a relative clause ('situations [which are] to do with ...'), or it may function as a projected clause (e.g. 'the order to leave immediately').

§   Refer to Exercise 9.1.

9.1.2 VERBAL GROUPS

While the nominal group has a mix of grammatical and lexical items, reflecting the different kinds of meanings expressed in it (identity, qualities, classification, etc.), the **verbal group** has only one lexical item: the main verb, which expresses the **Event** (cf. the Thing in nominal groups). Any other items in the group (auxiliary verbs) express choices from the same logical system, **tense**: they indicate the conceptual location of the Event in terms of past, present or future. There may be more than one choice, but then the choices are cyclical in function. As pointed out in Chapter 4, the first choice, the Finite, signals the relation of the Event to the here-and-now of the speech situation: for example, 'he *didn't* take it' indicates that the '(not) taking' is valid for the past. Any tense choice following the Finite takes its reference point from the time established by the Finite. For example, the Perfect forms ('have' + '-en') indicate pastness; so 'he hadn't (past Finite) spoken (past Event)', signals two steps into the past: past from the time of speaking, and then past from that point. This double time shift may be made explicit:

> [The letter *came* [past in relation to now] after *I'd left*. [past in relation to that past point]]

The same type of **cyclical time reference** is shown with the Present Perfect, though perhaps less obviously. In 'he's disappeared', the Finite ('has') is present, but the Perfect form relates this to past time – and this in fact expresses very well what the clause means: it is talking about the present situation (he isn't in sight) which is the result of a past event (he disappeared).

The simple equation of tense and time assumed so far does, of course, need to be modified, since the relationship is by no means straightforward. Pastness needs to be interpreted more generally as 'distance'; distance from the here-and-now is transferred, for example, to distance from reality, and hence the past tense can be used to express unreal meanings even when they relate to present time:

> I wish I *knew* some French. [= I don't know French]

> If I *had* a hammer ... [= I don't have a hammer]

Similarly, the future is closely connected with modality (the future is uncertain until it happens), and 'will' expressing futurity therefore shades over into expressing concepts like 'predicted certainty in the future about a present-time event':

> She'*ll* be at home now. [= I predict future confirmation of her being at home now]

The different meanings realised by the tense forms can, however, be seen to make sense, and to be derived in understandable ways from the basic tense-as-time meanings. If we keep in mind that 'past', 'present' and 'future' are therefore shorthand terms for sets of complex meanings, we can use them to capture the general logical cyclicity of tense choices in the verbal group.

To do this, we need to establish the basic meanings of the different items which can appear in the verbal group. The two main **auxiliaries** are 'be' (+'-ing': usually, misleadingly, called the Continuous form) and 'have' (+ '-en'). The first combination (the auxiliary 'be' plus the form it imposes on the following item) encodes presentness, while the second, as mentioned above, encodes pastness. If the auxiliary is in initial position in the group, it fuses with the Finite meaning, which adds pastness or presentness. We have already seen that 'he has disappeared' expresses presentness plus pastness. Similarly, 'he is disappearing' is present plus present (i.e. 'doubly' present – happening as I speak): compare 'he was disappearing', which is past plus present (i.e. go back to a past point, and in relation to that point the event is present). Halliday (1994: 198) suggests labelling the steps from the last step backwards: thus the groups we have looked at so far are labelled as follows:

He has disappeared	'past in present'
He had disappeared	'past in past'
He is disappearing	'present in present'
He was disappearing	'present in past'

We can combine these choices (in the fixed order Perfect^Continuous):

I've been practising since you went away.	'present in past in present'
She *had* clearly *been crying*.	'present in past in past'

For the full picture of the possibilities, we need to add three more elements. First, there are certain forms which are sometimes called **semi-auxiliaries**, e.g. 'be going to', which perform the same kind of function as the main auxiliaries.

I *was going to keep* it a surprise.	'future in past'
He *is about to jump*.	'future in present'

With these included, the number of times that we can make tense choices in a single verbal group is increased to a theoretical maximum of five. There are certain constraints on combinations of choices; and Halliday therefore calculates that we end up with a possible 36 forms, though many of these rarely occur in natural language use. The greatest degree of tense elaboration is represented by forms such as the following:

has been going to have been taking   'present in past in future in past in present'

For a full list of the forms, see Halliday (1994: 202–3).

Second, we need to allow for **passive** forms ('be/get' + '-en'). These are not strictly speaking tense-related forms: in principle, for every tense form in English there is a parallel passive form, which is always expressed as the last in the cycle of choices in the verbal group (i.e. immediately before the Event).

He *was sent* to Spain as manager.   'passive: past'

England *had been jolted* into becoming ...   'passive: past in past'

New wealth *was being created*.   'passive: present in past'

The parallel passive forms bring the number of forms in the verbal group that are theoretically possible to 72. Understandably, though, it would be extremely difficult to find authentic examples of many of these, especially in written text: in a corpus of 20,000,000 words (mostly written texts) I found no examples of the combination 'been being' + '-en', i.e. forms like 'has been being treated' are completely absent.

Finally, and most importantly, we must bring in **modality**. This is typically expressed in the Finite, and the initial tense choice in the modal operator itself is usually neutralised (see 4.4.2), although it is possible to encode pastness. Any subsequent choices mirror those of non-modal forms. Note that if the main verb follows the modal verb in the base form, it may be interpreted as expressing an Event in the present ('Patients *may complain* of fatigue') or, more commonly, in the future ('They *may arrive* late this evening').

She *ought to congratulate* me.   [modulated present view of future event]

Lady Emma *might have sown* the seed.   [modalised present view of past event]

You *must be joking*.   [modalised present view of present event]

I *could have been shot*.   [modalised present view of passive: past event]

He complained that she *should have written*.   [modulated past view of past event]

She *could have been going to rush out*.   [modalised past view of future in past event]

Sometimes, modal meanings are expressed in a way which requires a normal expression of primary tense:

Her children *seem to have been* fond of her.   [modalised present view of past event]

She *seemed to be getting* better.   [modalised past view of present – i.e. same-time – event]

Certain modal meanings may also appear later in the verbal group:

They *were having to force-feed* her.   'present (modulated) in past'

We *won't be able to finish* in time.   'future (modalised)'

It *was going to have to be wiped* from her mind.   'passive: future (modulated) in past'

9.1.3 OTHER TYPES OF GROUP

Brief mention should be made of two other types of group. The first type is the *adverbial group*, which has an adverb as Head, and which, like the nominal group, has optional Pre- and Postmodifiers, see Figure 9.3.

more quite far	regularly appropriately frankly faster	than I'd expected
Premodifier	**Head**	**Postmodifier**

Fig 9.3 Adverbial groups

The final type are **adjectival groups**, which Halliday (1994: 194) includes as a sub-category of the nominal group. Like nominal groups, they have a range of structural possibilities, expressing different kinds of meaning related to the Head (realised by an adjective), many of which are comparable to the functions of the Pre- and Postmodifier in nominal groups. Figure 9.4 shows a few of the possibilities.

Note that in some cases the Postmodifier in a nominal group can be seen as related to an adjective in the Premodifier rather than directly to the Head:

The *important* thing *for any particular animal* is to avoid trying to do both at once.

This is simply another example of the phenomenon identified above, that the Postmodifier may work together with an element in the Premodifier such as the Deictic to specify the Head in some way.

Premodifier	Head	Postmodifier
too	happy close hotter	to call than before
so very just about as	noisy happy stupid	that they called the police with the accommodation as I'd expect from him

Fig 9.4 Adjectival groups

9.2 Prepositional phrases

Prepositional phrases consist of a preposition followed by a nominal group. They do not fit into the same Head + Modifiers pattern as groups – they have a structure which is more like that of clauses. As I said in Chapter 2, groups may consist of a single word, whereas phrases must consist of at least two elements: the Head of a group can be used (e.g. in telegraphese) to represent the whole group, but in phrases both the preposition and the Head of the following nominal group need to be kept. I have already mentioned (5.2.6) Halliday's description of prepositions as 'minor processes', and he argues (1994: 180) that 'whereas a group is an expansion of a word, a phrase is a contraction of a clause'. The nominal group in a phrase can be seen as dependent on the preposition, but it clearly does not modify it in the same way as the Postmodifier in a group modifies the Head: the relationship is more like that between a (non-finite) Predicator and a Complement in a clause.

As we have seen, prepositional phrases function as Adjuncts in the clause and as Postmodifiers in the nominal group. Adjuncts, of course, typically act as circumstances for the process (even textual Adjuncts like 'on the other hand' and modal Adjuncts like 'in my opinion' can be seen as metaphorical circumstances, though for the clause as a whole rather than just the process). Many Postmodifiers act as a kind of circumstantial Attribute for the Head – they can often be clumsily paraphrased in the form of a defining relative clause:

> Embryos are put together by all the working genes [which are] in the developing organism.

Others, though, act more like circumstantial Adjuncts, especially when the Head is a noun which is either a nominalisation or has process-like characteristics:

> Of all possible speculations *about the origin of life*, most can be ruled out.

> Each step *in the pathway* needs an enzyme.

The most common preposition introducing a Postmodifier, 'of', has a rather different function. If, as Halliday argues, prepositions are like 'minor processes', 'of' in most of its uses is closest to the relational process: it simply indicates that there is a relationship of some kind between the Head and the nominal group in the prepositional phrase. As we saw in Chapter 8, this relationship may be that of identifying a participant in the nominalised process:

> ... the evolution *of life and intelligence* [life and intelligence evolved]

> ... the best estimate *of the probability* [someone estimates the probability]

However, 'of' is not restricted to this kind of context: the relationship may be of almost any kind. Some typical uses, deliberately expressed in terms that recall the descriptions of relational processes in Chapter 5, are: 'a stroke of luck' (the relationship between a single instance and a general category); 'the point of the argument' (a kind of possessive relationship); 'no hope of duplicating it' (identifying what the hope is).

9.3 Group complexes

Most **group complexes** are relatively unproblematic: they mirror the kinds of relationships that are possible in clause complexes (see Chapter 10), though in a less fully developed way. In most cases, both groups in the complex are of equal status (i.e. coordinated or '**paratactic**'):

> She was wearing [*plimsolls\and white socks*].

> His eyes [*glowed\and gleamed*] with imminent laughter.

> The sky had been [*grey,\then yellowish,\then almost white*].

The same is true of prepositional phrase complexes (note that the complex may 'branch' before or after the preposition):

> The cast had made a noisy procession [*from the Hall\to the pub*].

> They had walked up [*through the poplars\and the vineyard*].

However, there is one type of group complex which is rather trickier to handle. This is the kind of **verbal group complex** where one part of the complex is dependent on the other. In the example above, 'glowed and gleamed' are both finite, and both main verbs; but in the examples below the relationship is different:

> This [*tends\to be*] the mark of a rather literary style.

> Immediately, she [*began\to scream*].

> [*Try\turning*] it the other way.

In these cases, it is the second verb in the complex which expresses the Event (in transitivity terms, the processes are 'be', 'scream' and 'turning'). The function of the first verb is to modify the Event in some way: 'tends' is related to modality (usuality or frequency in this case); 'began' is related to the unfolding of the Event (starting, continuing and stopping); and 'try' is related to the possible outcome of the Event (attempting, succeeding, failing).

At first sight, it may seem odd that the first verb, which is semantically subordinate, is the finite one, and therefore structurally dominant; but in fact in any verbal group only the Finite is finite, and any other elements are non-finite. This is especially clear in examples like the following, where the Event is unarguably the final non-finite verb:

> We [are going to have to *rethink*] this.

As this example suggests, there is no distinct line between a simple verbal group with auxiliaries and a verbal group complex. This is predictable, since the existing central auxiliaries ('be', 'have', 'do') have evolved from full verbs; and the process is continuing in modern English: for example, 'tend to', which is extremely common in informal spoken language, is well on the way to becoming a modal operator; and 'keep' in groups like 'kept hitting' is also indeterminate in status. At the other end, verbal group complexes shade over indistinctly into separate clauses in a clause complex, especially when there is projection of some kind through a mental process expressed in the finite verb:

> I *didn't like to ask*.
>
> He *decided to read* history.
>
> He *wanted us to know*.

Halliday (1994: 290) suggests that the line is probably best drawn where the second verb has a different Subject, as in the last example. This fits with clear cases of clause complexes involving projection where the process is a verbal one:

> He *ordered them to fire*.

However, it is important to bear in mind that the boundaries between verbal group, verbal group complex and clause complex are inherently blurred.

You may have noticed that the non-finite verb in verbal group complexes is often the **'to'-infinitive** form; but it is sometimes the **'-ing'** form. Broadly speaking, the 'to'-infinitive signals that the Event is in some way unreal: it may still be in the future in relation to the Finite tense (e.g. the 'deciding' came before the 'reading history'); or it may look at the Event from the perspective of moving from unrealised to realised ('began to scream'); or it may be uncertain ('tends to be'). As this last point in particular suggests, 'to' is closely linked with modality, and it is possible to see 'to' as the non-finite equivalent of the modal verbs. The '-ing' form, on the other hand, signals reality or contemporaneous validity: 'try turning' means that the trying is done by turning – one involves the other – whereas 'try to turn' means that there is trying, but there is no guarantee that the turning happens (i.e. it is still unreal). Similarly, 'remember doing' means that the 'doing' happened, with the 'remembering' coming later; while 'remember to do' means that the 'doing' is not yet realised at the time of the remembering. It should be borne in mind, though, that these correlations between grammatical form and realness/unrealness are both only general tendencies, and there are unexpected or less easily explained uses:

> He had suggested *meeting* in the park. [the 'meeting' is unreal at the time of suggesting]

This is only a very brief outline of a complex area; for a fuller account, see Halliday (1994: 278–91). To conclude, I will simply give a couple of examples which illustrate the extra degree of elaboration that can be expressed about the Event by this type of modification of the main process:

> I *have to try to get to know* him.

> We *are going to have to start eating* rats.

> He *could have been wanting to communicate* something important.

> The city *seems to be going to be allowed to retain* its Circus much as it is.

> §   Refer to Exercise 9.2.

EXERCISE 9.1

Below are some of the sentences from the medical textbook extract that you analysed in Exercise 8.2 (p. 177). Pick out all the nominal groups; identify the Head of each; then label the functional constituents in the Premodifier (D, D_2, E, C); and finally identify all cases of embedding in the Postmodifier – use [ ] for embedded prepositional phrases and [[ ]] for embedded clauses. If an embedded element has other embedded elements in it, identify those as well. Label nominal groups in embedded elements in the same way. For example:

a preceding episode [of a silent or overt cardiac infarct]
D D_2 *Head*   D   E   E   C   *Head*

1   'Frozen shoulder' is a clinical syndrome which can probably be produced by a variety of pathological processes in the shoulder joint.
2   It is a condition affecting the middle-aged, in whose shoulder cuffs degenerative changes are occurring.
3   The outstanding feature is limitation of movements in the shoulder.
4   Restriction of movements is accompanied in most cases by pain, which is often severe and may disturb sleep.

5   There is frequently a history of minor trauma, which is usually presumed to produce some tearing of the degenerating shoulder cuff, thereby initiating the low-grade prolonged inflammatory changes responsible for the symptoms.

6   In some cases the condition is initiated by a period of immobilisation of the arm, not uncommonly as the result of the inadvised prolonged use of a sling after a Colles' fracture.

7   In some cases where pain is a particular problem, hydrocortisone injections into the shoulder cuff may be helpful.

8   In a few cases, once the acute stage is well past, manipulation of the shoulder under general anaesthesia may be helpful in restoring movements in a stiff joint.

EXERCISE 9.2

Identify all the verbal groups in the following sentences, and group them into three categories: finite (including modal), non-finite, and verbal group complexes. For all the finite groups, label them in terms of any choices between past, present and future reference. For non-finite groups, decide to what extent the past/ present/ future labels can be applied; and for group complexes, label the finite member of the group and decide what kind of meaning it is contributing (e.g. attempting, succeeding, failing).

1   Benn's strategy was shaped by his analysis of Britain's economic problems and the political situation as he saw it.

2   The reasons for the difference tend to confirm the analysis of Chapter VI.

3   I had been inoculated against hepatitis before leaving New Zealand, so I had never considered it as a risk.

4   I was bound to entertain this as an ever-present possibility.

5   Since the middle of June the joint shop-stewards' committee had been examining the issue of direct action.

6   So we're going to have to try to cope for a while without her.

7   She had been about to say that she had not expected Gareth to react quite so violently.

8   They'll probably have been worrying themselves sick about the delay.

10

Clauses in combination

10.1 Units of analysis

In discussing ranks (2.2), I mentioned the problem of using sentences as the basis of grammatically oriented text analysis. The fact that sentences are so clearly signalled in written text reflects the users' feeling that there is a unit in the language above the clause – one which in some ways is more important in communicating meanings than the clause (since sentences are always marked off by punctuation, etc. whereas not all clauses are). This certainly needs to be taken into account; but at the same time we need a principled way of showing how clauses relate to each other which is not restricted to written forms of the language. The unit that we will be working with, therefore, is the **clause complex**: a combination of two or more clauses into a larger unit, with their interdependence normally shown by explicit signals such as conjunctions.

The clause complex has the advantage that it is neutral with regard to any potential differences in the way meanings are organised in speech and writing. It is true that, in written language, we can typically equate the graphological sentences with clause complexes. However, keeping the two concepts separate allows us, for example, to handle clause complexes which are split by the punctuation: instead of simply dismissing them as 'ungrammatical', we can examine the effects of playing the grammar against the punctuation. More importantly, in analysing spoken language we obviously have no punctuation; and intonation and pausing frequently do not correspond in any straightforward way to the larger grammatical units in utterances. We therefore rely mainly on the signals of interdependence to identify boundaries within utterances – in other words we are working with clause complexes.

Adopting the clause complex does not, of course, mean that all our problems are solved. One particular difficulty arises with long strings of **coordinate clauses**. Do we treat them all as part of one clause complex or not, and, if we want to split them, how do we decide where to make the split? Coordinate clauses are equal in status and there is a fuzzy line between two equal clauses combined in a clause complex and two equal clauses treated as separate – the frequent use of coordinating conjunctions like 'but' at the start of written sentences and of spoken utterances reflects this indeterminacy. In written text we normally follow the punctuation: if a sentence starts with 'But' we count it as a new clause complex (since the punctuation presumably reflects how the writer wanted us to read it). But in spoken discourse coordination raises difficulties that are harder to resolve. The following utterance would presumably be analysed as a single clause complex since there are coordinating conjunctions at all the points where a division could be made (in italics); yet it is equally possible to see the main function of the conjunctions as just signalling that the speaker has not yet finished her utterance:

> I said to her in the summer I said I'd better pay the phone bill separately because I thought I bet it's going to be big *and* she said oh I don't know *and* then she said then the first time it came she said you're going to pay aren't you *but* then it was quite large *and* I thought I don't really think I ought to be paying all of this *and* so I had a word with her about it *but* she wasn't very sympathetic.

We can take a different approach to this area of fuzziness: the **T-unit**, mentioned in relation to Theme analysis (6.5). Whereas the clause complex approach essentially distinguishes at the first level between clauses linked by a conjunction, whether coordinating or subordinating, and those not so linked, the T-unit approach makes the first 'cut' between independent clauses and dependent clauses. The single clause complex above would thus be analysed into seven T-units, with breaks at each of the conjunctions in italics (I am ignoring for the moment the question of the quotes in the utterance, see 10.4.1 below). One implication of using T-units is a slightly different perspective on the items which signal conjunction (see 7.3). If we re-word part of the example above, we can see that the clause complex approach links the two following versions (both are clause complexes):

> *Although* I had a word with her, she wasn't very sympathetic

> I had a word with her *but* she wasn't very sympathetic

It separates them from this version:

> I had a word with her. *However* she wasn't very sympathetic.

In other words, it emphasises the functional similarities between subordinating and coordinating conjunctions. The T-unit approach, on the other hand, links the two last versions (both comprise two T-units) and separates them from the first (one T-unit). It therefore emphasises the similarities between coordinating conjunctions and conjunctive Adjuncts.

The clause complex and T-unit approaches are compatible and in many respects complementary: the choice of one or the other depends largely on the kind of discourse you are analysing and what you want your analysis to explore. You may well find that in analysing spoken language the T-unit is a more manageable unit than the clause complex, and not only for Theme analysis. In what follows, however, I will keep to the clause complex approach, mainly using relatively clear-cut cases where the boundaries are easy to establish (so that it is less necessary to consider the alternative T-unit analysis).

§   Refer to Exercise 10.1.

10.2 Types of relations between clauses

Although this was not their primary purpose, the reworded versions of the example above reflect the two basic dimensions that need to be considered in analysing how clauses relate to each other. The dimension that is focused on in the rewordings is **logical dependency**: whether one clause is dependent on or dominates another, or whether they are of equal status. The second dimension is implicit: all the rewordings are intended to express the same kind of **conjunctive relation** (in this case a concessive relation). The same variations in logical dependency could be illustrated for different conjunctive relations – cause and effect, comparison and contrast, and so on. Halliday (1994: 218) refers to the first of these two dimensions as **taxis** (dependency) and to the second as **logico-semantic** relations.

It should be emphasised that the various types of relationships that we identify between clauses can also be used to describe relations between many types of linguistic elements which combine into a larger unit. Although there is no space to follow up these parallels in detail here, we have already seen this in an informal way in the discussion of circumstances in Chapter 5 (see especially Figure 5.29) and of group complexes in 9.3. This generalisability is predictable, since we are in fact dealing with the fourth metafunction, the logical metafunction: this operates most saliently between clauses (rather than within the clause), but, as with all the metafunctions, we would expect to find it operating at other levels as well.

10.2.1 LOGICAL DEPENDENCY RELATIONS

We have already come across the two possible types of logical dependency: dependence or equality, or, in Halliday's (1994: 221) terms, **hypotaxis** and **parataxis**. In the following example, where two friends are discussing precious stones in Brazil, we have two paratactic (equal) clauses:

> why don't we look at some and I can have them set for you here

Since they are equal, we only need to distinguish them by the order in which the speaker has chosen to say them. Thus, we can indicate their paratactic status simply by numbers, 1 and 2, separating them by a double slash:

> ||| why don't we look at some || and I can have them set for you here |||
>   1   2

However, the original utterance included a clause that is dependent on clause 2:

||| why don't we look at some || and if you're serious | I can have them set for you here |||

Note that the dependent clause precedes the dominant one (though it could equally well follow it). In other words, the order does not reflect the dependency relations, so we need a different type of labelling for hypotactic (unequal) relations. Halliday suggests using Greek letters to show dependency: a dominant clause is α, while a dependent clause is β. Thus the example can be labelled as followed (separating the dependent and dominant clauses by a single slash):

||| why don't we look at some || and if you're serious | I can have them set
      1   2β 2α
for you here |||

In fact, the complete utterance had another clause dependent on clause 2:

||| why don't we look at some || and if you're serious | I can have them set for you here | because it'd be much cheaper than in England |||

The final 'because' clause seems in some ways more closely attached to the dominant clause, since the condition in the 'if' clause applies to both (though later I will suggest an alternative interpretation). We can show this by adding a second layer of dependency labels:

||| why don't we look at some || and if you're serious | I can have them set
      1   2β $2\alpha\alpha$
for you here | because it'd be much cheaper than in England |||
                $2\alpha\beta$

This labelling shows the two 2α clauses as dominant in relation to the 2β 'if' clause, and it also shows that, within the 2α grouping, the 'having them set' clause is dominant in relation to the 'because' clause.

In the example above, the two paratactic clauses (1 and 2) were independent clauses. However, parataxis can also occur within dependent clause groupings. Before looking at the analysis of the next example, you might like to try to analyse it yourself.

if Labour get in and bring in the minimum wage I'll have to get rid of you

Here is my version:

||| if Labour get in || and bring in the minimum wage | I'll have to get rid
     $\beta 1$ $\beta 2$ α
of you |||

As we will see in 10.4 below, **reported clauses** also can be analysed in terms of parataxis and hypotaxis: in the most straightforward cases, a reporting clause and a quote are equal in status, whereas a reported clause is dependent on the reporting clause:

||| they said || oh yes we sell refills |||
　　　1　　　　　　　2

||| I asked | how much two aquamarines would be |||
　　α　　　　　　　　　　　　　　　β

The quote or reported clause itself may, of course, include a clause complex:

||| she said || well bring the pen in || and we'll see |||
　　1　　　　　2 1　　　　　　　2 2

||| We were told | the change had been made | because Les was off form |||
　　α　　　　　　　βα　　　　　　　　ββ

You will inevitably come across cases where it is difficult to decide exactly what the hierarchy of clause dependency is. In the next example, does the initial 'when' clause relate to the first paratactic clause ('I paid you for the week I was in') or to both, i.e. the rest of the utterance?

when I first got here I paid you for the week I was in and then I paid you twice in the same week for the next week

In other words, which of the following analyses do you think is preferable?

||| when I first got here | I paid you for the week [[I was in]]|||
　　1β　　　　　　　1α

and then I paid you twice in the same week for the next week |||
　　2

or

||| when I first got here | I paid you for the week [[I was in]]|||
　　β　　　　　　　α1

and then I paid you twice in the same week for the next week |||
　　α2

(Fortunately, such ambiguity typically only occurs when, as in this case, either reading makes equally good sense: the problem is therefore one for the analyst rather than the language user, and is thus relatively unimportant.)

Embedded clauses (see 2.2) do not form clause complexes, since they function as constituents in other clauses; and therefore the categories of hypotaxis and parataxis do not apply to them as a whole (although there may be hypotaxis and parataxis within the embedding, i.e. an embedded clause complex). However, they do play a part in the analysis of clause complexes, if only because they need to be identified so that they can be assigned to their appropriate role. Halliday (1994: 242) suggests using [[ ]] to mark embedded clauses if necessary. Here are two examples marked in this way, the first a single clause with an embedded clause and the second a clause complex with an embedded clause complex:

||| There is some support for his argument [[that modern agents have to be ruthless]] |||

||| Peter Robinson said | that the Chancellor has the opportunity [[to
$$\qquad\quad \alpha \qquad\qquad\qquad\qquad\qquad\qquad \beta$$

stimulate the housing market, | hopefully by targeting first-time buyers]] |||
[[α β]]

In looking at clause complexes in text, we ideally need to be able to explain why the speaker/writer has chosen to present two messages as equal or as unequal. This is an extremely complex area, and there is only space here to indicate the kinds of issues involved. Essentially, there are two main factors that we need to examine: which, if either, of the messages is presented as **subordinate** to the other (generally, grammatical dependence reflects the lower functional importance of the message); and in which **order** the messages are presented (generally, the end position reflects greater functional importance). When I write comments on students' work, I often find myself hesitating between options like the following:

1. Although you make many good points, the line of argument is not always clear.
2. The line of argument is not always clear, although you make many good points.
3. Although the line of argument is not always clear, you make many good points.
4. You make many good points, although the line of argument is not always clear.
5. You make many good points, but the line of argument is not always clear.
6. The line of argument is not always clear, but you make many good points.

Which of these is the most damning and which the most encouraging – and why?

So far I have implied that hypotaxis and parataxis are watertight categories, and that all ranking (i.e. non-embedded) clauses can be assigned to one or other. However, it will not surprise you to find that this is an oversimplification. There are a number of borderline cases where the distinction does not work easily. I shall mention just one, to give you an idea of the difficulties. When certain dependent clauses are 'tagged on' in final position in a complex, they can often feel more like paratactic clauses: I find that in analysing spoken discourse I often hesitate about whether to treat them as separate T-units (i.e. as independent clauses) because of the function they seem to be serving. In one example above, I have analysed the final 'because' clause as dependent because of the grammatical signals:

> ||| why don't we look at some || and if you're serious | I can have them set for you here | because it'd be much cheaper than in England |||

However, it would also be possible to analyse the clause as if it were a new start – the intended meaning might be not 'have them set here because it's cheaper' but something like 'I'll now explain why I've suggested looking and having them set here: because it's cheaper', which would be a comment on the whole utterance. This would imply that it should be labelled 3 instead of $2\alpha\beta$.

Incidentally, of the options for comments on students' work above, for me 1 is the least flattering, because it puts the praise in the subordinate clause and in the less important position, and 3 is the most positive, because it reverses this. The other options show delicate gradations between these two points.

> §   Refer to Exercise 10.2.

10.2.2 LOGICO-SEMANTIC RELATIONS

As was mentioned in the discussion of conjunction in 7.3, there is a very wide range of possible relationships that can be signalled between clauses; and, as usual, the task facing an analyst taking a functional approach is to try to discern some general pattern in a confusing mass of meanings. The first distinction that Halliday (1994: 219) proposes in order to allow a pattern to emerge is between two basic types of relationships which function in very different ways: **expansion** and **projection**. In expansion, one clause expands on the meaning of another in various ways; for example, the first clause below adds specification concerning the location in time of the process in the second, dominant, clause

> ||| When you sleep, | all the muscles of the mouth relax |||

In projection (which covers much of the same area as what is traditionally called reported speech, but from a different perspective), the relationship is conceptually more complex: one clause projects another in the sense that it indicates that the other clause is a 'second-order' use of language, i.e. that, in the prototypical cases, what is said in the projected clause has already been said somewhere else. This is clearest in the case of quotes like the following, where the reporter signals that she is bringing into her text the actual wording used by someone else:

> ||| The manager said, || 'Do you want a joint account?' |||

Both these types of relationships can be construed between equal or unequal clauses, and can also be applied to embedded clauses. Figure 10.1 shows examples of the various possibilities.

	Expanding	Projecting
Paratactic	‖‖ They are not hairdressers, ‖ they are funeral directors ‖‖‖	‖‖ I said: ‖ 'No, I can't do it.' ‖‖‖
Hypotactic	‖‖ If you start trouble, | we'll finish it ‖‖‖	‖‖ A top official denied | that the meeting took place ‖‖‖
Embedded	‖‖ It depicts a little boat [[sailing through stormy seas]] ‖‖‖	‖‖ I told him about Koornhof's offer [[to sponsor the trip]] ‖‖‖

Fig 10.1 The basic logico-semantic relations

In the rest of this chapter, I will briefly discuss expansion and projection in turn. For a more detailed overview, see Halliday (1994: 225–73).

10.3 Expansion

Within the relationship by which one clause expands another, Halliday identifies three broad semantic groupings: *elaboration*, *extension* and *enhancement*. The central examples of each are fairly easy to identify, but – as always – there are borderline cases which are more difficult to pin down, not least because the same conjunction may be used to signal different semantic relations, or there may be no explicit signal. In most such cases, you will find it helps if you paraphrase the complex using unambiguous conjunctions or conjunctive Adjuncts, and see which paraphrase seems to correspond most closely to the meaning of the original.

10.3.1 ELABORATING

An elaborating clause does not add any essentially new element to the message, but gives more information about what is already there. It may relate to the whole message, or just to one part of the message; and it may restate it; or it may clarify or exemplify it; or it may add extra information about its attributes, including the speaker's comment. As with all clause complexes, the paratactic-hypotactic distinction applies.

Many paratactic elaborating clauses are traditionally said to be in **apposition** to the preceding clause, especially when they restate the same message in different words, or make a nonspecific message more specific. For example:

‖‖ I've had no nastiness ‖ *everyone's been fabulous* ‖‖‖

‖‖ When you set out to fail, \| one thing is certain – ‖ *you can't be disappointed* ‖‖‖

||| I had a job | when I first left school at Jacobs biscuits: || *I was a packer* |||

Generally, the relationship in paratactic elaboration can be paraphrased as 'in other words', 'to be precise' or 'for example' (Halliday 1994: 226). In spoken discourse, paratactic elaborating clauses are often difficult to distinguish from separate clause complexes since, as the examples show, there may be no explicit conjunctive signal of the relationship – the two clauses are simply juxtaposed. The main clue is in the intonation: if the speaker intends the clauses to be an elaborating complex, they will both have the same intonation pattern.

Hypotactic elaborating clauses are those that are traditionally called **non-defining relative clauses**, which add extra information about one element in the message. They normally follow that element immediately, wherever it occurs in the clause; and they thus represent a kind of interpolation, suspending the dominant clause temporarily. In the first example below, it is part of the Subject which is elaborated, while in the second it is part of the Adjunct:

||| Luisa, | *with whom Kate is still on good terms,* | made Kate welcome |||

||| I was further upset by his voice, | *which was loud, harsh and hoarse* |||

As well as the usual relatives 'who', 'which' and 'whose' (but not 'that', which is normally used only in defining – i.e. embedded – relative clauses) the conjunctive signal may be 'where' or 'when':

||| She spent the summer | working at Butlins in Minehead, | *where she met a local journalist.* |||

Less frequently, the elaboration may refer to the whole of the preceding clause rather than just one element in it. In this case, the relative is 'which':

||| And you don't have to talk to actors, | *which suits me at my stage of the game* |||

Non-finite clauses may also serve as hypotactic elaborations. In the following example, the elaborating clause specifies the kind of work the speaker did:

||| I once worked on a project in Plymouth | *helping to feed the homeless* |||

Non-finite clauses have an in-built indication of their dependent status – the fact that they are non-finite; but they frequently do not have a conjunctive element signalling the type of relationship. Thus it can be difficult to decide on exactly which relationship is intended. The second clause in the following sentence could be elaborating (specifying in what way the speaker was 'scared'), or enhancing (saying why she was scared), or just possibly extending (telling us about another reaction in addition to being scared):

||| I was scared of the changes, | *not knowing what life would be like* |||

10.3.2 EXTENDING

If one clause extends another, it adds to it by simple addition (the 'and' relation), or by replacement (the 'or' relation). Note that, in one of its meanings at least, 'but' can be included under the 'and' relation, see the example below; and the 'or' relation has two aspects: replacive and alternative. (Labelling the relations 'and' and 'or', as I have done here, is only a convenience: these do not have to be the conjunctions which signal the relations, even with parataxis.)

Paratactic extension covers most of what is traditionally called **coordination**. The most straightforward kind is signalled by 'and' (but see enhancing 'and', 10.3.3):

||| I gave the kids all a treat || *and I gave close friends a reasonable amount* |||

The meaning of 'but' which comes into this grouping is the one where both clauses are presented as true but opposite in some way:

||| The Vikings had mixed in with the English on more or less equal terms, || *but the Normans formed a separate caste* |||

Halliday (1994: 230) glosses this relation as 'X and conversely Y' (a meaning which comes out particularly clearly in the correlative structure 'not only ... but also'). The two 'or' relations are exemplified below: the first example shows the replacive relation, while the second shows the alternative relation.

||| He's been pestering me ever since – || *or rather his mates have* |||

||| Do you turn the page? || *Or do you ring our number?* |||

There is one type of replacive relation where there is no conjunctive signal: when the extending clause provides a positive wording to replace the first, negative clause. This is very close to the elaborating relation of the 'in other words' type – the second example below could be analysed as either:

||| It's not the noise [[I object to]], || *it's the smell* |||

||| He wasn't entitled to anything, || *he was just being greedy* |||

Hypotactic extension is most obviously signalled by 'while' or 'whereas' (like the extending use of 'but', they combine addition with contrast).

||| But *whereas some people claim not to revise,* | others finish || and then have a fixed number of revisions |||

||| In such cases the Germanic word tends to be more popular, | *while the French word is often more formal* |||

The alternative type of extension can be signalled by a particular kind of 'if' clause with a negative (which can be paraphrased by 'either ... or'):

||| *if they haven't arrived by six,* | we're leaving |||

Some non-finite clauses can be fairly definitely analysed as extending, particularly if they can be paraphrased by a finite clause with 'and':

||| He stormed out, | *slamming the door behind him* |||

10.3.3 ENHANCING

With enhancement, it is easier to start with hypotactic examples. These are clauses which are traditionally called **adverbial clauses**: they correspond very closely in function to Adjuncts (see 6.5 on Theme in clause complexes), specifying aspects of the dominant process such as the time, reason, condition, etc.; and in many cases there is an equivalent prepositional phrase or adverb (see Figure 5.29). Here are a few examples – you might like to consider whether an equivalent non-clausal Adjunct exists:

||| *When their father goes off to market,* | the older sisters demand fine dresses |||

||| Six hundred years had passed | *since the Anglo-Saxons had invaded Britain* |||

||| I'd love to travel | *now we can afford it* |||

||| *Although taxonomists mostly study animals or plants,* | all sorts of other things can be classified |||

||| *If we ever opened a restaurant,* | he'd be very good at front of house |||

||| We were waved through | *because we had a reservation* |||

||| They store them in their minds, | *so that they can spit them back out on demand* |||

Some non-finite clauses are fairly clearly enhancing, especially where the relationship can be paraphrased as 'after' and/or 'because':

||| Guests, | *having done the circuit of the rooms,* | did the circuit of the grounds |||

||| Marjorie and Dorothy shared a natural intimacy, | *being closer together in age* |||

Paratactic enhancement is basically the same as coordination – i.e. extension – but with a circumstantial flavour in the relation. The relation may be signalled by a conjunction such as 'so', 'yet' or 'but' (when this has a concessive meaning and can be paraphrased as 'although'); or by a conjunction group such as 'and then', 'and yet'. Increasingly, certain conjunctive Adjuncts such as 'however' and 'therefore' are being used to signal a paratactic enhancing relation (rather than to show the relation between two separate clause complexes). The following examples show some of the possibilities:

||| The dough was fine in texture, || *but its taste was bland* |||

||| I got behind on the gas || *so they put in a meter* |||

||| It had been set up with all the glitz and fireworks, || *and then it had been such a mega-flop* |||

||| The writing generally addresses the task relevantly, || *however, it could be more fully developed* |||

In narratives, 'and' by itself may be paraphrasable as 'and then', and thus be more enhancing rather than extending – though the exact line is hard to draw:

||| I wrote 10 on a piece of paper beside us || *and put a check beside it* |||

As with other uses of 'and', if the complex includes more than one paratactic extending clause, 'and' may be used to introduce all of them, or only the final clause in the sequence; or it may not be used at all:

||| He took off his mac || *and rolled it up inside out* || *and put it under Jesse's head* |||

||| He ascended two steps, || *fell back three,* || *and crashed once more into a bin* |||

||| I kneaded it, || *flattened it,* || *stretched it into a long thin piece,* || *tore it into smaller pieces* |||

In Chapter 5, we distinguished between circumstantial Adjuncts, which relate to the 'real-world' context in which the process takes place, and textual and interpersonal Adjuncts, which 'place' the clause in relation to the on-going speech event. In analysing clause complexes, you may find yourself hesitating over tagged-on or interpolated clauses which have a signal of enhancement but which express the writer/speaker's interpersonal comment on the preceding message rather than a relationship between processes in the outside world. In the following example, the final clause seems to express the writer's conclusion rather than the authorities' purpose in carrying out the changes, and to be elaborating ('so that' = 'which means that') rather than enhancing ('in order to'):

||| The authorities have constructed new hotels || and upgraded others, | *so that a visit to Cuba is rewarding and comfortable* |||

This is related to the question of whether the 'because' clause in the example discussed in 10.2.1 is hypotactic or paratactic (note that the more paratactic analysis is the interpersonal one, with the 'because' clause as comment). The problems posed by such examples suggest that we may eventually need to revise our view of clause complexes to allow for a greater functional difference between circumstantial and interpersonal clauses, just as we do with Adjuncts.

10.4 Projection

The relationship of **projection** is clearly very different from that of expansion: for one thing, it is always an essential part of the meaning of a projected clause that it is projected, whereas typically an expanded clause would not change its meaning radically if the expansion were taken away. Compare the following examples and rewordings:

‖‖ He got up hastily ‖ and plunged down the bank ‖‖	He plunged down the bank
‖‖ When he thought of this | he felt a pang of admiration ‖‖	He thought of this (then)
‖‖ He repeated, ‖ 'It's impossible.' ‖‖	It's impossible
‖‖ He made it clear | that she had suffered ‖‖	She had suffered

Although the rewordings of the last two examples can stand on their own, their function is very different: they are now statements made by the writer, whereas the original projected clauses are explicitly signalled as having a different source. We use language to talk about phenomena in the world; but one group of phenomena that can be talked about is stretches of language. If we include in our message the wording or the meaning of the original language event, we are not directly representing '(non-linguistic) experience' but giving a 'representation of a (linguistic) representation' (Halliday, 1994: 250). The effect of projection comes from this double layer of representation: on the one hand, the language is signalled as, in some sense, not our own; but on the other hand it clearly differs from the original utterance (even if we quote it verbatim) in that it is now incorporated into our present message rather than coming straight from the original source. This characterisation of projection applies most clearly to the prototypical kinds: a report of what someone else said or thought at a different time from the present. However, it underlies all the functions of projection, even where no other language event can be identified to be 'reported'.

10.4.1 QUOTES AND REPORTS

When we **quote**, we signal that we are re-using (more or less exactly) the wording of the other language event. This means, amongst other things, that the projected paratactic quote does not need to fit in with the projecting clause in Mood, reference, register, dialect, etc.

‖‖ *'Well, what about her, your London woman?'* ‖ she said \| after they had started to eat ‖‖

‖‖ *'Speak English,'* ‖ said Curran ‖‖

||| They forget how to deal positively with life, | to think and say, || '*I get it!*' |||

||| Meurig said readily: || '*He come with me.*' |||

With a hypotactic **report**, on the other hand, we project not the wording but the meaning of the original language event. Because a report is more fully incorporated into our own message, there is a greater degree of fit with the projecting clause: the Mood choices reflect our present context and purpose, as do the reference items; and there is typically consistency of register and dialect. Specific features of face-to-face interaction in the original language event, such as 'Yes' and 'Oh', are normally not re-used. In the following reports, the Mood choices of the original, which were most probably interrogative and imperative, have not been reproduced – unlike the original speakers, the reporter is not asking or ordering, but stating, and the Mood choice is therefore declarative. Similarly, in the finite clauses in the first example the tense choices are made in relation to the context of the report, not of the original speech event.

||| I asked Moody | *if he thought* | *other businesses could use Microsoft as a model* |||

||| He told me | *to give you the following instructions* |||

So far the examples have all involved speaking; but we can also report thoughts. For convenience, we can distinguish between **locutions** (projected verbal events) and **ideas** (projected mental events). In the case of ideas, there is normally no actual stretch of language to re-represent – certainly none in the outside world, since the thinking went on inside someone's mind. However, the link between thought and language is inherently so strong for us that the same relation of projection is used: whether or not the thought was in fact formulated partly or wholly in words, the way we can talk about it construes it in terms of language. Since there is no original wording, the norm for projecting thoughts is by means of reports; but, in narratives especially, quotes can also be used.

||| Anne was about to refuse the drink || but then thought | *she had better accept it* |||

||| '*She's nobody's fool,*' || I thought |||

Even the first example here could be understood to mean that something like the words 'I'd better accept it' passed through Anne's mind. In other cases, however, it is at least likely and at most certain that no original wording exists. Nevertheless, the expression choices open to us still construe the mental act of meaning in terms of projection, i.e. in terms of a language phenomenon.

||| You'd think | *there'd be a warning* |||

||| I secretly and guiltily believed | *him to be right* |||

||| Judy wished | *she didn't have to go in again* |||

||| He wanted | *me to draft the first year exam* |||

Once we take into account the fact that projections may also be embedded (see Figure 10.1 above), we have the basic possibilities shown in Figure 10.2.

	Locution (verbal)	Idea (mental)
Quote (paratactic)	||| 'Haven't seen much of you lately,' || continued John Franklin |||	||| Not || I reflected || that she would solve my problems for me |||
Report (hypotactic)	||| The Report points out	that milk fat is mostly saturated fat |||	||| He hoped to goodness	that the LA flight would be called soon |||
Embedded	||| All I wanted was an admission [[that she was there]] |||	||| Her decision [[to come back]] was to do with Bill |||

Fig 10.2 Basic categories of projection

The examples given so far illustrate the main types of hypotactic projected and embedded clauses. The type that is used depends largely on the Mood of the (real or hypothetical) original: 'that' clauses report declaratives, 'if/whether' clauses report 'yes/no' interrogatives, WH-clauses report WH-interrogatives and exclamatives; and 'to'-infinitive clauses report imperatives and future-oriented modality such as occurs in offers ('Shall I help?' – He offered *to help*.) This categorisation applies both to locutions and ideas.

There are many other aspects of projection which could be explored, such as the varied functions of different reporting verbs, or the use of **'self-projection'** to make clear to your hearer your purpose in saying something:

I promise I won't keep you a moment longer.

I have only discussed the central types of projection, but there are many others. For example, reports are normally hypotactic, but we find reports that seem to be paratactic, where the projecting clause follows or interrupts the projected clause:

She wanted desperately to finish the novel, *she told Alexis.*

There are also many blended types of reports, where, for example, a quote appears as part of a report, or where a report retains some of the interactive features of the original speech event:

||| He admitted | *that he adopted the name simply* | '*because it occurred to me at the moment*' |||

||| She said | *no* she goes through to Liverpool |||

The last example particularly represents what is often called '**free indirect speech**': reports which deliberately echo some of the wording of the reported speaker. In analysing the extract from 'Clay' on p. 63, we identified a number of signals which echo Maria's wording, though none of the text is actually quoted. These also represent free indirect speech – in this case mostly without a projecting clause ('She thought to herself'). Although I have implied that reports and quotes are identifiably separate types of projection, it would be truer to say that they are extremes on a cline, and that there are many intermediate cases.

10.4.2 FACTS

In Figure 10.2, I gave an example of an embedded idea functioning as Postmodifier to a reporting noun 'decision'. This is still recognisably linked to the basic types of projection since there is, at some level, a 'decider' (the Senser of the mental process). However, there is a type of embedded projection where no Sayer or Senser is involved. Halliday (1994: 264) calls these **facts**:

The publicity value of their ideas has nothing to do with the fact [[*that they might be right*]].

They were aware of the possibility [[*that the whole project might collapse*]].

Facts are information (i.e. pieces of language) treated as existing in something like the way that pieces of written or spoken language exist: even though no-one has necessarily expressed that meaning previously, the grammar construes the meaning as having already been established in some way. Like other projections, therefore, facts are phenomena which happen to consist of language. (It is important to realise that 'facts' as used here have nothing to do with truth: facts are, if you like, ideas without a thinker.)

This is perhaps clearer in cases where the embedded fact stands alone rather than as Postmodifier to a noun like 'fact' or 'possibility'. The most common case is with anticipatory 'it' (see 4.3.2):

It's odd [[*that he didn't say anything about this one*]].

It is perfectly possible [[*not to feel excluded*]].

Here, the fact in the embedded clause is treated as an entity to which a quality – of being 'odd' or 'possible' – is being attributed (in transitivity terms, the fact is the Carrier). The structure can therefore be seen as a way of commenting on or labelling the status of the fact in interpersonal terms. This formulation also helps us to see that in the first pair of examples the postmodified noun equally functions as an evaluative label for the fact: it is a 'fact' or a 'possibility'. Although this does not always happen, there is a strong tendency for facts to be associated with modal or evaluative labels.

We can begin to see why this association exists if we compare facts with **nominalisations**. In 8.2, I mentioned that a meaning may be brought into the text as an independent **proposition**, or it may be treated as an already established entity and brought (back) in as a nominalisation. Facts represent a half-way house: whereas nominalisations are propositions that are fully packaged as 'things', facts are semi-packaged propositions. The following rewordings may make this clearer:

> *The whole project might collapse.*

> What I'm worried about is *that the whole project might collapse.*

> *The possible collapse of the whole project* means a radical rethink of our plans.

In the second version, the proposition expressed in the fact is new information; but it is brought in as 'something I'm worried about', in other words, it is treated as an idea floating around 'out there' which can affect me. This helps to explain the link with interpersonal labelling: expressing a proposition as a fact allows me to stand back from it and to comment on it as I bring it into my text, which means that, if I want to comment on a proposition as I bring it in, I am more likely to express it as a fact. At the same time, because it is only semi-packaged it is usually possible to challenge the proposition expressed in the fact (e.g. 'But it won't') without having to reconstitute it; whereas if I wanted to challenge the nominalised wording in the third version above I would have to turn it back into a clausal proposition (e.g. 'But it/the project won't collapse', see 4.3.3). Thus facts combine the 'thinginess' of nominalisations with the negotiability of propositions.

§   Refer to Exercise 10.3.

10.4.3 PROJECTION IN TEXT

In looking at projection in text, certain threads emerge as particularly worth investigating. There is the question of the reporter's **attitude** towards what is reported: for example, the choice of the reporting verb 'point out' indicates that the reporter accepts what the other person said as true, whereas 'claim' suggests scepticism. There is the more general question of **source**: which propositions in the text are explicitly assigned to someone else (and why)? At what points in the text does the reporter use quotes rather than reports (and why)? What kind of people are reported in different contexts (and why)? How close are quotes to the original wording (and why have any changes been made)? What kinds of changes have been made in projecting the original meaning in a report (and why)? On this last point, compare the following reports with what was originally said:

> On foreign policy issues he held out little hope of an early rapprochement with the US, insisting that the Labour Party's nuclear-free policy remained intact.

> 'We want to talk to the Americans, we want to talk to anybody. But our policy has not changed and it will not change. Being nuclear-free is a matter which is in the hearts and minds of New Zealanders now.'

> She appealed for more understanding and, though the language was coded, appeared to hint that changes might be on the way.

> 'We are all part of the same fabric of our national society, and that scrutiny – by one part of another – can be just as effective if it is made with a touch of gentleness, good humour and understanding. This sort of questioning can also act, and should act, as an effective engine for change.'

(The analysis indicates the need to take account of the reporter's decision to use projection or some other structure, e.g. 'appealed for more understanding'.)

Another perspective on projection in text is from the interpersonal angle. I have already mentioned source, which is also relevant to the exploration of modal and evaluative meanings (4.4.5 and 4.5), and the frequent co-occurrence of facts with modal or evaluative labels. We have seen that projecting clauses of the 'I think' kind are actually modal signals (8.3); while 'self-projection' as with 'I promise' (10.4.1) signals the speaker's purpose and therefore has an interpersonal function. (In analysis, it is usually best to take the 'I think' kind as modality – i.e. not a separate projecting clause – and cases of self-projection as clause complexes; but the line between them is obviously fuzzy.) Thus it is often revealing to examine the contribution of projection to interpersonal meanings.

§   Refer to Exercise 10.4.

EXERCISE 10.1

Look back at the extracts from a doctor's consultation that you analysed in Exercise 4.3 (p. 74). I put vertical strokes at 'natural breaks'. In the light of the discussion of clause complexes and T-units, are there any points where alternative analyses are possible? If you follow first a strict T-unit approach, then a strict clause-complex approach, what differences will appear in the analysis?

EXERCISE 10.2

Analyse the following in terms of the dependencies, marking any embedded clauses. If it is a clause complex which is embedded, analyse the dependencies within the embedded element.

As a reminder, the symbols you should use are:

||| clause complex boundary

|| paratactic clause boundary – label the clauses 1, 2 etc.

| hypotactic clause boundary – label the clauses $\alpha\beta$ (you will also need to use γ to label third-level dependencies in one or two places)

[[ ]]   embedded clause

1   At the trial Mr Justice Judge said if he didn't admit what police said he admitted he was the 'victim of an outrageous and unacceptable conspiracy by a large number of policemen'.

2   They had wrangled about parts and benefits, quarrelled over contracts and money; she had suffered from his deep-seated suspicion of actresses, he had been frightened by the tenacity with which she had extracted her salary; but they had been part of the same team and the same world.

3   She skims over her early life; mainly to protect her family, but also, one suspects, because her life as we now know it did not come into existence until she became a television star in the Eighties.

4   Well you see she wrote this letter saying that she'd been ringing and what we couldn't understand when we spoke to Liz was she knew you were going to Peru and she knows you don't put the cats in the cattery when you go away so it was obvious where we were.

5   While this handbook will give intending applicants the information they need, students must, in order to obtain up-to-date, full and official information about entrance requirements and courses, write direct to the institutions of their choice at least a year before they hope to begin their studies, so that they will have decided to which institutions they wish to seek admission, and obtained the necessary application form, well before the closing date for receipt of applications.

6   *The 'frozen shoulder' text in Exercise 8.2 (p. 177) – analyse only the sentences consisting of clause complexes, not of single clauses.*

EXERCISE 10.3

Look back at your analyses for Exercise 10.2 and label the type of relationship in each case – expanding (elaborating, extending or enhancing) or projection (with locution or idea) – including in embedded clause complexes. Identify any embedded clauses which are facts.

EXERCISE 10.4

Here are two extracts from British newspapers with opposite political views, both published on the day of a General Election. Identify any cases of projection; then identify any information which could have been reported (i.e. which clearly comes from another source) but is presented as first-hand information. What does the analysis tell us about the two texts? Consider issues like the arguability of projected propositions, the kind of source relied on, etc.

BRITAIN is heading back to economic growth this year and a strong recovery in 1993 – if the nation sticks with responsible Tory policies. This election day boost for John Major [*the Tory leader*] comes from the prestigious International Monetary Fund.

The latest optimistic forecast coincides with a survey from British bosses showing business recovery is well under way. The survey also predicts a slump in the pound if Neil Kinnock [*the Labour leader*] gets in.

The IMF analysis of Britain's economic prospects claims Chancellor Norman Lamont is being too modest about the return to growth this year. It forecasts a growth rate of one and a half per cent, compared with Treasury estimates of one per cent, indicating that the worst is past. By next year, claims the IMF, Britain will enjoy a healthy three per cent growth rate as it leaves the recession far behind. The forecast is based on the assumption that Britain sticks with the same policies.

The Institute of Directors gives strong backing to the rising feeling that the economy is on the mend. But the bosses' organisation makes it clear Labour's high-tax plans would significantly damage the recovery. The number of directors reporting rising order books is up to 43 per cent from 28 per cent in February.

(From the *Daily Express*, Thursday 9 April 1992)

Despairing Julie Cleminson cuddled her newborn son Paul yesterday ... and prayed he will be given the chance to be happy that she has never had. Just 18, Julie has spent most of her life under Tory rule. And she has ended up with precious little.

Julie, whose mother died in a fall four years ago, knows little about politics. But she believes that if the Tories win, the odds could be stacked against Paul from the very start.

Her only hope is that a new dawn of a Labour government will be a new dawn for Paul, too. She said: 'My baby is so beautiful and I love him so much.'

'I know he's not getting the best start in life. I just want somewhere where we can all be together and where he can cry without upsetting anyone.'

(From the *Daily Mirror*, Thursday 9 April 1992)

Implications and applications of Functional Grammar

11.1 Three-dimensional analysis of texts

With the detailed discussion in Chapters 4 to 10, we have moved a fair way from the broad overview with which I started this book; and I am sure that at times it has been hard to keep in mind how everything fitted in. As a way of beginning to draw the threads back together again, I will sketch a three-dimensional analysis of two texts that you have already come across in the exercises: the conversation in the doctor's surgery (Exercise 4.3, p. 74); and the extract from a medical textbook (Exercise 8.2, p. 177). The discussion which follows is based on an analysis of the following grammatical features in both texts: Mood and modality; transitivity; Theme; cohesion; grammatical metaphor; and clause complexes. The exercises have asked you to do each of these types of analysis on one or other of the texts, but, before reading on, you may find it useful to carry out the analyses that are 'missing' e.g. Mood and modality in the textbook extract.

The reason for choosing these texts to compare is that they both deal with closely related topics (back/shoulder pain) but in very different ways. Some of the differences are obvious (e.g. the fact that the conversation is produced by two interactants, whereas the textbook has only one producer) but that does not make them less interesting to explore, in order to see both exactly how these differences are realised in the wordings and how they reflect the cultural and ideological expectations of the producers and their audience.

In the conversation, the best path in to exploring the meanings is the way the interaction is carried on. The range of **Mood** choices is clearly greater than in the other text: here we have declaratives, interrogatives and imperatives, as well as Mood tags and 'queclaratives' (4.6), e.g. 'so it got worse overnight'. As one might expect, the imperatives are from the doctor to the patient. The established roles allow the doctor to issue the commands with little or no modal softening (such as 'I wonder if you'd mind …'): it is accepted by both interactants that the doctor has the authority to control the patient's behaviour, since it is for her own good. This power imbalance is also reflected less obviously in the questions: the patient asks exclusively interrogative questions – e.g. 'what is it' – whereas nearly all the doctor's questions are queclaratives. The patient is therefore signalling that she is genuinely seeking information that she does not have, whereas the doctor is signalling that he wants confirmation of something he already knows. The function of the queclaratives is typically to present his (authoritative) wording of what the patient has told him in lay terms. Even when he does use his sole interrogative – 'how long did you say again' – it is to check the patient's wording rather to elicit information. (In the parts of the conversation not included here, the doctor does use two interrogatives, but to give commands, e.g. 'can you climb on the couch'; and, when he is seeking information, he uses either queclaratives or imperatives, e.g. 'tell me where the tender spot is'.) The patient responds to all this not as bossiness but as sympathy and reassurance: a doctor is expected to be in control and to take responsibility from the patient who is, by definition, in a vulnerable position.

In terms of **modality**, most of the realisations are easily explicable: the patient talks about what she can't/couldn't do because of the pain, and the doctor states the medically established facts ('it'll try and go into spasm'), and sets out his own course of action ('I'll give you some painkillers') and the patient's obligations ('you don't have to finish the course'). As far as the final outcome of this specific case is concerned, however, he is careful to hedge a little ('it should recover', 'I think you're going to be off work'). There is a particularly revealing exchange of modality at one point: 'you wouldn't think it was so painful would you' 'oh no it is'. The patient advances a tentative, modalised view, and the doctor de-modalises it and confirms it as categorically valid.

The most frequent **Subjects** are 'I' and 'you', highlighting the personal interaction (note that this is not inevitable just because the conversation is face-to-face: we could imagine the discussion focusing more exclusively on the problem). Other Subjects tend to be pronouns rather than full nominal groups, e.g. 'it' referring (often rather vaguely) to the patient's problem. On the one occasion when there is a heavy nominal group as Subject it is in fact split up to make the message easier for the patient to process: 'the tablets I'm going to give you a common side-effect' (instead of 'a common side-effect of the tablets I'm going to give you'). The doctor's knowledgeable, authoritarian role is being tempered by consideration for the (relatively ignorant) patient on a personal level.

The same impression of keeping the discussion at a manageable level of complexity is given by the **Themes**, which are nearly all unmarked: Subject (and therefore mainly pronouns in this case), or WH-element ('how long', 'what') or Predicator in imperatives. The signals of conjunction, most of which appear as textual elements in Theme, are those which are most frequent in unplanned conversation, especially 'so', which is used either to signal the doctor's reformulations ('so it's pain in the lower back') or to mark a new stage in the interaction ('so the first thing is rest'). There are four marked Themes (I am excluding '*there's* your note', which is the unmarked Theme in this idiomatic expression). Of these, two are preposed Themes ('the bottom of my spine', 'the tablets I'm going to give you'), which function to establish a topic clearly before going on to discuss it. The other two are temporal subordinate clauses ('as soon as you move', 'simply when your back is fine'). In many cases, circumstantial Themes like these would have a text-structuring function (see, for example, the repeated 'in ... cases' Themes in the textbook extract); here, however, they seem to be prompted by more local, interactive considerations (the doctor's wish to emphasise specific points).

There are a good many **cohesive signals**. The frequent ellipsis (e.g. 'oh no it is [so painful]') reflects the cooperative nature of the meaning construction that is going on; while the pronominal reference, which often extends over long stretches without the full referent being explicitly specified or needing to be repeated (e.g. 'it' = the problem), reflects the constant focus on the same topic (this is not just a casual conversation), and the fact that both interactants expect the other to cooperate in accepting a fair degree of inexplicitness.

In terms of **clause complexes**, the utterances are mostly relatively simple: there is little of the syntactic complexity that Halliday (1985b) argues is characteristic of much speech. The patient typically extends: that is, she adds on further chunks of information, without indicating any connections between them apart from addition ('I can't bend forward and I can't like turn sideways'). The doctor, on the other hand, elaborates – he restates the information and instructions he gives, presumably to ensure that the patient understands ('they don't speed up the healing, it's just to make life comfortable for you'). He also enhances, filling in the background conditions, and explaining actions in terms of their purpose ('take them with food just to protect yourself'). This again reflects their relative roles in the interaction: the patient feeds in the raw data, as it were, which the doctor restates ('so') and then interprets and places in context, in a way which reflects his simultaneous role as 'teacher'.

If we look finally at **transitivity**, we have, as we might expect, mainly material and attributive relational processes: accounts of the patient's actions ('couldn't stand up') and the doctor's proposed response ('give you some painkillers'); and descriptions of the problem ('it got worse'). We also find identifying relational processes at key points in outlining the treatment (e.g. 'the first thing is rest'), creating a comforting feeling of resolution as to the course to take (though this is balanced by the modal hedging in expressing the final outcome that I mentioned above). The wordings are almost entirely congruent rather than metaphorical: what little **grammatical metaphor** there is is mainly interpersonal (e.g. 'I think') rather than experiential. Although the doctor needs to show that he is in command of his subject (which could be done by the use of technical experiential nominalisations), he also needs to keep his meanings accessible to a non-expert. Equally importantly, he needs to avoid 'objectifying' her experience too much, since this might stress too strongly his role as 'scientific observer' – to whom illness and pain are professionally interesting rather than humanly distressing – at the expense of his role as 'healer'. The congruent expression is the more natural, and thus in this context more human, one.

I hope that it has become clear that a number of constant threads run through these analyses: we are seeing the same phenomena from different perspectives. Perhaps the most salient is the doctor's need to balance a reassuringly authoritative display of his expertise with a concern to be understood by the non-expert and to show appropriate consideration for her on a personal level. This impacts on a number of different kinds of lexico-grammatical choices. It is also noticeable that the patient is as skilled at fulfilling the linguistic demands of the role of patient as the doctor, with more overt training, is at fulfilling those of his role. There is therefore little need for the kind of 'steering' by the expert from topic to topic that we will see in the textbook. The necessary information is exchanged in the conversation, but in an explicit framework of cooperation and negotiation: interpersonal meanings play as great a role (if not greater) in the success of the communication as experiential ones.

If we now turn to the textbook extract, the contrasts with the conversation are very obvious. This is language which sets out to reduce interaction to a minimum, at least at the overt level; and thus it seems more promising to start the analysis from the **experiential** meanings. Perhaps the most striking feature, given that the topic is medicine, is the almost total absence of people: it is the objective science face of medicine that is being presented here. The only overt mention of people is in terms of an impersonal classificatory group: 'the middle-aged'. The removal of human involvement or agency is carried out by resort to **nominalisations** (e.g. 'treatment' – by doctors; 'rotation' – by patients) and **passive clauses** ('these can seldom be differentiated' – by doctors). In the place of humans, we get disembodied bits – shoulders, arms, joints – which are typically represented as the location or Goal of processes (which are themselves often nominalised): e.g. 'movements in the shoulder', 'manipulation of the shoulder'.

The entities which comprise the main participants in the text are inanimate medical concepts, in many cases nominalised processes or states: the symptoms (e.g. 'restriction of movements'), the causes (e.g. 'inadvised prolonged use of a sling') and the possible treatments (e.g. 'manipulation of the shoulder'). This list shows that the text is in fact covering very much the same topics as the consultation, though the similarities may be obscured by the differences in expression. Many of the processes are attributive relational, reflecting the main purpose of the text, which is to describe the condition. Identifying processes are used at two keys points: to sum up the little that is definitely known about the condition ('the outstanding feature is …'); and to indicate the little that can be done about it ('the main aim of treatment is …', '… are the mainstay of treatment').

There is also a relatively high number of existential processes – three in this short extract – which helps give the impression of the text as a 'checklist' (existential processes are typically used to bring a new participant into the text). This checklist character is reinforced when we look at the function of the extensive **grammatical metaphor** in the text. Apart from 'This restriction' in the fifth sentence, which encapsulates the preceding Rheme, the nominalisations overwhelmingly have indefinite deixis, even where cohesively definite deixis could easily be used (e.g. 'Restriction of movements' in sentence 6): in other words, they do not represent encapsulations of propositions which have been mentioned earlier. The impression is of a series of independent points about frozen shoulder (try re-ordering the sentences: in many cases this has little effect on the overall coherence). Within each sentence, we do find logical linking in terms of cause and effect, often realised by the processes, which are either metaphorical wordings of the logical relation between nominalised processes (e.g. 'initiating') or resultative material processes (e.g. 'produce', 'restore'). But the linking is chiefly within rather than between sentences: if we go back to the three existential processes, for example, it is remarkable that none of the three new participants (the Existents) is actually picked up again in the following sentences.

Rather than being used for encapsulation, experiential grammatical metaphor in this text is used primarily for depersonalisation and condensation (try unpacking the ninth sentence beginning 'In some cases the condition ...'), and for fixation (see 8.2). The writer actually admits in the second sentence that little is known about frozen shoulder; but this does not hinder him from describing it in terms of concepts such as 'a period of immobilisation of the arm' which are represented as fixed and classifiable (as we will see, this fixedness contrasts markedly with the modal meanings).

As noted above, relatively little use is made of grammatical resources for signalling **cohesion**. When definite deixis occurs, it is mostly generic rather than cohesive (e.g. 'the shoulder' is equally well interpreted as 'any shoulder' rather than 'the shoulder mentioned earlier'). Lexical repetition occurs extensively, but typically each repetition is treated as if it were a new start, because of the absence of cohesive deixis. For example, 'movements' occurs in six of the fourteen sentences; but even in the last sentence there is no explicit signal that the word has occurred earlier. Though less extreme than the repetition in the extract from the children's textbook (7.4), there is a similarly unusual degree of explicitness within each sentence. This explicitness suggests that the writer is relying very little on cooperation from the reader in constructing meanings by supplementing the information in one sentence with information carried over another; but it contrasts somewhat oddly with the fact that he clearly does expect the reader to be knowledgeable enough to see how the information chunks fit together – there are, for example, no conjunctive Adjuncts at all to signal any connection between sentences. The writer seems to be projecting a reader who is familiar with the typical pattern of information in texts like this and who can make the necessary connections, but who lacks the specific information to complete each slot in the pattern for the particular condition of frozen shoulder.

In the **clause complexes**, the dominant relationship is extension – the 'adding on' relationship – which again reflects the impression of the text as a series of detachable information chunks. (I am including the non-defining relative clauses as extending rather than elaborating, see Halliday, 1994: 229.)

Even where it would be possible to add a note of enhancement, the writer tends not to do so explicitly: for example, the fact that the condition is commoner on the left side is clearly linked to the fact that it often follows a heart attack, but this is not spelt out in the conjunction 'and'. This mirrors the absence of inter-sentence conjunctive signalling mentioned above.

The **Theme** analysis picks up most of the few cases where cohesive pronouns and demonstratives occur ('These', 'It', 'This restriction', 'It'), indicating that we should not overemphasise the self-contained nature of the sentences in the text. Nevertheless, the other Themes do reinforce the impression that the text is moving systematically through all the important aspects of the condition separately one by one. The first unmarked Subject Theme, 'Frozen shoulder', sets up the main topic, while the others, apart from the four noted above, all signal new sub-topics ('treatment', 'Restriction of movements', 'Radiographs of the shoulder', etc.), as do the two existential Themes. All but one of the marked Themes have exactly the same basic pattern 'in ... cases' (five times). Once again, these signal different aspects of the topic: note that these are not contrastive groupings of 'cases' ('in some cases' vs. 'in other cases'), which would be cohesive (see 7.2.1 on comparison as a signal of cohesion); each set of cases is independent of the others.

If we turn finally to the interpersonal meanings, it is the **modality** which stands out as the main type. As mentioned above, there is a great deal of uncertainty about the causes of and appropriate treatment for frozen shoulder; and the writer hedges constantly, using a wide range of modalising resources, often in reinforcing combinations (e.g. 'can probably', 'is usually presumed to', 'not uncommonly', 'almost always'). From this perspective, the 'in ... cases' mentioned under Themes can also be seen as modal resources, since they limit the validity of the writer's claims. The impression is of an established general framework of explanatory concepts expressed through the nominalisations, but of uncertainty as to which are the appropriate concepts to call on in the case of this particular condition. We can note in passing that this uncertainty is unusual for textbooks: unlike, say, research article writers, who are expected to be cautious in advancing their claims of new knowledge (see Myers, 1989), textbook writers are normally expected to treat their topic as fully understood and unproblematic.

I started the analysis of this text by saying that there is little overt interaction; but, of course, there cannot be communication without interaction of some kind. In this case, the writer has made the conventional (in this context) choice of depersonalising the interaction just as he depersonalises the topic: unrelieved declaratives are matched by an absence of direct address. The effect of this choice comes out more clearly if we imagine a textbook for the same audience in which, say, sentence 2 was worded in a different way: 'You may find it difficult to decide exactly what has produced the frozen shoulder in particular patients, and you should be ready to try out various forms of treatment until you hit on the best one.' (Note that interactivity, as usual, involves sacrificing brevity, not least because it tends strongly to be accompanied by relatively congruent – i.e. unpacked – wordings.)

Overall, the main threads that have emerged from this text are depersonalisation, information focus, and 'chunking'. The writer uses a range of resources to 'hide' behind the information and to make it sound as authoritative and fixed as possible. Unlike the doctor in the conversation, there is every reason for him to play wholeheartedly the role of dispassionate scientific observer, since he is communicating with other experts (or at least people training to be experts) whose interest in the topic is professional rather than personal. He also avoids overt interaction, projecting a reader who, like himself, is interested above all in the compact, efficient transfer of necessary information within a framework – symptomsˆcausesˆtreatment – which is familiar enough to need little or no overt signalling. Less predictably, perhaps, he breaks the information into self-contained chunks. This seems to be due partly to the desire for compactness (like interactiveness, reader-friendly textual guidance takes up space), and, perhaps, partly to the fact that his book may be used as a reference book for rapid consultation by inexperienced doctors in the middle of medical examinations. (Its main use as a textbook may also influence the chunking: the writer may be aware that testing in medical training relies heavily on the memorisation of facts – each sentence typically presents a memorisable gobbet.)

Having read these analyses, you might find it useful to try the same kind of three-dimensional analysis, relating lexico-grammatical choices both across to each other and outwards to the context, on the letter and response from a medical advice column of a magazine given in Exercise 2.1 (p. 24). If you want to try out this kind of analysis on other texts as well, you will often find that a contrastive study of two texts that are similar in, say, topic but not in audience will help to highlight key features in each. It is not always easy to find spoken and written pairs like those above, but one fairly accessible source is television material with written spin-off – e.g. newspaper commentary on television interviews, or cookery programmes with an accompanying book. Other possible pairings are: reports of the same event from quality and popular newspapers; advertisements aimed at different kinds of consumers; texts for or by experts vs. texts for or by novices, e.g. research papers or advanced level textbooks vs. school textbooks or reports from magazines for the general public such as *New Scientist*; texts for 'outsiders' vs. texts for 'insiders', e.g. a persuasive publicity leaflet for a bank account vs. the regulatory small print of the contract for the account; or even an original of, say, a short story and a translation.

11.2 A summary review of Functional Grammar

The analyses above have not by any means covered everything that could be said: for example, I have not touched on tense and polarity, which function very differently in the two texts. However, I hope that they have provided a practical demonstration of two fundamental features of Functional Grammar which I stressed in the opening chapters and which have underpinned all the detailed discussion of grammatical systems: **multifunctionality** in the clause, and the determining role of **context** in the kinds of choices that are made. The view from different perspectives illuminates different but equally important aspects of the meaning construction going on (and, when combined, each perspective throws light on the others); and the description that we end up with leads us smoothly and inevitably to an explanation in terms of the wider context of situation.

This intimate link between language and context is also the source of a third crucial point about Functional Grammar which has been constantly emphasised: it is designed for use on **text** (i.e. language in use), not simply on isolated, decontextualised sentences. Part of the meaning of any clause is its function in relation to other clauses around it (to take an obvious example, it is part of the meaning of an answer to a question that it is an answer); and the grammar of the language reflects this (e.g. by allowing certain kinds of ellipsis in answers, where part of the question is treated as carried over). Equally, the clause only makes sense – performs its function of expressing meaning – if we look at it in its whole context of use. The fact that English has different declarative and interrogative clause structures, for example, can only be fully understood in terms of the reasons why speakers need to differentiate between the functions that those structures perform (i.e. to make statements or to ask questions – to give or to demand information).

It is important, though, to reiterate that in terms of analysis this is not a one-way process, from context to use. The exploration can go both ways: we can learn more about the general grammatical resources of the language by looking at how they are used in text (e.g. we might investigate what the role of Subject 'means' by examining many instances of Subjects in text); and we can understand how texts work by applying what we know about the meaning of grammatical resources (e.g. we might apply our definition of Subject as 'the entity responsible for the validity of the proposition' – see 4.3.3 – to specific texts in order to show how the interaction develops).

The overall approach is summed up by Halliday's description of language as a system of **'meaning potential'**, which is only realised in use. This focus means that 'rules' in Functional Grammar are expressed as sets of possible options, as systems of **choices**. In any context, there are a number of meanings that speakers might express, and a number of wordings that they might use to express them. There are also factors which make it more or less likely that specific kinds of meanings or wordings will be chosen. Note that unless we do see language as choice there is no principled way in which we can link it with context: if context determines the language likely to be used, different linguistic choices must be available to reflect different contexts. As I said in 1.1.2, choice does not necessarily mean conscious choice – it is unlikely that the doctor in the consultation would be aware of his use of queclaratives rather than interrogatives. We can, however, identify at least some of the socio–cultural factors which make that wording more likely to occur in that context than others. We could then go on to hypothesise that in other similar contexts that option might be statistically more likely to present itself as the most appropriate to the speaker: we might, for example, think it possible that teachers will use more queclaratives than their pupils, and we can look at classroom interaction to see if this is true. Note that this can be reversed: if we find that in other contexts the same linguistic choices are made, we can hypothesise that there are shared socio-cultural features of the contexts which we may not have been aware of. For example, if we do find that doctors and teachers both use queclaratives, we can then examine the similarities in their social roles which lead to their making similar linguistic choices.

Many approaches to linguistic description take a strictly **modular** view: structure (syntax) is dealt with separately from meaning (semantics), which is dealt with separately from use (pragmatics). Thus the syntactician would describe the doctor's 'So it got worse overnight' as structurally declarative (with all the constituents in their expected places); the semantician might talk about comparative change of state encoded in 'got worse'; and the pragmatician would comment on the use of the declarative form for an interrogative purpose. This 'divide and conquer' approach clearly has advantages in making each module more manageable; but it also has the disadvantage that it is much less easy to see the links between each part of the description. For language users, meaning is the central fact about language, and meaning emerges from a seamless union of wording and context. Functional Grammar attempts to face that uncomfortable fact head-on and to establish a **unified** model of language which in principle allows the links to be made within the same description.

11.3 Using Functional Grammar

The way I have summed up Functional Grammar above implies throughout that it is designed for **application**. It is, of course, intended to help us understand more fully the theoretical issue of how language itself is structured; but it expressly does this in a way which encourages the investigation of wider practical issues relating to the uses that we make of language. In this section, I want briefly to indicate some of the areas in which you may find it useful to apply Functional Grammar.

As an approach, it is clearly in harmony with the aims of **discourse analysis**. Halliday (1994: xvi) argues forcefully that 'a discourse analysis that is not based on grammar is not an analysis at all'; and this view has become increasingly accepted. Not all discourse analysts use Functional Grammar as set out here, but the vast majority rely on recognisably similar models of language. As probably the most fully developed version of a text-oriented functional approach, Functional Grammar has the great advantage that it is there ready for use by analysts whose main focus may be on different aspects such as the text structure of newspaper editorials, the functions of citations in academic articles, or the major themes running through a poem.

As this last example suggests, Functional Grammar can be applied in the particular branch of discourse analysis traditionally known as **stylistics**, which tends to concentrate on literary texts. Literature is one of the clearest cases of a 'constitutive' use of language (by definition, literature can only be realised through language, whereas, for example, in face-to-face giving of instructions language may have an ancillary role, helping the interactants to get things done but not constituting the whole of the social action). Therefore it is clear that any interpretation of literary text needs to be firmly based on an understanding of what is happening at the lexico-grammatical level: all the effects of literature are created by the language used.

An important aim of stylistics is not just to describe but to **evaluate** the text: to show why it is (or is not) worth valuing. In this respect, it has much in common with testing and assessment of language performance: deciding, for example, whether a university student's assignment is good enough to pass, or a doctor has the necessary interactional skills to handle consultations effectively and sympathetically, or a business manager can respond persuasively to letters of complaint. Because Functional Grammar allows us to describe objectively the appropriate patterns of language use in specified contexts, it can help to clarify the often intuitive and subjective criteria on which assessment (including that of literary texts) is based.

Equally importantly, Functional Grammar can help to decide what language to teach: it can provide the basis for **educational** decisions about what the university student, or the doctor, or the business manager needs to know about successful communication in their field. This applies equally to students of the mother tongue and of a foreign language. One of the areas where Functional Grammar has had an immensely powerful effect is in the Teaching of English as a Foreign Language. This does not mean, happily, that foreign learners are taught to label the three metafunctions; but the overall view of language from the FG perspective has fuelled the Communicative Language Teaching movement, and, in many cases, insights on specific areas such as cohesion, modality and Theme choice have in fact been adapted for practical use in the classroom.

On a wider scale, linguists working in the FG tradition, especially in Australia, have undertaken a sustained critical investigation of the **language of education** itself. They have started from the insight that the process of education is very largely a process of learning how to handle the specialised conventions of the language in which education is conducted (see 8.2): for example, how to understand textbooks or how to write essays. Once these conventions are made explicit, it becomes possible both to train children linguistically to cope with education more assuredly, and to bring to light the unspoken ideological assumptions underlying the educational process – and thus, if necessary, to challenge them.

This brings us to the final area of application that I want to mention: **critical discourse analysis**. Over the last 15 or so years, there has been increasing interest in looking at the often hidden ideology construed (i.e. reflected, reinforced and constructed) by text. As well as educational texts, the use of language in the media has been the focus of special attention; but the scope has widened more recently to include many kinds of institutional practices in science and medicine, business, the law, politics, and so on. Since Functional Grammar is deliberately designed to look outwards from specific instances of linguistic choices to the socio-cultural – and, eventually, ideological – factors influencing their existence and use, critical discourse analysis is a natural extension into practical application.

This list of possible applications is far from complete: a longer list is given in Halliday (1994: xxix). However, I hope that it has suggested lines of enquiry that you may want to follow up in more detail, exploring for yourself the central claim that Functional Grammar is a **grammar of use for application**.

11.4 Closing

I will close, as I began, with an old joke. It is the middle of a very dark night. A policeman comes across a man crawling around at the foot of a lamppost, and asks him what he is doing. 'I've lost my keys.' The policeman gets down on his knees and begins searching with him. After a few minutes, when they have still found nothing, the policeman asks, 'Are you sure you dropped them around here?' 'No, it was over the other side of the road.' 'Then why are you looking here?' 'Because there's no light over there.'

In doing Functional Grammar, you will often feel that you are groping round in the dark, unsure of whether you are interpreting the meaning of a wording correctly, or identifying the differences in meaning between two different wordings accurately. I have frequently mentioned uncertain or fuzzy cases where two analyses (or a blend of them both) seem equally appropriate; and the descriptions have often been couched in terms of clines and tendencies rather than absolutely separate categories. There is sometimes uncertainty in the analysis of authentic utterances even in terms of their 'objective' constituent structure (e.g. whether a reported clause which precedes the reporting clause is dependent or not, see 10.4.1). Once we bring in inherently messy issues such as the relationship between speakers or the influence of the preceding clause on the wording of the present one, the uncertainty increases exponentially. There are two responses to this. You can limit your investigation to the relatively well-lit areas that you feel able to describe in definite yes/no terms, labelling isolated, decontextualised bits of language, and ignoring as far as possible the confusion that meaning and function inevitably introduce; or you can accept the fuzziness as an inherent and central feature of language, without which it could not function effectively as a system of communication, and build this into your linguistic description in as ordered and generalisable a way as is possible. As you have seen, functional grammarians take the latter course. They know that the keys are on the other side of the road in the dark: the search conditions may be worse than under the lamppost, but the results are much more rewarding.

Answers to exercises

Exercise 1.1

The following comments simply confirm the context and indicate some of the features that could be explored in greater depth.

1 Buying a train (or coach) ticket. The roles of the two participants are fixed in advance, so there is little need to spell out aspects like 'Give me [a day return]', or to negotiate politeness. If the speaker started 'I wonder if you could ...' the ticket seller would assume a non-standard request (e.g. for help) was coming.

2 From an advertisement. The only modality, 'can', comes when the writer is not talking about the product (the Heineken slogan '*Probably the best lager in the world*' played precisely on the expectation that advertisers do not modalise or hedge their claims). The punctuation separates parts that are grammatically linked, probably to suggest the unplanned afterthoughts of speech rather than writing. The deliberate use of 'we' rather than 'the company' suggests a more personal, human interaction with the reader/customer.

3 From an informal conversation. There are some discourse markers that belong to informal speech ('Well you see'); 'this' used for what is clearly the first mention of the letter is typical of oral narratives (including jokes); and the repeated 'she' is unlikely to occur in more formal writing. It is syntactically fairly complex (you will be analysing it in detail in Chapter 10): this is actually typical of speech, see Halliday (1985b), as is the use of 'simple' conjunctions ('and', 'so') to hold together the complexity.

4 From a novel, *Monk's-Hood* (Ellis Peters, 1980). Clearly a narrative, because of the past tense and the personal details (i.e. it is not, for example, a history textbook). A written rather than an oral narrative because of the amount of detail: the way the character is named; the purely 'scenic' detail ('nodding his head') – in an oral narrative, details, if given, are normally evaluative or advance the storyline; the piling up

of attributive clauses (e.g. 'stubbly chin jutting') and of adjectives. The writer is clearly determined to let the reader 'see' the scene.

5 From a handbook for overseas students planning to study in Britain. The addressees are clearly students but they are referred to in the 3rd person rather than as 'you'. The verbal group 'must write' is interrupted by a long interpolation setting out exact details of the requirements; where there are choices in structural and lexical forms the formal option is chosen ('will have decided' rather than 'decide'; 'to which institutions they wish to seek admission' rather than 'the institutions (that) they want to apply to') – one aspect of the formality is a preference for nominalisations rather than verbs ('admission', 'receipt').

6 From a recipe. There is a typical pattern of purpose ('to make') followed by unsoftened commands ('divide', 'press', etc.). Step-by-step instructions are given, but with little explicit sequencing ('next'): writer and reader expect each step to follow in order. It is also accepted, though, that equipment ('an unfloured surface') need not be brought in as a separate step. Some signs of informal chattiness ('nicely') tend to occur in the middle of an otherwise relatively neutral style.

7 From a textbook, *University Physics* (H.D. Young, 8th edition, 1992). The technical terminology stands out, often consisting of nominal groups with densely packed information in front of the main noun (e.g. 'a two-source interference pattern' rather than 'a pattern of interference from two sources'). The use of 'we' reflects the writer/teacher cooperatively taking the reader/student through the steps of the operation; and the future-oriented discussion ('we may', 'we have to'), guiding the reader's actions, is more typical of textbooks written by experts for non-experts than of research papers written for other experts.

8 A cheat: it's from 'Song at the Beginning of Autumn', by Elizabeth Jennings; but to make it a bit less obvious that this was a poem, I didn't keep the original layout. There are unusual collocations ('evocations in the air'); the present tense does not refer to habitual actions as usual but is used for 'instantaneous narration'; there is a tension between the highly personal content and the relatively formal style, which suggests literature rather than conversation (which is the other likely context for talk of memories, etc.); and the reader needs to make an effort to construct coherence in the text – the connections between the statements are not immediately obvious (poetry shares with informal conversation the readiness of interactants to do more collaborative work on interpreting meanings).

Exercise 2.1

Don't worry too much about the details of the conventions used to show the boundaries of clause, etc. – we will come back to them more systematically in

Chapter 10. The main thing here is to check that you have identified the constituents.

||| [Recently], [I] ['ve had] [a very painful shoulder [[[which] [makes]
    A   S   P   O   S   P

[lifting my arm][almost impossible]]]. |||
    O   C

The 'which' clause is embedded as part of O. I have analysed SPOCA in that clause as well: note the Object + Complement structure following 'make'. The O in the embedded clause – 'lifting my arm' – itself consists of an embedded clause (P O).

||| [My GP] [diagnosed] [a 'frozen shoulder'], || [prescribed]
    S   P   O   P

[painkillers] || and[told][me] | [to stay] [off work] [for a week]. |||
    O   P   O   P   A   A

This is a clause complex consisting of three coordinate main clauses and a non-finite subordinate clause ('to stay ...'). I have labelled 'me' as O: at a more delicate level, it could be labelled IO (Indirect Object).

||| [What] [causes] [it] || and [will] [it] [get] [better]? |||
    S   P   O   (P)   S   P   C

This is a clause complex consisting of two coordinate main clauses. The verbal group functioning as P in the second clause is interrupted by the S.

||| [Frozen shoulder] [can result] [from muscle sprain or wear and tear].|||
         S   P   A

The A consists of a nominal group complex within the prepositional phrase.

||| [It] [may happen] [after surgery to the chest, or a heart attack]. |||
    S   P   A

Again, the A consists of a nominal group complex within the prepositional phrase. Note that 'to the chest' is a prepositional phrase embedded in the nominal group 'surgery to the chest'.

||| [Movement] [is] [usually] [painful and difficult]. |||
      S   P   A   C

The C consists of an adjectival group complex.

||| [It] [can be treated] [with pain-killers, anti-inflammatory pills, or –
    S   P   A

in severe cases – a steroid injection in the shoulder]. |||

The A consists of a nominal group complex within the prepositional phrase. The group complex itself consists of three nominal groups, with an interpolated prepositional phrase 'in severe cases'.

||| [Physiotherapy] [aids] [recovery]. |||
       S   P   O

||| [Recovery time] [varies] [from a week to over a year]. |||
      S   P   A

This time the A consists of a prepositional phrase complex.

Exercise 4.1

1 Kate // didn't
2 the universe // should
3 Tears // [past]
4 they // [past]
5 the four we have // don't
6 That // might
7 The other few items in the printing history of this work // are
8 the titles of works which we have had to cite fairly frequently // have
9 It = that one can describe the position of a point in space by three numbers, or coordinates // is
10 It = I'm worried about // isn't

Exercise 4.2

1

He	[past]	picked up	ideas about form	from his teachers
S	F	P	C	Circumstantial A
Mood		Residue		

2

He	had	already	been	over the house
S	F	Mood A	P	Circumstantial A
Mood			Residue	

3

Where	have	all the flowers	gone?
Circumstantial A	F	S	P
	Mood		
	Residue		

4

Of course	Tim	could not	really	banish	care
Comment A	S	F	Mood A	P	C
Mood				Residue	

5

The relatively well-educated and literate soldiers of these countries	most willingly	[*past*]	accepted	their own death
S	Mood A	F	P	C
Mood			Residue	

6

In her waking hours	she	would	never	let	us	out of her sight
Circumstantial A	S	F	Mood A	P	C	Circumstantial A
	Mood					
	Residue					

7

The union involved	certainly	has to	face	criticism	for its lack of activity on health and safety over many years
S	Mood A	F	P	C	Circumstantial A
Mood			Residue		

8

Put simply,	you	will	probably	find	it		difficult	to find a job as a student
Comment A	S	F	Mood A	P	$C_1 =$	C_2	C_1	
Mood				Residue				

9

Meanwhile	B G's days at Liverpool	could	be	over	this week
(Conjunctive A)	S	F	P	C	Circumstantial A
	Mood		Residue		

10

Right now	however	you	might	have to juggle	your finances	around
Circum. A	(Conjunct. A)	S	F	P	C	Circum. A
		Mood				
	Residue					

Exercise 4.3

Subjects are in bold, and expressions of modality are in italics. The symbols ? (?) and ! are used to mark interrogative, queclarative and imperative clauses respectively. The discussion of the interaction will come in Chapter 11.

P   I *can't* bend forward and I *can't* like turn sideways it's like **the bottom of my spine** it *just* feels like I'm sitting on a pin
D   (?)so **it**'s pain in the lower back
P   lower back just about there
D   ok ?how long did **you** say again
P   *I mean* all last night I *couldn't* turn on my side I *couldn't* stand up I *couldn't* go to the toilet
D   (?)so **it** got worse overnight
P   yeh …
D   so **the first thing** is rest secondly **I**'*ll* give you some painkillers **they** don't speed up the healing **it**'s *just* to make life comfortable for you while **it**'s healing now **it**'s

P ?what is **it** ?is **it** like a thing **I**'ve got with my spine or

D **it**'s a torn muscle in your back yeh **it** *should* recover

P **you** *wouldn't* think **it** was so painful ?*would* **you**

D oh no **it** is but **it**'s all right as long as **you** don't move as soon as **you** move **it**'*ll* try and go into spasm to stop you using those muscles **you**'ve injured

P ?how long *will* **it** take to um

D *I think* **you**'re going to be off work at least a week

P a week

D *possibly* two weeks ...

D **there's** your note the tablets **I**'m going to give you a **common side-effect** is indigestion !so take them with food *just* to protect yourself **it**'s one three times a day **they** don't make you drowsy **you** *don't have to* finish the course *simply* when **your back** is fine !*just* stop them

P ok

D **it**'s not like an antibiotic

Exercise 5.1

In some cases possible alternative analyses are given in brackets.

1

She	bought	the car	from him	for £3000
Actor	Pr: Material	Goal	Circ: Location?	Circ:?

2

He	sold	her	the car	for £3000.
Actor	Pr: Material	Beneficiary	Goal	Circ:?

3

She	paid	him	£3000	for the car.
Actor	Pr: Material	Beneficiary	Range	Circ: Purpose

4

He	got	£3000	for the car.
Actor	Pr: Material	Goal (or Range?)	Circ: Purpose

5

The car	cost	her	£3000.
Carrier	Pr: Relational	Beneficiary	Attribute

6

The car	was sold	to her	for £3000.
Goal	Pr: Material	Beneficiary	Circ: ?

7

The cat	's eaten	all the fish.
Actor (or Behaver)	Pr: Material (or Behavioural)	Goal (or Range)

8

All our pasta	is made	daily.
Goal	Pr: Material	Circ: Extent

9

This decision	was	the most difficult of her life.
Identified/Token	Pr: Relational	Identifier/Value

10

A car	backfired	outside	in the street.
Actor	Pr: Material	Circ: Location	Circ: Location

11

They	finally	announced	their engagement	to the press.
Sayer		Pr: Verbal	Verbiage	Receiver

12

The house	stands	beside the River Weaver.
Carrier	Pr: Relational	Attribute (circumstantial)

13

I	worry	about her health.
Senser	Pr: Mental (cognition)	Circ: Matter

14

Her illness	worries	me.
Phenomenon	Pr: Mental (affection)	Senser

15

It was snowing	heavily	outside.
Pr: Material	Circ: Manner	Circ: Location

16 (= they like jelly + ice-cream)

Most children	like	jelly with ice-cream.
Senser	Pr. Mental (affection)	Phenomenon

or (= they like jelly when they have ice-cream)

Most children	like	jelly	with ice-cream
Senser	Pr: Mental (affection)	Phenomenon	Circ: Accompaniment

Exercise 5.2

Recently	I	've had	a very painful shoulder which ... impossible
Circ: Time	Carrier	Pr: Rel	Attribute

which	makes	lifting my arm	almost impossible
Initiator	Pr: Rel	Carrier	Attribute

(Halliday suggests the transitivity label Initiator for cases where causation is explicitly expressed by verbs like 'make' or 'cause' as here.)

My GP	diagnosed	a 'frozen shoulder'
Sayer/Senser	Pr: Verbal/Mental	Verbiage/Phenomenon

(One slightly problematic process here is 'diagnosed', which seems to involve a mental decision and the verbal expression. I have coded it as both.)

[my GP]	prescribed	painkillers
[Sayer]	Pr: Verbal	Verbiage

and told	me	to stay	off work	for a week
Pr: Verbal	Receiver	Pr: Material	Circ: Place	Circ: Time

What	causes	it	and will	it	get	better?
Actor	Pr: Material	Goal	Pr:-	Carrier	−Rel	Attribute

Frozen shoulder	can result	from muscle sprain or wear and tear
Actor	Pr: Material	Circ: Reason

It	may happen	after surgery to the chest, or a heart attack
Actor	Pr: Material	Circ: Time

Movement	is usually	painful and difficult
Carrier	Pr: Rel	Attribute

It	can be treated	with pain-killers, anti-inflammatory pills, or – in severe cases – a steroid injection in the shoulder
Goal	Pr: Material	Circ: Means

Physiotherapy	aids	recovery
Actor	Pr: Material	Goal

Recovery time	varies	from a week to a year
Actor	Pr: Material	Circ: time

Exercise 5.3

As usual, non-experiential elements such as conjunctive Adjuncts are ignored in the analysis. Non-defining relative clauses are analysed separately, not as embedded clauses within a nominal group. Some of the analyses given could be disputed – you may well think of good reasons for preferring a different analysis in some cases.

Now however	to get onto that programme which starts in 1995	you	have to bid	for a preliminary programme referred to by the initials JEP
	Circ: Purpose	Sayer	Pr: Verbal	Circ: Matter

to get	onto that programme	which	starts	in 1995
Pr:	Circ: Location (place)			
Material		Actor	Pr: Material	Circ: Loc. (time)

(a preliminary programme)	referred to	by the initials JEP
[Target]	Pr: Verbal	Verbiage (or Circ: Means)

and that	was	50 thousand ecus	which	is	about 30 grand
Identified/ Value	Pr: Rel	Identifier/ Token	Identified/ Token	Pr: Rel	Identifier/ Value

Now	this	has come	from Gareth
	Actor	Pr: Material	Circ: Location (place)

whose	of course	general view	is	if there is money there get it you know and then worry about it later on
Ident-		-ified/Value	Pr: Rel	Identifier/Token

if	there	is	money	there	get	it	you know
Circ: Condition					Pr:	Goal	
		Pr: Existential	Existent	Circ: Loc. (place)	Material		

and then	worry	about it	later on
	Pr: Mental (cognition)	Circ: Matter	Circ: Loc. (time)

which	has caused	him	a few hiccups	from time to time
Actor/Agent	Pr: Material	Beneficiary	Goal/Medium	Circ: Extent (duration)

but	I	feel	there	is	probably	something	in this
	Senser	Pr: Mental (cognition)		Pr: Existential		Existent	Circ: Loc. (place)

he	called	Linda and Dennis	to see		him
Sayer	Pr: Verbal	Receiver	Circ: Purpose		
		(Actor)		Pr: Material	Range

'Linda and Dennis' is labelled Actor in brackets to show that this is its role in relation to the process in the clause of purpose. In that clause 'see' is interpreted as equivalent to 'meet' (i.e. material not mental).

and	said
	Pr: Verbal

Look	I think	you	should put	a bid	together	under this general heading	just in principle
	[Modal-see Ch 8]	Actor	Pr:-	Goal	-Material	Circ: Loc. (place)	Circ: Behalf

Linda	obviously	because	it	's		Russian-related
Receiver (?)		Circ: Reason				
			Carrier	Pr: Relational		Attribute

and Dennis	because	it	talks	about the economic things
Receiver (?)	Circ: Reason			
		Sayer	Pr: Verbal	Circ: Matter

They	kindly	then	deputed	me	to make	it	happen
Sayer		Circ: Loc. (time)	Pr: Verbal	Receiver (Initiator/Agent)	Pr:-	Actor/ Medium	-Material

'me' functions as Initiator/Agent for the process in the projected clause.

Exercise 6.1

1   This *(declarative, unmarked)*
2   In this same year *(declarative, marked)*
3   What *(WH-interrogative, unmarked)*
4   Don't you *(yes/no interrogative, unmarked)*
5   Print *(imperative, unmarked)*
6   More heads at independent schools *(declarative, unmarked)*
7   *(elliptical, no Theme)*
8   How many times a week *(WH-interrogative, unmarked)*
9   Actions which are inconsistent with an individual's usual behaviour and which give rise to some concern *(declarative, unmarked)*
10 For enquiries relating to this offer *(imperative, marked)*
11 Don't forget *(imperative, unmarked)*
12 With a CharityCard *(declarative, marked)*
13 Out of the pub *(declarative, marked)*
14 What sort of car *(WH-interrogative, unmarked)*
15 A £2 million, two-hour adaptation of *Emma*, Austen's fourth novel, planned for ITV's autumn 1996 season, *(declarative, unmarked)*

Exercise 6.2

1   What often happens *(thematic equative)*
2   It is vital *(thematised comment)*
3   It's not only our engine *(predicated Theme)*
4   These mass parties *(pre-posed Theme)*
5   This *(marked alternative to thematic equative)*
6   All I want *(thematic equative)*
7   What we didn't realise *(thematic equative)*
8   That book you were talking about *(pre-posed Theme)*
9   It was with an infinite feeling of tolerance *(predicated Theme)*
10 Eating at home *(marked alternative to thematic equative)*

Exercise 6.3

1   If she were to survive,
2   The workmen ‖ and she
3   While drinking it,
4   He
5   When talking about people in industrialised countries with problems in reading or writing,
6   As long as the Chancellor funds tax cuts by cutting spending
7   To find out more about this unique, new way of giving and how you can make the most of your generosity,
8   Eventually, when the region got small enough, ‖ and in this way

Exercise 6.4

1   Now *(textual)* at first sight *(experiential)*
2   However, *(textual)* I *(experiential)*
3   Surprisingly, *(interpersonal)* however, *(textual)* this tendency *(experiential)*
4   And *(textual)* no doubt *(interpersonal)* he *(experiential)*
5   Well, *(textual)* perhaps *(interpersonal)* he *(experiential)*
6   The first three letters
7   Oh, *(textual)* Alice, *(interpersonal)* you *(experiential)*
8   The coming of print in Europe at this point in history

Exercise 7.1

The Themes are shown in bold. Some of the Themes in the spoken extract are tricky because the utterances are incomplete or the speaker changes tack in the middle of a clause. I have marked such cases with #. Minor clauses (e.g. 'Yeh') are ignored. The other symbols are those used in Figure 6.34, see p. 142.

The cohesive signals operating between clause complexes are in italics. Several of the occurrences of 'it' and 'the' could be seen as either anaphoric or exophoric, but I have included all these as cohesive (i.e. I have treated them as anaphoric). Cohesive ellipsis is marked +; contextually-determined (i.e. non-cohesive) ellipsis is marked ϕ. Lexical repetition is not marked, and neither is clear exophoric reference.

Recently, I've had a very painful shoulder which makes lifting my arm almost impossible.
My GP diagnosed a 'frozen shoulder',
* prescribed painkillers
and * told me to stay off work for a week.
What causes *it*
and will *it* get better?
Frozen shoulder can result from muscle sprain or wear and tear.
It may happen after surgery to the chest, or a heart attack.
Movement is usually painful and difficult.
It can be treated with pain-killers, anti-inflammatory pills, or – in severe cases – a steroid injection in the shoulder.
Physiotherapy aids recovery.
Recovery time varies from a week to over a year.

P   **I** can't bend forward
    and I can't like turn sideways
    #**it's like the bottom of my spine** it just feels like I'm sitting on a pin
D   *so* **it**'s pain in the lower back

P   φ lower back just about there
D   ok
    ?**how long** did you say again +
P   **I mean all last night** I couldn't turn on my side
    I couldn't stand up
    I couldn't go to the toilet
D   *so it* got worse overnight
P   yeh +
D   *so the first* thing is rest
    secondly I'll give you some painkillers
    they don't speed up *the* healing
    it's just to make life comfortable for you while *it*'s healing
    #*now* it's
P   ?**what** is *it*
    ?is *it* like a thing I've got with my spine
    #or
D   *it*'s a torn muscle in your back yeh
    it should recover
P   you wouldn't think
    it was *so* painful would you
D   oh no *it is* +
    but it's all right as long as you don't move
    as soon as you move *it*'ll try and go into spasm to stop you using
    those muscles you've injured
P   how long will *it* take to um φ
D   **I think** you're going to be off work at least a week
P   + a week
D   + possibly two weeks
D   there's your note
    the tablets I'm going to give you a common side-effect is indigestion
    so take *them* with food just to protect yourself
    it's one three times a day
    they don't make you drowsy
    you don't have to finish *the* course
    simply when your back is fine just stop *them*
P   ok +
D   *it*'s not like an antibiotic

Exercise 8.1

The most salient examples of grammatical metaphor are: 'views' (a nominalised mental process); 'conversion' and 'drive' (nominalised material
processes). There are less obvious metaphors in 'boasts' (which is not a
verbal process when it is followed by a direct Object, as here, but a relational

process meaning 'has something which someone can be proud of'); and 'serviced' (it is the *people* of Frodsham who use the services). You may well also have picked up on the more traditional kind of metaphor in 'Providing' with the inanimate 'house' as the Actor. Note that this process has 3 inherent participants: Actor, Goal and Beneficiary. The Beneficiary is not made explicit here.

The common theme is the absent (human) participant – the person who views, the Beneficiary of 'providing', the converter and driver, and the person who can feel proud of the rooms on the ground floor. This chimes in with 'useful' and 'available', both of which imply a kind of Beneficiary role. As often with advertising, 'you' are invited to fill the missing roles. The basic process type in the text might be characterised as 'you-oriented attributive': it describes the house but in a way that involves you as Senser, Actor and Beneficiary (i.e. ideally as owner).

Exercise 8.2

The nominalisations are in italics, and the 'logical' verbs are in bold. I have also marked one or two features which do not fall strictly into these two categories but which are functioning in similar ways.

'Frozen shoulder' is a clinical syndrome which can probably be produced by a variety of pathological processes in the shoulder joint. These can seldom be differentiated and *treatment* is empirical. It is a condition affecting the middle-aged, in whose shoulder cuffs *degenerative changes* are occurring. The outstanding feature is *limitation of movements in the shoulder*. *This restriction* is often severe, with *virtually no gleno-humeral movements* possible, but in the milder cases *rotation, especially internal rotation*, is primarily affected. *Restriction of movements* **is accompanied** in most cases by pain, which is often severe and may disturb *sleep*. There is frequently *a history of minor trauma*, which is usually presumed to produce *some tearing of the degenerating shoulder cuff*, thereby **initiating** *the low-grade prolonged inflammatory changes* **responsible** for the symptoms. Radiographs of the shoulder are almost always normal. In some cases *the condition* **is initiated by** a period of *immobilisation of the arm*, not uncommonly as the result of *the inadvised prolonged use of a sling after a Colles' fracture*. It is commoner on the left side, and in an appreciable number of cases there is *a preceding episode of a silent or overt cardiac infarct*. If untreated, pain subsides after many months, but there may be *permanent restriction of movements*. **The main aim** of *treatment* is to improve the final range of *movements in the shoulder*, and *graduated shoulder exercises* are the mainstay of *treatment*. In some cases where pain is a particular problem, *hydrocortisone injections* into the shoulder cuff may be helpful. In a few cases, once the acute stage is well past, *manipulation of the shoulder under general anaesthesia* **may be helpful in restoring** *movements* in a stiff joint.

Exercise 9.1

1 'Frozen shoulder'
    C   Head
a clinical syndrome [[which can probably ... in the shoulder joint]]
D C   Head
a variety [of pathological processes [in the shoulder joint]]
D Head   C   Head   D   C   Head

2 It
Head
a condition [[affecting the middle-aged]]
D Head   D   Head
whose shoulder cuffs
D   C   Head
degenerative changes
  E (? or C)   Head

3 The outstanding feature
D   E   Head
limitation [of movements [in the shoulder]]
  Head   Head   D   Head

4 Restriction [of movements]
  Head   Head
most cases
D   Head
pain
Head
sleep
Head

5 a   history [of minor trauma]
  D   Head   E   Head
some tearing [of the degenerating shoulder cuff]
D   Head   D   E   C   Head
the low-grade prolonged inflammatory changes [[responsible for the
D   E   E   E (? or C)   Head   D
symptoms]]
  Head
I have analysed the Postmodifier as a clause here even though there is no
verb, because I am taking it as a reduced relative clause: 'which is
responsible ...'.

6 some cases
D   Head
the condition
D   Head

a period [of immobilisation [of the arm]]
D Head   *Head*   *D Head*
the result [of the inadvised prolonged use [of a sling] [after a Colles'
D Head   D   E   E   Head   D Head   D   C
fracture]]
  Head

In 'a Colles' fracture' the apostrophe makes it look misleadingly as
though we have a possessive Deictic (cf. 'a man's arm', where 'a man' is
Deictic). The use of possessive proper names as Classifiers is fairly rare
and is almost unique to scientific registers: compare, say, 'a Dickens
novel', where the apostrophe is not used. Note that 'after a Colles'
fracture' postmodifies 'use', not 'sling'.

7 some cases [[where pain is a particular problem]]
   D   Head   *Head D   D₂   Head*
   hydrocortisone injections [into the shoulder cuff]
        C   Head   *D   C   Head*

8 a few cases
      D Head
   I have analysed 'a few' as a complex Deictic. Alternatively, 'few' could
   be labelled D₂.
   the acute stage
   D   E   Head
   manipulation [of the shoulder [under general anaesthesia]]
      Head   *D   Head*   *C   Head*
   movements [in a stiff joint]
      Head   *D E Head*

Exercise 9.2

(a) = finite; (b) = non-finite; (c) = complex

1	was shaped	(a) passive: past
	saw	(a) past
2	tend to confirm	(c) present – 'tend' = modalisation of present event
3	had been inoculated	(a) passive: past in past
	leaving	(b) 'present' at the past time in relation to which 'inoculated' is past
	had considered	(a) past in past
4	was bound to entertain	(a) modulated past view of 'future' (in relation to the 'being bound') event
5	had been examining	(a) present in past in past
6	're going to have to try to cope	(c) modulated future in present view of 'future' (in relation to the 'having to') event – 'try' = attempting

7	had been about to say	(a) future in past in past
	had not expected	(a) past in past
	to react	(b) 'future' in relation to the time of 'expecting'
8	'll have been worrying	(c) modalised present view of present in past event (NB: the 'probably' indicates that 'will' is expressing certainty rather than futurity here)

Exercise 10.1

This activity obviously applies only to the longer utterances. The clause complex analysis is problematic in a number of places where we could argue that there is intended to be implicit conjunction tying two clauses into a complex. The following shows the most 'generous' analysis, i.e. wherever possible, clauses are treated as combined in a complex; where needed, a conjunction is added in square brackets to show the possible link.

The strict T–unit analysis uses all the clause complex boundaries (shown by three vertical slashes), but adds others (shown by two vertical slashes).

P   I can't bend forward || and I can't like turn sideways ||| it's like the bottom of my spine it just feels like I'm sitting on a pin

P   I mean all last night I couldn't turn on my side || *[and]* I couldn't stand up || *[and]* I couldn't go to the toilet

D   so the first thing is rest ||| secondly I'll give you some painkillers ||| they don't speed up the healing || *[but]* it's just to make life comfortable for you while it's healing ||| now it's

P   what is it ||| is like a thing I've got with my spine || or

D   it's a torn muscle in your back yeh ||| it should recover

D   oh no it is || but it's all right as long as you don't move || *[to be precise]* as soon as you move it'll try and go into spasm to stop you using those muscles you've injured

D   there's your note ||| the tablets I'm going to give you a common side–effect is indigestion || so take them with food just to protect yourself ||| it's one three times a day ||| they don't make you drowsy ||| you don't have to finish the course || *[but]* simply when your back is fine just stop them

Exercise 10.2

1 ||| At the trial Mr Justice Judge said | if he didn't admit [[what police said |
                α   ββ   [[α
he admitted]] | he was the 'victim of an outrageous and unacceptable
    β]]   βα
conspiracy by a large number of policemen' |||

Note that in the embedded clause 'what' is the Complement of 'he admitted' – in transitivity terms it is the Verbiage.

2 ||| They had wrangled about parts and benefits, || quarrelled over contracts
                 1 1 1   1 1 2

and money; || she had suffered from his deep-seated suspicion of actresses,
                 1 2 1

|| he had been frightened by the tenacity [[with which she had extracted
          1 2 2

her salary]]; || but they had been part of the same team and the same
                                    2

world |||

The punctuation indicates that the writer intends this as a single clause complex, which is how I have analysed it.

3 ||| She skims over her early life; | mainly to protect her family, || but also, ||
        α   β1

one suspects, || because her life [[as we now know it]] did not come into
  β 2 1   β 2 2 α

existence | until she became a television star in the Eighties |||
          β 2 2 β

I have analysed the 'because' clause as being in a paratactic relation to 'one suspects', though neither that nor a hypotactic analysis seems entirely adequate.

4 ||| Well you see she wrote this letter | saying | that she'd been ringing || and
                    1α   1β   1γ

[[what we couldn't understand | when we spoke to Liz]] was [[she knew |
     [[α   β]]   2   [[1α

you were going to Peru || and she knows | you don't put the cats in the
    1β   2α   2β

cattery | when you go away]] || so it was obvious [[where we were]] |||
       2γ]]   3

I have ignored 'you see', taking it as an interpersonal discourse marker rather than a real clause; I have analysed 'saying' as equivalent to 'and she said' rather than 'which (= the letter) said'; and I have analysed the final 'so' clause as a comment on the whole utterance, rather than as part of the embedded explanation of 'what we couldn't understand'. None of these decisions is entirely certain!

5 ||| While this handbook will give intending applicants the information
                β

[[they need]], | students must, | in order to obtain up-to-date, full and
                        αβ

official information about entrance requirements and courses, | write
                                  αα

direct to the institutions of their choice at least a year [[before they hope to begin their studies]], | so that they will have decided [[to which
                                      γ1

institutions they wish to seek admission]], ‖ and obtained the necessary
γ2

application form, well before the closing date for receipt of applications ‖‖

Note that 'hope to begin' and 'wish to seek' are verbal group complexes rather than clause complexes.

6   Some of the sentences consist of one-clause complexes. In this case, I have omitted them here unless they include an embedded clause.

a   ‖‖ 'Frozen shoulder' is a clinical syndrome [[which can probably be produced by a variety of pathological processes in the shoulder joint]] ‖‖

b   ‖‖ These can seldom be differentiated ‖ and treatment is empirical ‖‖
1   2

c   ‖‖ It is a condition [[affecting the middle-aged]], | in whose shoulder cuffs
α

degenerative changes are occurring ‖‖
β

d   ‖‖ This restriction is often severe, | with virtually no gleno-humeral movements
1α   1β

possible, ‖ but in the milder cases rotation, especially internal rotation, is primarily affected ‖‖
2

The 'with virtually no ...' clause is a special type of non-finite clause: there is no verb in it. This can happen following 'with' when the omitted verb is 'be', as here.

e   ‖‖ Restriction of movements is accompanied in most cases by pain,
α

| which is often severe ‖ and may disturb sleep ‖‖
β1   β2

f   ‖‖ There is frequently a history of minor trauma, | which is usually
α

presumed to produce some tearing of the degenerating shoulder cuff,
β

| thereby initiating the low-grade prolonged inflammatory changes
γ

responsible for the symptoms ‖‖

g   ‖‖ It is commoner on the left side, ‖ and in an appreciable number of
1

cases there is a preceding episode of a silent or overt cardiac infarct ‖‖
2

h   ‖‖ If untreated, | pain subsides after many months, ‖ but there may be
β   α1   α2

permanent restriction of movements ‖‖

i   ‖‖ The main aim of treatment is [[to improve the final range of
1

movements in the shoulder]], ‖ and graduated shoulder exercises are
$$2$$
the mainstay of treatment ‖‖

j   ‖‖ [[In some cases where pain is a particular problem]], hydrocortisone
injections into the shoulder cuff may be helpful ‖‖

k   ‖‖ In a few cases, | once the acute stage is well past, | manipulation of
$$\beta$$
the shoulder under general anaesthesia may be helpful in [[restoring
$$\alpha$$
movements in a stiff joint]] ‖‖

Exercise 10.3

1 $\alpha-\beta$:   projecting (locution)
       $\beta\alpha-\beta\beta$:   enhancing (condition)
       $[[\alpha-\beta]]$:   projecting (locution)

2   1 1 1–1 1 2:   extending
       1 1–1 2:   extending
       1 2 1–1 2 2:   extending
       1–2:   enhancing (concession)

3 $\alpha-\beta$:   enhancing (purpose)
       $\beta1-\beta2$:   extending
       $\beta\,2\,1-\beta\,2\,2$:   projecting (idea)
       $\beta\,2\,2\,\alpha-\beta\,2\,2\,\beta$:   enhancing (temporal)

4 $1\alpha-1\beta$:   extending
       $1\beta-1\gamma$:   projecting (locution)
       1–2:   extending
       $[[\alpha-\beta]]$:   enhancing (temporal)
       $[[1\alpha-1\beta]]$:   projecting (idea)
       $[[1-2]]$:   extending
       $[[2\alpha-2\beta]]$:   projecting (idea)
       $[[2\beta-2\gamma]]$:   enhancing (temporal)
       2–3:   enhancing (cause/effect)

The second embedded clause complex ('she knew ... when you go
away') is a fact.

5 $\beta-\alpha$:   extending
       $\alpha\beta-\alpha\alpha$:   enhancing (purpose)
       $\alpha-\gamma$:   enhancing (cause/effect)
       $\gamma1-\gamma2$:   extending

6

a   (embedded clause only)
b   1–2:   extending (or enhancing = 'and so'?)
c $\alpha-\beta$:   elaborating

d	$1\alpha-1\beta$:	extending
	$1-2$:	extending
e	$\alpha-\beta$:	elaborating
	$\beta1-\beta2$:	extending
f	$\alpha-\beta$:	extending
	$\beta-\gamma$:	enhancing (means)
g	$1-2$:	extending
h	$\beta-\alpha$:	enhancing (condition)
	$\alpha1-\alpha2$:	extending
i	$1-2$:	extending (or enhancing = 'and so'?)
j	(embedded clause only)	
k	$\beta-\alpha$:	enhancing (temporal)

Exercise 10.4

Projected clauses (including embedded projections) are in bold. Clauses which could have been reported are in italics: I have included anything where it is possible that the information comes from a different source, so you will need to decide whether you agree in all cases. Nominal groups functioning as Verbiage are not included, even though they may reinforce the manipulation carried out by the projections (e.g. 'predicts a slump in the pound ...').

BRITAIN is heading back to economic growth this year and a strong recovery in 1993 – if the nation sticks with responsible Tory policies.

This election day boost for John Major comes from the prestigious International Monetary Fund.

The latest optimistic forecast coincides with a survey from British bosses showing **business recovery is well under way**. The survey also predicts a slump in the pound if Neil Kinnock gets in.

The IMF analysis of Britain's economic prospects claims **Chancellor Norman Lamont is being too modest about the return to growth this year**. It forecasts a growth rate of one and a half per cent, compared with Treasury estimates of one per cent, indicating **that the worst is past. By next year**, claims the IMF, **Britain will enjoy a healthy three per cent growth rate as it leaves the recession far behind**. The forecast is based on the assumption **that Britain sticks with the same policies**.

The Institute of Directors gives strong backing to the rising feeling **that the economy is on the mend**. But the bosses' organisation makes it clear **Labour's high-tax plans would significantly damage the recovery**.

The number of directors reporting rising order books is up to 43 per cent from 28 per cent in February.

Despairing Julie Cleminson cuddled her newborn son Paul yesterday ... and prayed **he will be given the chance to be happy that she has never had**.

Just 18, Julie has spent most of her life under Tory rule. And she has ended up with precious little.

Julie, *whose mother died in a fall four years ago*, knows little about politics. But she believes **that if the Tories win, the odds could be stacked against Paul from the very start.**

Her only hope is **that a new dawn of a Labour government will be a new dawn for Paul, too.** She said: '**My baby is so beautiful and I love him so much.**'

'**I know he's not getting the best start in life. I just want somewhere where we can all be together and where he can cry without upsetting anyone.**'

The following is only a brief indication of some of the points that could be developed.

In the first report, there is little arguability possible: several projections are embedded inside nominalisations (we cannot be sure whose 'assumption' or whose 'rising feeling' is being reported); the projecting verbs are often those which assume that the information in the projected clause is true (e.g. 'show', 'indicate'). The strong claim in the opening sentence is in fact a report of the IMF's view, but this is not made clear until the following sentence; it therefore looks like a factual account direct from the journalist. The sources are all official bodies: the newspaper is taking the 'informed official sources' tack to impress its readers with objective, authorised 'facts'.

In the second report, the source is an individual: this newspaper is trying the 'human interest' tack. The projections are mostly presented as arguable in theory but some of them are so personal (e.g. 'My baby is so beautiful') that readers will hardly be able or want to disagree. The controversial projections are humanised and emotional ('prayed ', 'believes'). The only unarguable projection ('a new dawn' – grammatically a fact) is also controversial but is tagged as 'her only hope', thus linking in with this humanised emotional line. Quotes – there are none in the first extract – let the individual voice come through. The Labour viewpoint is being constructed as that of the ordinary people rather than of institutions.

Further reading

As I mentioned in the Foreword, one way of using this book is as preparation for reading Halliday's *Introduction to Functional Grammar*, and if you want a fuller exposition of any of the ideas here you should turn first to that source. Two other books that provide full accounts of the approach, each useful in different ways, are Bloor and Bloor (1995) and Eggins (1994): the first is particularly good on the detailed analysis of clauses, looking upwards from that to meanings in text; while the second focuses more on the concepts of register and genre, looking downwards to the clause-level choices which realise the generic choices. For each chapter below, I will indicate any parts of these three books which are relevant.

In addition, I will suggest other titles that you can read if you want to follow up on a particular issue. The list is naturally far from complete: I will generally give just one or two representative references for each area, selecting as far as possible those which are easily available and accessible in content.

Chapter 1

On the general rationale for a functional approach, the Introduction to Halliday (1994) is well worth reading twice: first as an introduction and later as a review. Berry (1975) includes a discussion of the main features which make Systemic Functional Grammar (SFG) different from other approaches. Bloor and Bloor (1995) Chapter 12 shows how FG relates to other schools of linguistics. There are many introductions to Transformational Generative grammar: the one I find most useful is the first chapter of Horrocks (1987).

Chapter 2

Halliday (1994) Chapter 2 looks at different ways of analysing clause constituents, and the idea of functional labels, but the discussion becomes fairly complex: Bloor and Bloor (1995) Chapter 2 provides a simpler outline. In Eggins (1994), the relevant chapter is Chapter 5. Huddleston (1984) defines word classes and looks at areas of mismatch between the traditional categories and actual use. Two descriptive grammars of English within a functional framework are the *Collins Cobuild English Grammar* (1990) and Downing and Locke (1992).

Chapter 3

In the first part of Halliday and Hasan (1985), Halliday gives a clear overview of the FG model of clause grammar; in the second part, Hasan does the same for register and genre. Eggins (1994) also deals very thoroughly with register and genre in Chapters 1–3. Although the title of Halliday (1985b) – *Spoken and Written Language* – does not seem directly related to the model as a whole, the book does provide an interesting view of it from a side-angle. An early summary of the three metafunctions is given in Halliday (1970); and Halliday (1976) brings together a number of his writings up to that point. Martin (1992) is by no means an easy read, but it represents a sustained attempt to show exactly how lexico-grammatical choices interact with contextual factors. Two very useful sources of papers on all aspects of SFG are: *Occasional Papers in Systemic Linguistics*, published since 1987 by the Department of English Studies at the University of Nottingham; and the journal *functions of language* (published by John Benjamins), which first appeared in 1995.

Chapter 4

The relevant chapters are Halliday (1994) Chapter 4, Bloor and Bloor (1995) Chapter 3 and Eggins (1994) Chapter 6. Simpson (1990, 1993) is good on modality in text, and Thompson and Thetela (1995) discuss in more detail the aspects of interpersonal management shown in Figure 4.21. Berry (1987) and Ventola (1987) analyse interaction in dialogue; Hasan and Cloran (1990) look particularly at exchanges between mothers and children. Lemke (1992) is a complex theoretical discussion of evaluation as interpersonal meaning, while Hunston (1993) looks at evaluation in scientific writing in a more concrete and accessible manner.

Chapter 5

On transitivity, the relevant chapters are Halliday (1994) Chapter 5, Bloor and Bloor (1995) Chapter 6 and Eggins (1994) Chapter 8. The basic model of transitivity is first set out in Halliday (1967–8, parts 1 and 3). Hasan (1987) pushes transitivity analysis towards the more delicate levels at which individual lexical choices are made. Halliday's analysis of William Golding's novel *The Inheritors* (most easily accessible in Halliday, 1973) is a classic example of transitivity/ergativity analysis in action on text. Davidse (1992) presents highly complex arguments in favour of regarding ergativity as a different phenomenon from transitivity.

Chapter 6

The relevant chapters are Halliday (1994) Chapter 3, Bloor and Bloor (1995) Chapters 4 and 5, and Eggins (1994) Chapter 9. Halliday (1967–8, part 2) is the first full exposition of his ideas on Theme. Fries has written extensively and lucidly on Theme in text (e.g. 1981/83, 1994, 1995), and also on other aspects of texture and cohesion (e.g. 1992). Other interesting treatments of Theme include Davies (1988) and Francis (1989). Halliday and Martin (1993) contains several chapters on Theme in academic text. On the particular issues of thematising structures (which he calls 'special operations clauses') and interpolation, see Winter (1982).

Chapter 7

The classic treatment of cohesion is Halliday and Hasan (1976). Halliday (1994) Chapter 9 is a more concise version of this, while Hasan, in Halliday and Hasan (1985 – Chapter 5), sets out to explore the links between cohesion and coherence. See also Bloor and Bloor (1995) Chapter 5, and Eggins (1994) Chapter 4. Salkie (1995), despite the misleadingly broad title, is a useful basic introduction to the mechanics of cohesion. Parsons (1990) is a book-length treatment of cohesion in scientific text; a paper drawn from this is in Ventola (1991). S. Thompson (1994) explores the interaction of different cohesive resources in speech; see also Fox (1987) on anaphoric reference in spoken and written text. Francis (1994) looks at the cohesive function of labelling. Hoey (1991a, b) makes a powerful case for lexical repetition as the most important cohesive resource. On the clause relational approach to conjunction, see Hoey (1983) and Winter (1994).

Chapter 8

The relevant chapter in Halliday (1994) is Chapter 10. Martin (1992 – especially Chapters 3, 5 and 6) explores the all-pervasiveness of grammatical metaphor. Ravelli (1988) gives a systematic account of how grammatical metaphor works, while Halliday (1985b) shows how it is typical of written language. A number of chapters in Halliday and Martin (1993) explore grammatical metaphor in scientific text; see also Halliday (1988) and Martin (1991).

Chapter 9

The relevant chapters are Halliday (1994) Chapters 6 and 7A; and Bloor and Bloor (1995) Chapters 7 and 8.

Chapter 10

On clause complexes, see Halliday (1994) Chapter 7, and Bloor and Bloor (1995) Chapters 9 and 10. Haiman and Thompson (1989) covers a range of different approaches to clause complexes, including the Hallidayan approach. S.A. Thompson (1985) discusses reasons for the ordering of subordinate clauses in relation to the dominant clause; while Schleppegrell (1992) is interesting on the difficulties of separating parataxis and hypotaxis. For a full description of reporting in English, including analyses of its function in text, see G. Thompson (1994).

Chapter 11

There is a huge range of writing on functional text analysis and applications of Functional Grammar, and the list here can only scratch the surface. Halliday (1994) Appendix 1 and Eggins (1994) Chapter 10 both have detailed analyses of texts. Other analyses include Francis and Kramer-Dahl (1992 – medical case histories); Drury (1991 – students' summaries); and Fries (1993 – advertisements). Mann and Thompson (1992) contains twelve analyses in functional terms of the same text. For functional approaches to literary text, see Hasan (1985) and Birch and O'Toole (1988). For educational applications of Functional Grammar, see Hasan and Martin (1989) and Martin (1985/89); and for its application in foreign language teaching in particular, see Hasan and Perrett (1995). For Critical Discourse Analysis, see especially Hodge and Kress (1993), and many of the papers in the journal *Discourse and Society* published by Sage.

References

BERRY, M. 1975: *Introduction to Systemic Linguistics: Volume 1 Structures and Systems.* London: Batsford (reprinted by the Department of English Studies, University of Nottingham, 1989).

BERRY, M. 1987: Is teacher an unanalysed concept? In HALLIDAY, M.A.K., and FAWCETT, R. (eds), *New Developments in Systemic Linguistics Volume 1: Theory and Description.* London: Pinter, 41–63.

BIRCH, D., and O'TOOLE, M. 1988: *Functions of Style.* London: Pinter.

BLOOR, T., and BLOOR, M. 1995: *The Functional Analysis of English: A Hallidayan Approach.* London: Arnold.

Collins Cobuild English Grammar 1990. London: Collins.

COULTHARD, M. (ed.) 1994: *Advances in Written Text Analysis.* London: Routledge.

DAVIDSE, K. 1992: Transitivity/ergativity: the Janus-headed grammar of actions and events. In DAVIES, M., and RAVELLI, L. (eds), *Advances in Systemic Linguistics: Recent Theory and Practice.* London: Pinter, 105–35.

DAVIES, F.I. 1988: Reading between the lines: thematic choice as a device for presenting writer viewpoint in academic text. *ESPecialist* 9, 173–200.

DOWNING, A., and LOCKE, P. 1992: *A University Course in English Grammar.* New York: Prentice Hall.

DRURY, H. 1991: The use of systemic linguistics to describe student summaries at university level. In VENTOLA, E. (ed.), *Functional and Systemic Linguistics: Approaches and Uses.* Berling and New York: Mouton de Gruyter, 431–56.

EGGINS, S. 1994: *An Introduction to Systemic Functional Linguistics.* London: Pinter.

FOX, B.A. 1987: *Discourse Structure and Anaphora: Written and Conversational English.* Cambridge: Cambridge University Press.

FRANCIS, G. 1989: Thematic selection and distribution in written discourse. *Word* **40** (1–2), 201–21.

FRANCIS, G. 1994: Labelling discourse: an aspect of nominal-group lexical cohesion. In COULTHARD, M. (ed.), *Advances in Written Text Analysis.* London: Routledge, 83–101.

FRANCIS, G., and KRAMER-DAHL, A. 1992: Grammaticalizing the medical case history. In TOOLAN, M. (ed.), *Language, Text and Context.* London: Routledge, 56–90.

FRIES, P.H. 1981: On the status of theme in English: arguments from discourse. *Forum Linguisticum* 6 (1), 1–38 (reprinted in PETÖFI, J.S., and SÖZER, E. (eds) 1983, *Micro and Macro Connexity of Texts.* Hamburg: Helmut Buske, 116–52).

FRIES, P.H. 1992: Lexico-grammatical patterns and the interpretation of texts. *Discourse Processes* 15, 73–91.

FRIES, P.H. 1993: Information flow in written advertising. In ALATIS, J.E. (ed.) *Language, Communication and Social Meaning: Georgetown University Round Table on Languages and Linguistics 1992*. Washington, D.C.: Georgetown University Press, 336–52.

FRIES, P.H. 1994: On Theme, Rheme and discourse goals. In COULTHARD, M. (ed.), *Advances in Written Text Analysis*. London: Routledge, 229–49.

FRIES, P.H. 1995: Themes, methods of development, and texts. In HASAN, R., and FRIES, P.H. (eds), *On Subject and Theme: From the Perspective of Functions in Discourse*. Amsterdam and Philadelphia: John Benjamins.

HAIMAN, J., and THOMPSON, S.A. (eds) 1989: *Clause Combining in Grammar and Discourse*. Amsterdam and Philadelphia: John Benjamins.

HALLIDAY, M.A.K. 1967–8: Notes on transitivity and theme in English, parts 1–3. *Journal of Linguistics* 3 (1), 37–87, 3 (2), 199–244, 4 (2), 179–215.

HALLIDAY, M.A.K. 1970: Language structure and language function. In LYONS, J. (ed.), *New Horizons in Linguistics*. Harmondsworth: Penguin, 140–65.

HALLIDAY, M.A.K. 1973: *Explorations in the Functions of Language*. London: Edward Arnold.

HALLIDAY, M.A.K. 1976: *System and Function in Language* (ed. KRESS, G.). Oxford: Oxford University Press.

HALLIDAY, M.A.K. 1985a: *An Introduction to Functional Grammar* (1st edn). London: Edward Arnold.

HALLIDAY, M.A.K. 1985b: *Spoken and Written Language*. Geelong, Vic.: Deakin University Press (republished by Oxford University Press, 1989).

HALLIDAY, M.A.K. 1988: On the language of physical science. In GHADESSY, M. (ed.), *Registers of Written English*. London: Pinter, 162–78.

HALLIDAY, M.A.K. 1994: *An Introduction to Functional Grammar* (2nd edn). London: Edward Arnold.

HALLIDAY, M.A.K., and HASAN, R. 1976: *Cohesion in English*. London: Longman.

HALLIDAY, M.A.K., and HASAN, R. 1985: *Language, Context and Text: Aspects of Language in a Social-semiotic Perspective*. Geelong, Vic.: Deakin University Press (republished by Oxford University Press, 1989).

HALLIDAY, M.A.K., and MARTIN, J.R. 1993: *Writing Science: Literacy and Discursive Power*. London: Falmer Press.

HASAN, R. 1985: *Linguistics, Language and Verbal Art*. Geelong, Vic.: Deakin University Press (republished by Oxford University Press, 1989).

HASAN, R. 1987: The grammarian's dream: lexis as most delicate grammar. In HALLIDAY, M.A.K., and FAWCETT, R. (eds), *New Developments in Systemic Linguistics Volume 1: Theory and Description*. London: Pinter, 184–211.

HASAN, R., and CLORAN, C. 1990: Semantic variation: a sociolinguistic interpretation of everyday talk between mothers and children. In GIBBONS, J., NICHOLAS, H., and HALLIDAY, M.A.K. (eds), *Learning, Keeping and Using Language: Selected Papers from the 8th World Congress of Applied Linguistics*. Amsterdam and Philadelphia: John Benjamins, 67–99.

HASAN, R., and MARTIN, J.R. (eds) 1989: *Language Development: Learning Language, Learning Culture*. Norwood, NJ: Ablex.

HASAN, R., and PERRETT, G. 1995: Learning to function with the other tongue. In ODLIN, T. (ed.), *Perspectives on Pedagogic Grammar*. New York: Cambridge University Press.

HODGE, R., and KRESS. G. 1993: *Language as Ideology* (2nd edn). London: Routledge.

HOEY, M.P. 1983: *On the Surface of Discourse*. London: George Allen and Unwin (reprinted by the Department of English Studies, University of Nottingham, 1991).

HOEY, M.P. 1991a: *Patterns of Lexis in Text*. Oxford: Oxford University Press.

HOEY, M.P. 1991b: Another perspective on coherence and cohesive harmony. In VENTOLA, E. (ed.), *Functional and Systemic Linguistics: Approaches and Uses*. Berlin and New York: Mouton de Gruyter, 385–414.

HORROCKS, G. 1987: *Generative Grammar*. London: Longman.

HUDDLESTON, R. 1984: *Introduction to the Grammar of English*. Cambridge: Cambridge University Press.

HUNSTON, S. 1993: Evaluation and ideology in scientific writing. In GHADESSY, M. (ed.), *Register Analysis: Theory and Practice*. London: Pinter, 57–73.

LEMKE, J.L. 1992: Interpersonal meaning in discourse: value orientations. In DAVIES, M., and RAVELLI, L. (eds), *Advances in Systemic Linguistics: Recent Theory and Practice*. London: Pinter, 82–104.

MANN, W.C., and THOMPSON, S.A. (eds) 1992: *Discourse Description: Diverse Linguistic Analyses of a Fund-raising Text*. Amsterdam and Philadelphia: John Benjamins.

MARTIN, J.R. 1985: *Factual Writing: Exploring and Challenging Social Reality*. Geelong, Vic.: Deakin University Press (republished by Oxford University Press, 1989).

MARTIN, J.R. 1991: Nominalization in science and humanities: distilling knowledge and scaffolding text. In VENTOLA, E. (ed.), *Functional and Systemic Linguistics: Approaches and Uses*. Berlin and New York: Mouton de Gruyter, 307–37.

MARTIN, J.R. 1992: *English Text: System and Structure*. Philadelphia and Amsterdam: John Benjamins.

MYERS, G. 1989: The pragmatics of politeness in scientific articles. *Applied Linguistics* 10 (1), 1–35.

PARSONS, G. 1990: *A Comparative Study of the Writing of Scientific Texts Focussing on Cohesion and Coherence*. University of Nottingham: Department of English Studies.

QUIRK, R., GREENBAUM, S., LEECH, G., and SVARTVIK, J. 1985: *A Comprehensive Grammar of the English Language*. London: Longman.

RAVELLI, L. 1988: Grammatical metaphor: an initial analysis. In STEINER, E.H., and VELTMAN, R. (eds), *Pragmatics, Discourse and Text: Some Systemically-inspired Approaches*. London: Pinter.

SALKIE, R. 1995: *Text and Discourse Analysis*. London: Routledge.

SCHLEPPEGRELL, M. 1992: Subordination and linguistic complexity. *Discourse Processes* 15, 117–31.

SIMPSON, P. 1990: Modality in literary-critical discourse. In NASH, W. (ed.), *The Writing Scholar*. Newbury Park: Sage Publications, 63–94.

SIMPSON, P. 1993: *Language, Ideology and Point of View*. London: Routledge.

THOMPSON, G. 1994: *Reporting: Collins Cobuild English Guides 5*. London: HarperCollins.

THOMPSON, G., and THETELA, P. 1995: The sound of one hand clapping: the management of interaction in written discourse. *Text* 15 (1), 103–27.

THOMPSON, S. 1994: Aspects of cohesion in monologue. *Applied Linguistics* 15 (1), 58–75.

THOMPSON, S.A. 1985: Grammar and written discourse: initial versus final purpose clauses in English. *Text* 5 (1–2), 55–84.

VENTOLA, E. 1987: *The Structure of Social Interaction: A Systemic Approach to the Semiotics of Social Encounters*. London: Pinter.

VENTOLA, E. (ed.) 1991: *Functional and Systemic Linguistics: Approaches and Uses*. Berlin and New York: Mouton de Gruyter.

WINTER, E. 1982: *Towards a Contextual Grammar of English*. London: George Allen & Unwin.

WINTER, E. 1994: Clause relations as information structure: two basic text structures in English. In COULTHARD, M. (ed.), *Advances in Written Text Analysis*. London: Routledge, 46–68.

Index